CLIFFORD ODETS

GOLDEN BOY
AWAKE AND SING!
THE BIG KNIFE

WITH AN INTRODUCTION BY
ERIC MOTTRAM

PENGUIN BOOKS

Penguin Books Ltd, Harmondsworth, Middlesex
AUSTRALIA: Penguin Books Pty Ltd, 762 Whitehorse Road,
Mitcham, Victoria

—

Golden Boy first published in the U.S.A. 1937
Published in Great Britain in *Three Plays* by
Clifford Odets by Gollancz 1938
Copyright © Clifford Odets, 1937

Awake and Sing! first published in the U.S.A. 1935
Published in Great Britain by Gollancz 1936
Copyright © Clifford Odets, 1933, 1935

The Big Knife first published in the U.S.A. 1949
Published in Great Britain in *Famous Plays of 1954*
by Gollancz 1954
Copyright © Clifford Odets, 1949

—

This selection published in Penguin Books 1963

—

Made and printed in Great Britain
by Hazell Watson & Viney Ltd, Aylesbury and Slough
Set in Monotype Bembo

CONTENTS

INTRODUCTION

By Eric Mottram

FROM *Waiting for Lefty* (1935) to *The Flowering Peach* (1954) the plays of Clifford Odets expound a career which in a number of important ways represents the sensitive, socially responsible writer in America living through the Depression, the New Deal, and the Second World War and the Cold War, from Roosevelt through Eisenhower. Odets needed a theatre through which to give his early experience of the lower middle class in Philadelphia and the Bronx, the dramatic region of his awareness of the human plight under capitalism in the cities. That theatre was the Group Theatre and it became his creative home. The heart of his drama concerns homelessness, however, the loneliness of men in a time of disorder. Odets himself seems to have had a need for a creative framework, a 'home' to work in. After his membership of the Communist Party ended in 1934, he found that home in the Group. When the Group ended in 1951, he tried, with ambiguous success, to find creative security in Hollywood, where he first went after that extraordinary initial outpouring of plays in 1935 – the year of *Lefty, Awake and Sing!, Till the Day I Die,* and *Paradise Lost*. But Odets was primarily the finest product of the Group Theatre, which, founded between 1928 and 1931, came to focus the growing social purpose of the Depression and New Deal years.

Gradually Odets shifts the balance between personal and social emphases in his plays. In *Lefty* the bias of human deterioration lies with the social structure: only cooperative strike action can produce a better world. *Awake and Sing!* shows this in a more subtle and more extended dramatic form: the action moves towards awakening in a young man as he prepares to take his place in social change. *Paradise Lost* translates the implications of the first two plays into a somewhat Marxist analysis of social disintegration. The family's decadence is made the symbol of social decay. The proletarian philosophy – 'the

7

smell of decay may sometimes be a sweet smell' – precedes redemption and rebirth out of collapse, even if the small middle-class people do not understand why their comfort and assumed rights of status have come to an end in the Depression years. Leo Gordon, the man dispossessed of his home, manages to achieve the measure of faith and hope which enable him to go on living.

Golden Boy (1937) balances equally the need for change in the system and the need to awaken personally from lifelessness. The final death has a logic of suicidal despair, the only way out of the trap. In 1940, *Night Music* implies a ruinous city society but the emphasis now lies with the disorientated, unawakened characters, the homeless in their loneliness. *Rocket to the Moon* (1938) shows loneliness relieved by understanding: Odets writes a typically modern play of anguish, which is neither comic nor tragic but simply an awakening to reality to things and people as they are. The hero is redeemed into some kind of life, but the social problems and the outcome of his awakening remain unsolved. Odets stresses the change that is to take place inside the self, but, at the same time, the social system is not condoned.

In *The Big Knife* (1949) the scene has shifted from the frustrated lower middle class in cities to the seat of the entertainment industry, Hollywood with its loot and its self-pitying, once idealistic, stars, their agents, and their producers. This world apart abstractly reflects the tensions of social hypocrisy eating away at responsibility and conscience. The hero commits suicide within the trap set by men who want to own other men; Odets backs his theme of loneliness with the theme of slavery.

By 1941 and *Clash by Night*, Odets's very contemporary dilemma was clear: he had to decide between explaining his actions by critical social analysis or allowing his characters to explain themselves. A sharp division would, of course, be a false simplification, but the choice of dramatic emphasis remained a problem if only because the public is never too keen to acknowledge the close relationships between personal life in crisis and a particular crisis in society. *Clash by Night* still seems to evoke the despairing mood of the forties, and, in the words of Harold Clurman, 'the sense of a working class that was basically homeless, racked with inner tension, ignorant, baffled, pathetic, and dangerously close to that breaking-point of "mystic" hysteria and violence that often provides the spiritual soil for the seeds of Fascism'. The play ran briefly after the shock of Pearl Harbor 'silenced everything that wasn't entertainment or a contribution to the war effort'.

After the war Odets returned to the stage with *The Country Girl* (1950), a backstage drama about an actor's return to theatre life under the inspiration of his wife and the encouragement of a young director. Odets has whittled the external effects on the personal action to a minimum. It is the wife who succeeds in regenerating her husband; the action is private. Then, in 1954, Odets re-created the Noah story as a contemporary allegory which got right away from the Bronx, Hollywood, and theatre worlds the playwright knew from personal experience. *The Flowering Peach* is an ambiguous abstraction carried towards inconclusion and compromise. The once gifted and active Noah is now tired and in search of comfort in a violent time. He tries to forget the world but God makes him act again in a foredoomed disaster. Japheth believes in the individual's will for good constructing its own decent fate rather than in a vengeful God. Noah has to knock him out to get him into the ark. Once there, Japheth insists on a man-controlled rudder, while Noah will not interfere with God's programme. The mother reconciles them to compromise between human idealism and determinist fate. Shem's capitalist acumen may be redeemed if it is used for the good of family and community, and it is with Shem that Noah finds the comfort of his old age. Odets has come some distance from the conclusion of *Waiting for Lefty* with its cry of 'Tear down the slaughterhouse of our old lives!' and its famous call to 'Strike!' reiterated from the stage and the audience in unambiguous unison.

But the core of his feeling and the movement of his plays, which always reach out endearingly to his audience, remains steady: the awakening from loneliness into companionship and love which redeems men and women from frustration and slavery into a measure of understanding and dignity. From being half dead Odets's heroes pass through a stage of lively awareness which either gives them life or intensifies their despair into death.

For all his technical competence, Odets has never, since *Lefty*, engaged in theatrical innovation. His simple plots are subordinated to a display of human living and feeling. He may once have said: 'All plays, just like all literature, are essentially propaganda ... my problem and business in the world is to present truth dramatically, appealingly, and entertainingly'; but it is those cries from the heart which an audience remembers: in *Lefty*, Edna shouting at her taxi-driver husband – 'Stand up and fight for the crying kids and wives – Goddammit! I'm tired of slavery and sleepless nights' – and Florence: 'Someone wants us to be lonely like that – crawling alone in the dark. Or they want us to be trapped' – and the stenographer: 'I'm saying the meek shall not inherit the earth!' In *Awake and Sing!*, the old grandfather says: 'In my day the propaganda was for God. Now it's for success', and the grandson cries out: 'Is every house lousy with lies and hate? ... We don't want life printed on dollar bills!' – and later: 'Let me die like a dog if I can't get more from life.' In *Golden Boy*, Joe says: 'I'm alone ... Nobody, nothing stands in my way'; and later: 'No more fighting, but where do we go?' In *Paradise Lost* the hero exclaims: 'There is more to life than this! ... Men are understanding the bitter black total of their lives. ... They become an ocean of understanding! No man fights alone.' And in *Rocket to the Moon*, the girl Cleo appeals to Ben: 'Don't let me be alone in the world.'

The Expressionist theatre of Kaiser, Toller, and Wedekind seems to lie behind the staging of *Waiting for Lefty*, but Odets did not develop into a theatre experimentalist, as O'Neill, for instance, did. Yet *Lefty* contains the seeds of his career. The fifty-minute action concerns the New York taxi-drivers' strike of 1934 and moves between stage and auditorium in order to draw the audience into the propaganda theme of the play: strike action. *Lefty* was played throughout the country:

it was the most directly agitational of all working-class revolutionary plays of this period. The immediate plot shows the efforts of a treacherous alliance between union leader and capitalist boss to break down the workers' resistance to conditions which deny the minimum required for a decent life. Odets carefully constructs his action between private and public life by making the stage the assumed platform of a union meeting, with the audience (and plants in the audience) as the workers themselves. Into this structure is built a series of scenes from the current lives of taxi-men, an unemployed actor, and a young doctor. The strike action is shown to involve the undermining of business control in all professions and trades, in the name of a decent life according to American national principles. Odets ironically uses 'pop' lyric phrases to suggest the betrayal of men's desires, shows how acting is part of business investment, how a man's public impotence seems like emasculation to his wife, how a man can be betrayed by nationalist propaganda into becoming a false soldier-hero, and how a young Jewish surgeon can so easily be replaced by the incompetent son of a Senator. Only a stenographer in one short scene suggests an overtly Communist way through the mess. *Lefty* is not a Party piece all through: it is a radical's bitter plea for concerted action against anti-life forces. Lefty never turns up to assume his heroic leadership; he is murdered by the forces of reaction. It is up to the audience to take over.

Already the speech in this short play shows Odets's remarkable ear for city language, from the colourful and cynical mass idiom to the bitter lyrical idiom of metropolitan hopelessness. He spoke out, and through his common touch uniquely reached a large audience who understood his presentation of common life. *Lefty* had a purpose. Clurman writes that the Group Theatre's actors 'seemed to hanker after barricade dramatics, a sense of being in the fight rather than on the side-lines'. They rehearsed *Lefty* in their spare time. At the first performance, on 5 January 1935, Clurman reports: 'deep laughter, hot assent, a kind of joyous fervour seem to sweep the audience toward the stage. The actors no longer performed; they were carried along as if by an exultancy of communication such as I had never witnessed in the theatre before. Audience and actors became one'. Even though the audience was not taxi-drivers, of course, at the end of the play they 'responded to the militant question from the stage: "Well, what's the answer?" with a spontaneous roar of "Strike! Strike!"' To Clurman it is 'the birth-cry of the thirties'. Odets had voiced a deep need. Other acting groups took up his play in 'some sixty towns which had never witnessed a theatrical performance'. For its Broadway production, Odets added his anti-Nazi play *Till the Day I Die*, in which a young German Communist resists his Nazi torturers: the theme is a united front against Fascism. This double bill played in thirty-two towns simultaneously, and arrests and bans only increased its significance. Odets was practically a 'wanted man' as far as reactionary power was concerned.

He consolidated his blazing reputation with Clurman's Group Theatre production of *Awake and Sing!*, his finest play. As in *Lefty* and *Golden Boy*, the young hero with ambition and pretensions, the man who wants to make up his mind and act, to choose his own integrity, only reaches a point of change. He has a future or he dies; both ways he is a survivor and a victim, not the anti-hero of the 1950s and 60s but the typical hero of the thirties. *Awake and Sing!*, originally called *I Got the Blues*, was Odets's major effort to share the life of workers and lower middle class, perhaps the single most important drive behind his work. After its opening on 10 February 1935 the Press was decently impressed. The Leftists handled it carefully, seeing in it signs of a renegade reaction in their pet dramatist. *New Masses* and the *Daily Worker* failed to understand that Odets's plays were not political analyses but structures of emotion in which he tried to articulate shared feeling for the classes which suffered and were dislocated most by the Depression, and tried, too, to present their embryonic yearning for a better life, however tentative. Odets has never been the facile optimist with an applied social or personal panacea.

Awake and Sing! lives through Odets's handling of Jewish Bronx idiom in a range from naturalistic dialogue to brief lyrical expressions of tension and communication. The centre is a middle-class family on the threshold of decay, still clinging to assumed rights of comfort and security which have long ceased to have meaning. Jacob, the atheistic, patriarchal, Jewist Marxist quotes the Old Testament, Isaiah's 'Awake and sing, ye that dwell in dust, and the earth shall cast out the dead.' His plea for living, however, is backed by a programme and doctrine from Marx. He hands on to his grandson, Ralph, not Communist dogma, but a healthful urge towards change and a hope for developed life. Ironically, he is old, bullied, and reduced to an occasional barbering job. The Berger family has an extraordinary vitality of characterization; the family likeness breaks through in their dialogues again and again. Odets is deeply involved in their tensions, where distinct hate and love become blurred into habitual unexamined relationships, as they do in all families. His vision of moral compromise working against men and women penetrates his obvious affection for the Bergers. Beneath the warmth lies terror. The wolf-pack image Sam uses in Act Two suggests a range of human brutality between anti-semitic Cossacks and post-Depression American society. It is the mother, ironically, who is the tyrant. Bessie's hardened wit against her own family, in the name of their own good, is her defence against a fear of poverty and indignity which she won't examine. Odets balances sympathy for her with antipathy for a woman given over to the money-success ethic, to verbal cruelty, lies, and betrayals. Even her nostalgia and sacrificial stance in Act Three hardly change the tough line Odets takes with her.

The family apartment is claustrophobic – the white poodle, Tootsie, has to be taken out *on the roof*. The set, then, is an image of the closed world of a family fighting for life in the midst of Depression by growing inwards until it comes as ironic relief when Jacob bursts out in Act Two with: 'This is a house? Marx said it – abolish such families.' Odets carefully constructs his plot around the image of a possible Paradise, the traditional yearning for 'a new world': Moe's dream of a summer orange grove, Jacob's record of Caruso's 'O

Paradiso', Marx's Utopia, and that airmail plane off to Boston which is as far away as Chehov's Moscow:

JACOB: Caruso stands on the ship and looks on a Utopia. You hear? Oh, paradise! Oh paradise on earth! Oh the blue sky, oh fragrant air!
MOE: Ask him does he see any oranges?

Against Bessie's money-success ideal Jacob awakens Ralph to a life of work, responsibility, and social solidarity, the real Paradise. But the ironies of the plot counterpoint Paradise. Bessie cannot see beyond her sacrificial life to a society where not personal but social and cooperative criteria will be the helpful ones, not her acceptance of class weakness but a mutual working for strength which will not burden the individual life.

Odets calls his play 'a struggle for life amid petty conditions'. He gives the centre to 'a sentimental idealist' who has 'no power to turn idealism into action'. Moe, the embittered veteran, lost *his* idealism in the war and now his desire goes into Hennie absolutely. But on Jacob's wall is a picture of Sacco and Vanzetti and just after the curtain rises Ralph says: 'All I want's a chance to get to first base!' Life to Moe in his post-war disillusion is 'all a racket' which destroys 'the possibilities of life', but when Jacob recalls the industrial slavery of the workers, Morty, the cynical, comics-reading, 32-degree Mason and businessman howls with delight. So the ironies build to the point where Bessie smashes 'O Paradiso'. Ralph picks up the fragments but they will never play that music again. Ralph must create another future but Odets brings down the curtain before he tells us exactly how. In American drama since the twenties there is a strong streak of Saroyan sentimentality; Odets plays this optimism against his 'teams together all over' type of progressiveness, with the consequence that *Awake and Sing!* withstands changing fashion as few other plays of the thirties can.

Golden Boy takes up the money-success theme, and this time it is Ralph's generation who have bought it, not the parents. As J. W. Krutch observes, Odets's play is somewhere between melodrama and greatness in his 'power to suggest the lonely agony of imprisoned souls in their own private hells of frustrated desire and inarticulate love'. Odets, more than any American playwright, has the power to involve his audience in the suffering of his people, in the political implications of their agonies, and in their awareness of transience. The language of *Golden Boy* is alternately urban Italian and Jewish lower middle class and the brash hard talk of the boxing, gambling, sports-page world. Once again Odets raises his characters out of these idioms in brief passages of revealing lyrical tenderness. They have a sporadic human energy which redeems vulgarity.

It takes little more than sixteen months to bring the twenty-one-year-old New York–Italian city-boy from home to alienating success and back home again, dead. This ambitious play presents unsolved technical problems because of its very condensed action. Considering how much symbolic weight the violin-playing must carry, Odets does little to demonstrate Joe's talent. We have to take it on trust that he is good, unless the off-stage playing dares to show as much. (Odets's stage directions say nothing of the kind.) The main active positive to money-success is Frank's unionism, but it is no more than sketched. And Odets never faces the fact that the urge to fight your way up in competitive society is not the same desire as the urge to be a prize-fighter. The allegory is not flawless. But the play is serious and effective at its personal level: the ironic initiation of a boy into the manhood world of gold, brilliantly embodied in the homosexual gunman and gambler who eventually owns Joe Bonaparte, Eddie Fuseli.

Joe's family, its music, the violin, and the patriarchal father, is home. Fuseli is homelessness, chill loneliness, empty-eyed selfishness. Between these poles lies the frustration of identity and love through an insane belief in absolute personal triumph and immediate freedom through fast cars, paired with a pathetic belief in 'some city where poverty's no shame – where music is no crime! – where there's no war in the streets – where a man is glad to be himself, to live and make his woman herself'.

The condition of loneliness in the success world is there before Joe joins it, in the mutual lonely need of Lorna and the fight manager Tom Moody. Ironically, it is Joe who destroys their future by his own love and his own need. His aggressive self-confidence in Act One, scene 1, becomes destructive and deathly as the play progresses. Even the violin his father wants to give him is imaged as a baby's coffin, and Joe remarks later: 'If music shot bullets I'd like it better – artists and people like that are freaks today.' Joe's coffin is the car in which he 'burns up the night' with Lorna.

Like *Awake and Sing!*, *Golden Boy* is a highly organized pattern of bitter ironies. Joe is like Ralph when he says in Act One: 'Tomorrow's my birthday! I change my life!' – but this self-sufficiency becomes the illusion of a lonely ego rather than a step towards community. He wants a car like Gary Cooper's, something more 'real' than violin-playing. His love for Lorna springs from need and he cuts out Tom Moody from his plans with little thought. Joe accuses Lorna of being 'half-dead' and draws her into his need; but Tom's attitude is healthier: 'What the hell's all this struggle to make a living for if not for a woman and a home?' Joe turns love into ambition and destruction: 'When a bullet sings through the air it has no past – only a future – like me! Nobody, nothing stands in my way.' His broken hand is the symbolic turning-point of his career, the centre of the play, in Act Two, scene 4: his impotent hardness is proudly complete. He has become a killer and does in fact kill the Chocolate Drop. Odets's dramatic logic is accurate and terrible: the boxing killing prefigures Joe's own death. Joe wants to go on to where there is no more fighting, but the only place left on earth where a man is 'unconnected' and doesn't have to think, is death.

Golden Boy concludes with Frank's barely indicated life of service, the real music which is 'the pleasure of acting as you think . . . at harmony with millions of others'. Joe's tragedy is waste, even if he did in fact also act as he thought.

The year was 1937 and the play ran for 248 performances in New York, was sold to films for $70,000, and, during the London season of 1938, was used as an example by Opposition M.P.s in the House of

Commons. But some critics already detected Odets's self-repetition as a playwright – 'physically glued to the material of his first plays'. The critic was Mary McCarthy in 1937. She attacked Odets's narrow invention, monotonous subject-matter, 'the half-ludicrous, half-touching cultural aspirations, the malapropisms, the inarticulate longing for a sunny life, that make up the Odets formula of frustration'. The themes of *Golden Boy* are 'vulgarized out of all nobility' and Odets uses 'a fortuitous, melodramatic device to dissolve the elements of his play and bring it to its falsely tragic curtain (which is itself an *exposé* of the play's "serious" pretentions'.

What truth there is in this swamping excoriation lies in the fact that Odets works in a strictly popular medium. He needs to tell his social themes in the broad terms of popular theatre which is not inclined to attend to moral radicalism in any other form. His problem is still being tried by Arthur Miller and Jack Gelber in America, and by Arnold Wesker, John Arden, and John Osborne in Britain in the 1960s.

By 1949 Odets was ready to tackle the social–sexual theme in a Hollywood setting. *The Big Knife* is essentially a criticism of a degenerating life of compromise between idealism and personal weakness. The play has some of the bite, as well as the common theme, of Nathanael West's *The Day of the Locust* (1939) and Norman Mailer's *The Deer Park* (1955). Odets's simple central conflicts are those of scenes in *Waiting for Lefty* between the stenographer and the actor and between Joe, the taximan, and his wife Edna, in which threats to love arise from a competitive society which uses power inhumanely.

The action unfolds in the Ibsen manner: a corrupting accident in the past gradually corrupts the present, challenges the hero, and leads to death. Its logical course begins when the curtain goes up on the deteriorating Charlie Castle. In Act Two his choice is made between thoroughgoing decay of character by becoming an instrument of power, and the chance of redemption into manhood through love and personal integrity. In Act Three, the right choice is made but the hero is too weak to face its consequences. The final suicide and cry for help are logical.

Odets cannot use here his familiar Bronx voices, and instead he sharply contrasts the slick artificial Hollywood idiom of temporizing, shop, and gossip with the speech of painfully emerging truth which drops inflated language and shows the nearly exhausted private life beneath mechanical surface activity. Early in Act One the core of Odets's criticism is given by Charlie: 'Don't you see them pushing man off the earth and putting the consumer in his place?' His agent warns him: 'Business and idealism don't mix . . . you expect too much of yourself.' The 'atmosphere of loneliness', as Odets calls it, develops from that exchange. The polar characters are Charlie's wife, Marion, and the film tycoon, Marcus Hoff. Hoff is one of Odets's finest characterizations through speech: his idiom carefully reveals, behind the sodden clichés of pseudo-patriarchal kindliness and fake self-pity, the hypocritical tyrant who wields the gold fountain pen, once used by MacArthur to sign the end of the Second World War, to continue the war of money-success against those reluctant to be bought.

Unsubtle blackmail brings *The Big Knife* to its climax, but the inner climax is Marion's challenge to Charlie: 'Your sin is living against your own nature. You're denatured.' Years of compromise with the idealism that once isolated him, but made him a man to be reckoned with, have reduced him to 'common trash – coarsened down to something I don't even recognize'. Like Edna in 1935, Marion in 1949 cannot stand a husband who yields to tyranny. But now the emphasis lies more with Charlie's personal failure to use his opportunities to resist power: 'your passion of the heart has become passion of the appetites.' Marion is asking for change in a man who is no longer youthful and Odets's theme of loneliness arises from the betrayal of a grown man's character, not a boy betrayed by social ethics. Charlie is advised by Hoff's man, Smiley Coy: 'Don't study life – get used to it' – meaning yield to Hoff. And the writer Teagle advises him: 'Stop torturing yourself, Charlie – don't resist!' – meaning since 'half-idealism is the peritonitis of the soul – America is full of it', the happy life is impossible in a world where idealism is an irritating flaw of character. But both Coy and Teagle are biased men. Charlie must make his own decision when it comes to condoning murder in order to retain his status.

He chooses right and is defeated by his own character, becoming the typical hero of the thirties rather than the post-war years – the American failure whose defeat exposes his fundamental decency in a bad time. But Charlie's decency is so thin and it is not clear that Odets fully realizes how unpleasing his weakness appears. His suicide is too quickly motivated perhaps, and at too few levels of character, to be the tragedy that Odets intended. But, as Clurman wrote of the play at the time, 'Clifford Odets, in success or failure, is a man grappling with essential moods and problems of our American life. Very few people in our theatre do.'

His heroes and their women are victims or survivors in a world where strikes have made essentially little difference. Lefty will never come now, but his ghost is still around in Odets's plays. The trouble with Charlie is that he has no knowledge of who Lefty could be, no real social background. He left Philadelphia, Odets's own birthplace, while still a boy, and Sunset Boulevard and Beverley Hills are no substitute for home or, to draw the parallel closer, the Group Theatre. Too casual references to Hamlet and Macbeth cannot disguise Charlie's deep commitment to the money-success world in which he is a tool and therefore a nonentity. Only the confronting idioms of Hollywood and the truth of personal life give *The Big Knife* strength from act to act. The talent of Charlie Castle is as undemonstrated as Joe's violin prowess. Odets is still uncertain where the blame for disorientated gifts going to rot really lies. But his plays have always dramatized his feeling for human uncertainty and distress in a common plight.

*

In writing this introduction I am indebted to *The Fervent Years: The Story of the Group Theatre and the Thirties* by Harold Clurman (New York, 1945), *American Drama Since 1918* by J. W. Krutch (New York, 1957), and *Sights and Spectacles 1937-1958* by Mary McCarthy (London, 1959).

GOLDEN BOY

FOR LUISE

SCENES

Act One

Act Two

Act Three

ACT ONE

SCENE I

The small Broadway office of Tom Moody, the fight manager.

[*The office is scantily furnished, contains desk, chairs, telephone, and couch. With* MOODY *at present is his girl,* LORNA MOON. *There is a certain quiet glitter about this girl, and if she is sometimes hard, it is more from necessity than choice. Her eyes often hold a soft, sad glance. Likewise, Moody's explosiveness covers a soft, boyish quality, and at the same time he possesses a certain vulnerable quality which women find very attractive.*

The time is eighteen months ago.

As the lights fade in, we catch these two at the height of one of their frequent fights.]

MOODY: Pack up your clothes and go! Go! Who the hell's stopping you?

LORNA: You mean it?

MOODY: You brought up the point yourself.

LORNA: No, I didn't!

MOODY: Didn't you say you had a good mind to leave me?

LORNA: No, I said –

MOODY: You said you were going to pack!

LORNA: I said I feel like a tramp and I don't like it. I want to get married, I want –

MOODY: Go home, Lorna, go home! I ain't got time to discuss it. Gimme some air. It's enough I got my wife on my neck.

LORNA: What does she say?

MOODY: Who?

LORNA: Your wife – your sweet goddam Monica!

MOODY: She wants five thousand dollars to give me the divorce. [LORNA *laughs.*] I don't see that it's funny.

LORNA: Look, Tom, this means as much to me as it does to you. If she's out of the way, we can get married. Otherwise I'm a tramp from Newark. I don't like the feeling.

MOODY: Lorna, for Pete's sake, use your noodle! When I get rid of Monica, we'll marry. Now, do I have to bang you on the nose to make you understand?

LORNA: Go to hell! . . . But come back tonight.

[MOODY'S *answer is to look at her, then smile, then walk to her. They kiss.*]

MOODY: If I had the money, I'd buy you something – I don't know what – a big ostrich feather! If Kaplan wins tonight, I'll take you dancing at the Park.

LORNA: He won't win.

MOODY: How do you know? *I* don't know – how do *you* know?

LORNA: Are you crazy? Do you think your Mr Kaplan can go ten rounds with the Baltimore Chocolate Drop?

MOODY: How do I know?

LORNA: It's the twentieth century, Tom – no more miracles. [MOODY'S *face turns worried.* LORNA *smiles.*] You know what I like about you – you take everything so serious.

MOODY: Who will if I don't? I've been off the gold standard for eight years. This used to be a gorgeous town. New York was hot with money. Kaplan gets four hundred bucks tonight. In the old days, that was nothing. Those were the days when I had Marty Welch, the heavyweight contender – Cy Webster who got himself killed in a big, red Stutz. In twenty-seven and eight you couldn't go to sleep – the town was crawling with attractions.

LORNA: My mother died in twenty-eight.

MOODY: I haven't had a break in years. 'Carry me back to old Virginny' – that's how I feel. There isn't much of a future.

[*Suddenly despondent,* MOODY *goes back to his desk.*]

LORNA: I was fooling.

MOODY: What about?

LORNA: Do you think I'd leave you?

MOODY: Why not? I'm an old man. What can I give you?

LORNA: A bang on the nose for a start. But what can I give you?

MOODY: A boy who can fight. Find me a good black boy and I'll show you a mint.

LORNA: Are good boys so hard to find?

MOODY: Honest to God, you make me sick to my stomach! What do you think I took a trip to Philadelphia? What do you think I went to Chicago? Wasn't I up in Boston for a week? You think good boys are laying around like popcorn? I'd even take a bantamweight, if I found one.

LORNA: How about a nice lady fighter with a beard – [*Preparing to leave*] Well, I'll see you tonight, Moody.

MOODY [*thoughtfully*]: I'd give me right eye for a good black boy.

LORNA: Let me have your right eye for a minute. [*She kisses his eye. MOODY begins to embrace her – she eludes his grasp.*] That's to keep you hot. But if the truth were known – 'yours till hell freezes over'.

MOODY: I need you, I need you, Lorna – I need you all the time. I'd like to give you everything you want. Push your mouth over ...

[*LORNA holds her face to his; he kisses her. Suddenly a youth is standing at the office door. LORNA sees him and breaks away.*]

BOY [*breathing quickly*]: Mr Moody ...

MOODY [*spinning around*]: Don't you knock when you come in an office?

BOY: Sometimes I knock, sometimes I don't.

MOODY: Say your piece and get the hell out!

BOY: I just ran over from the gym ...

MOODY: What gym?

BOY: Where Kaplan trains. He just broke his hand ... [*MOODY stiffens to attention.*] It's a fact.

MOODY [*grasping the phone*]: Is Tokio over there? My trainer?

BOY: He's looking after Kaplan.

[*MOODY begins to dial the phone but abruptly changes his mind and replaces the phone.*]

MOODY: You can put me in the bug-house right now. Moody is the name folks – step right up and wipe your shoes! Ah, that Kaplan! That phonus bolonus! [*He sits at his desk in despair.*] Now I have to call up Roxy Gottlieb and cancel the match. His club's in the red as it is.

BOY: I don't think it's necessary to cancel, Tom.

MOODY [*aware of the Boy for the first time*]: Oh, you don't? Who the hell are you? And who the hell are you to call me Tom? Are we acquainted?

BOY: I wrote you a couple of letters. I can do that stretch.

MOODY: What stretch?

BOY: Why don't you let me take Kaplan's place tonight?

MOODY [*sarcastically*]: Go slow and tell me again . . . what?

BOY [*coolly*]: I can take Kaplan's place. . . .

MOODY: You mean you want to fight the Baltimore Chocolate Drop? *You?* [*The* BOY *remains silent.* MOODY *comes out from behind his desk and stands face to face with the Boy. With sudden discovery*] You're cock-eyed too.

BOY [*quietly*]: Can't you fix it up with Roxy Gottlieb?

MOODY [*suddenly*]: Looka, kid, go home, kid, before I blame Kaplan's glass mitts on *you.* Then you won't like it, and I won't like it, and Miss Moon here, she won't like it.

BOY [*turning to Lorna*]: How do you do, Miss Moon. [LORNA *smiles at the Boy's quiet confidence.*] I need a good manager, Mr Moody. You used to be tops around town – everyone says so. I think you can develop me. I can fight. You don't know it, but I can fight. Kaplan's been through for years. He may be the best fighter in your stable, but he's a stumble-bum for the younger boys, growing up. Why don't you give me this chance, Tom?

MOODY: I don't want you calling me Tom! [*He glares at the Boy and then returns to the desk and telephone.*]

BOY: I'm waiting for your answer.

[MOODY'S *answer is an exasperated glance as he begins to dial the phone. The* BOY *half approaches the desk.*]

There are forty-three thousand minutes in a month – can't you give me five?

MOODY: I'll give you this phone in the head in a minute! Who are you? What the hell do you want? Where do you fight?

BOY [*with cool persistence*]: We ought to get together, Tom.

MOODY: I don't want you calling me Tom. You're brash, you're fresh, you're callow – and you're cock-eyed! In fact, you're an insult to my whole nature! Now get out!

> [MOODY *turns back to the phone and begins dialling again. The* BOY *stands there, poised on his toes, not sure of his next move. He turns and looks at* LORNA. *She nods her head and gives him a faint smile of encouragement. On phone*]

This is Tom Moody . . . is Tokio there? . . . [*He hangs up the phone and holds the instrument thoughtfully.*] Tokio's on his way over.

BOY: The Baltimore Chocolate Drop is not as good as you think he is.

> [MOODY *suddenly whirls around and holds the telephone high over his head in a threatening gesture. The* BOY *steps back lightly and continues.*]

I've studied his style for months; I've perfected the exact punch to quench his thirst. Did you ever watch closely? [*Acting it out*] He likes to pull your lead – he hesitates for a second – he pulls your lead – he slips his face away and then he's in. Suppose you catch that second when he hesitates – he's open for the punch!

MOODY [*sarcastically*]: And what do you do with his left hook?

BOY [*simply*]: Avoid it.

MOODY [*lowering the phone*]: Looka, you idiot, did you ever hear of Phil Mateo?

BOY: I heard of him.

MOODY: The Chocolate Drop marked him lousy in twelve minutes and ten seconds. Was Kid Peters within your ken? And did you ever hear of Eddie Newton? The Chocolate gave him the blues in two rounds. And Frisco Samuels and Mike Mason . . .

BOY: Did you ever hear of me?

MOODY [*sarcastically*]: No, who are you? I would honestly like to know – who are you?

BOY [*quietly*]: My name is Bonaparte.

[MOODY *howls with laughter, and even* LORNA, *sympathetic to the Boy, laughs. The* BOY *continues.*]

I don't think it's funny. . . .

MOODY: Didn't that name used to get you a little giggle in school? Tell the truth, Bonaparte. Didn't it?

BOY: Call me Joe.

MOODY [*laughing*]: And your eyes . . . Didn't they used to get a little giggle too?

JOE: You don't seem as intelligent as I thought you were.

LORNA [*to the laughing* MOODY, *seeing the Boy's pain*]: Stop it, Tom.

MOODY [*laughing*]: You can't blame me, Bonaparte. . . . I haven't laughed for years.

JOE: I don't like it . . . I don't want you to do it. [*Suddenly* JOE *grabs Moody by the coat lapels.* MOODY, *surprised, shakes him off. At the same time, a small, quiet man enters the office. He is* TOKIO, *Moody's trainer.*] I'm sorry I did that, Tom. We ought to be together, Tom – not apart.

MOODY: Tokio, did you send this kid here?

TOKIO: No.

MOODY: Take him out before I brain him! [*He storms back to his desk.*]

TOKIO [*after looking at the Boy*]: You hear about Kaplan?

MOODY: This idiot told me. It's the end of everything! I'm off my top with the whole thing! Kaplan was our meal-ticket. I'm up to the throat in scandal, blackmail, perjury, alimony, and all points west!

TOKIO [*turning to Joe*]: You oughta be ashamed to show your face in this office.

JOE: If Kaplan's mother fed him milk, he wouldn't have those brittle bones.

MOODY: ? ? ? ?

TOKIO [*to Moody*]: This is the boy who did it to Kaplan.

MOODY: ? ? ?

TOKIO: I went down for an apple and I come back and Kaplan's sparring with this kid – picked him up in the gym. The next thing I know, Kaplan's down on the floor with a busted mitt.

JOE [*modestly*]: I took it on the elbow.

MOODY: ! ! [*Silence finally.*]

LORNA: Where do you come from, Bonaparte?

JOE: Here.

LORNA: How old are you?

JOE: Twenty-one – tomorrow.

MOODY [*after a look at Lorna*]: Fight much?

JOE: Enough.

MOODY: Where?

JOE [*fabricating*]: Albany, Syracuse ...

LORNA: Does Roxy Gottlieb know you?

JOE: I never fought at his club.

MOODY [*harshly*]: Does he know you?

JOE: No.

[TOKIO *and* MOODY *look at each other. The phone rings.*]

MOODY [*on the phone*]: Hello ... 'What's this you hear?' ... You hear the truth, Roxy. ... He bust his mitt again. ... I can't help it if you got *fifty* judgements on your club. ... The same to you. ... Your mother too! [*Keeping his eyes on Bonaparte*] If you tie up your big flabby mouth for a minute, I'll give you some news. I'm in a position to do you a big favour. I got a replacement – *better* than Kaplan ... Bonaparte. ... No, Bon-a-parte. [*Holds hand over mouthpiece and asks Boy*] Is that crap?

JOE: No, that's my name.

MOODY [*back at phone*]: That's right, like in Napoleon. ... [*Looks the Boy over appraisingly*] One hundred and thirty.

JOE: Three.

MOODY: Hundred and thirty-three. Your customers'll eat him up. I'll bring him right over ... you can take my word – the kid's a cock-eyed wonder ... *your* mother too! [*He hangs up and turns around.* JOE *is the focus of all eyes.*] It's revenge on somebody – maybe God.

JOE [*quietly*]: I think you'll be surprised.

MOODY [*sadly*]: Do your worst, kid. I've been surprised by experts.

JOE: Don't worry, Tom.

MOODY: Call me Tom again and I'll break your neck!!

Quick fadeout

SCENE 2

Later that night.

[*The combination dining- and front room of the Bonaparte home. A round dining-room table, littered with newspapers, is lighted from directly above like a billiard table. Plaster busts of Mozart and Beethoven are on the sideboard. A cage of love birds at the other side of the room. Sitting at the table are two men: MR BONAPARTE, the father of Joe, and a Jewish friend, a MR CARP, who owns the local candy and stationery store.*

As the lights fade in, MR BONAPARTE turns his newspaper. MR CARP is slowly pouring beer from a bottle. He begins to sip it as SIGGIE, Mr Bonaparte's son-in-law, enters from the kitchen. He is barefooted, dressed in an undershirt, trousers and hung-down suspenders. He brings his own beer and glass, which he begins to fill with an expert's eye. In the silence, MR CARP takes a long, cool sip of beer combined with a murmur of relish.]

CARP [*finally*]: I don't take it easy. That's my trouble – If I could only learn to take it easy. . . .

SIGGIE: What do you call it now, what you're doing?

CARP: Say, it's after business hours.

SIGGIE: That's a business? A man who runs a candy store is an outcast of the world. Don't even sell *nickel* candies – *penny* candies!

CARP: And your taxicab business makes you higher in the social scale?

SIGGIE: So I'm an outcast too. Don't change the subject. Like my father-in-law here – he's always changing the subject when I get a little practical on him. [*Putting his beer on the table and scratching himself under the arms like a monkey*] You – I'm talking about you, Mr Bonaparte.

MR BONAPARTE [*suddenly shooting out two words*]: Ha ha! [*He then resumes his reading.*]

SIGGIE: Every time I talk money, he gives me that horse laugh. Suppose you bought me a cab – I could pay it off by the week.

MR BONAPARTE [*who talks with an Italian accent*]: I don't go in taxi-cab business.

SIGGIE: I am married to your daughter and when you do this little thing, you do it for her and me together. A cab in two shifts is a big source of profit. Joe takes the night shift. I'm a married man so you don't expect me to take the night shift.

[ANNA, *Siggie's wife, in a nightgown, pokes her head in at the door.*]

ANNA: Come to bed, Siggie. You'll wake up the whole neighbourhood. [ANNA *disappears.*]

SIGGIE: See? I'm a married man! You don't expect me to take the night shift.

MR BONAPARTE [*having heard this talk for months*]: No, Siggie . . . no.

SIGGIE: No, what?

MR BONAPARTE: No taxicab.

SIGGIE: Don't you wanna help your own family, foolish? After all, Joe's your own son – he's a man, no kid no more –

MR BONAPARTE: Tomorrow's twenty-one.

SIGGIE: If he don't work he'll turn into a real bum. Look how late he's staying out at night.

MR BONAPARTE: I don't expects for Joe to drive taxi.

SIGGIE: He's got to do something. He can drive like a fire engine. Why not?

MR BONAPARTE: He gonna do something.

SIGGIE: What? Play his violinsky in the backyards?

ANNA [*looking in at the door again*]: Come to bed, Siggie! Poppa, don't talk to him so he'll come to bed! [ANNA *disappears again.*]

SIGGIE [*annoyed*]: Women! Always buzzing around.

[MR BONAPARTE'S *only answer is to turn over the newspaper on the table before him.*]

CARP [*reflectively*]: Women ... the less we have to do with women the better. As Schopenhauer says, 'Much ado about nothing ... the comedy of reproduction.' [*He wags his head bitterly.*] Women ... !

SIGGIE: I'm hungry, but I ain't got the heart to go in the kitchen again. It reminds me of how my wife slaves for this family of crazy wops! A fine future for an intelligent woman!

MR BONAPARTE: She'sa your wife, but also my daughter. She'sa not so intelligent as you say. Also, *you* are not so intelligent!

SIGGIE: You can't insult me, I'm too ignorant!

[ANNA *now comes fully into the room. She is buxom, energetic, good-natured, and adenoidal.*]

ANNA: Poppa, why don't you let Siggie come to bed? Looka him, walking around barefooted!

MR BONAPARTE: I don't stop him ....

SIGGIE: Sure he stops me – he stops me every night. I'm worried. I don't sleep. It's my Jewish disposition. He don't wanna help me out, your old man. He wants me to drive a company cab and submit to the brutalities of the foremen all my life. I could be in a healthy little enterprise for myself, but your old man don't wanna help me out.

ANNA: Why don't you buy Siggie a cab, Poppa? You got the cash.

SIGGIE: Buy it for Siggie and Joe.

ANNA: For Siggie and Joe – it don't have to be a new one.

SIGGIE [*after giving his wife a stabbing glance*]: Sure, even an old one – the way they recondition them now-a-days –

MR BONAPARTE: Children, gone to bed.

SIGGIE: Don't tell a lie – how much you got in the bank?

MR BONAPARTE [*with a smile*]: Millions.

SIGGIE: Four thousand?

34

MR BONAPARTE: No.

SIGGIE: Three? [MR BONAPARTE *shakes his head.*] Three? . . .

ANNA: What's your business how much he's got?

SIGGIE: Shut up, Duchess! Am I asking for my health? If I wanna take you out of the kitchen, is that the gratitude I get? You and your father, you get my goat! I'm sore!

ANNA: Come to bed, Siggie.

SIGGIE: 'Come to bed, come to bed!' What the hell's so special in bed. [ANNA'S *answer is a warm prolonged giggle.*] It's a conspiracy around here to put me to bed. I'm warning one thing: if matters go from worse to worse, don't ever expect me to support this family, I'm warning!

MR BONAPARTE [*smiling kindly*]: We have-a receive the warning. We are in a conspiracy against you – gone to bed.

[*He turns back to his newspaper,* SIGGIE *sees he has lost again and now turns on his wife.*]

SIGGIE: Who asked you to stick in your two cents about second-hand cabs? As long as I'm not gonna get it, I'll tell you what I want – a first-class job, fresh from the factory.

[*He suddenly swats her on the head with a rolled-up newspaper. She hits him back. He returns her blow.*]

ANNA: Don't be so free with your hands! [*He hits her again. She hits him back.*] You got some nerve, Siggie!

SIGGIE [*hitting her again*]: The next time I'll break your neck – I'm super-disgusted with you!

MR BONAPARTE [*standing up*]: Stop this . . .

SIGGIE [*turning to him*]: And with you, I'm super-finished! [*Turning back to his wife*] Sit out here with this Unholy Alliance – I'll sleep alone tonight.

[*He starts for the door.* MR BONAPARTE *puts his arm around* ANNA *who begins to sob.*]

MR BONAPARTE: Hit your wife in private, not in public!

CARP: A man hits his wife and it is the first step to fascism!

SIGGIE [*to Carp*]: What are you talking about, my little prince! I love

35

my wife. You don't stop talking how you hate yours. [*Now to Mr Bonaparte*] And as for you, don't make believe you care! – Do I have to fall on my knees to you otherwise? We wanna raise a family – it's a normal instinct. Take your arm off her.

ANNA [*suddenly moving over to* SIGGIE]: That's right, poppa. He can hit me any time he likes.

SIGGIE [*his arm around her*]: And we don't want you interfering in our affairs unless you do it the right way!

ANNA: That's right, poppa – you mind your g.d. business!

[MR BONAPARTE, *repressing a smile, slowly sits.*]

SIGGIE: In the bed, Duchess.

ANNA [*with a giggle*]: Good night.

MR BONAPARTE *and* MR CARP: Good night.

[*She exits. After a belligerent look at the pair at the table,* SIGGIE *follows her.*]

MR BONAPARTE [*bursting into hushed laughter*]: There'sa olda remark – never interfere in the laws of nature and you gonna be happy. Love! Ha ha!

CARP [*gloomily*]: Happy? A famous man remarked in the last century, 'Pleasure is negative.'

MR BONAPARTE: I feela good. Like-a to have some music! Hey, where'sa my boy Joe? [*Looks at his watch; is surprised.*] One o'clock ... don't come home yet. Hey, he make-a me worry!

CARP: You think you got worries? Wait, you're a young man yet. You got a son, Joe. He practised on his fiddle for ten years? He won a gold medal, the best in the city? They gave him a scholarship in the Erickson Institute? Tomorrow he's twenty-one, yeah?

MR BONAPARTE [*emphatically*]: Yeah!

CARP [*leaning forward and dramatically making his point*]: Suppose a war comes? Before you know it, he's in the army!

MR BONAPARTE: Naw, naw! Whata you say! Naw!

CARP [*wagging his head in imitation*]: Look in the papers! On every side the clouds of war –

MR BONAPARTE: My Joe gotta biga talent. Yesterday I buy-a him

36

present! [*With a dramatic flourish he brings a violin case out of the bottom part of the sideboard.*]

CARP [*as the case is opened*]: It looks like a coffin for a baby.

MR BONAPARTE [*looking down at the violin in its case*]: His teacher help me to picka him.

CARP [*the connoisseur*]: Fine, fine – beautiful, fine! A cultural thing!

MR BONAPARTE [*touching it fondly*]: The mosta golden present for his birthday which I give him tonight.

CARP: How much, if I'm not getting too personal, did such a violin cost you?

MR BONAPARTE: Twelve hundred dollars.

CARP [*shocked*]: What?

MR BONAPARTE: You're surprised of me? Well, I waita for this moment many years.

CARP [*sitting*]: Ask yourself a pertinent remark: could a boy make a living playing this instrument in our competitive civilization today?

MR BONAPARTE: Why? Don't expect for Joe to be a millionaire. He don't need it, to be millionaire. A good life'sa possible –

CARP: For men like us, yes. But nowadays is it possible for a young man to give himself to the Muses? Could the Muses put bread and butter on the table?

MR BONAPARTE: No millionaire is necessary. Joe love music. Music is the great cheer-up in the language of all countries. I learn that from Joe.

[CARP *sighs as* MR BONAPARTE *replaces the violin in the buffet.*]

CARP: But in the end, as Schopenhauer says, what's the use to try something? For every wish we get, ten remains unsatisfied. Death is playing with us as a cat and her mouse!

MR BONAPARTE: You make-a me laugh, Mr Carp. You say life'sa bad. No, life'sa good. Siggie and Anna fight – good! They love – good! You say life'sa bad ... well, is pleasure for you to say so. No? The streets, winter a' summer – trees, cats – I love-a them all. The gooda boys and girls, they who sing and whistle – [*Bursts into a moment of gay whistling*] – very good! The eating and sleeping, drinking wine – very good! I gone around on my wagon and talk to many people – nice! Howa you like the big buildings of the city?

CARP: Buildings? And suppose it falls? A house fell down last week on Staten Island!

MR BONAPARTE: Ha ha, you make me laugh, ha ha!

[*Now enters* FRANK BONAPARTE, *oldest son of the family, simple, intelligent, observant.*]

MR BONAPARTE: Hello, Frank.

FRANK: Hello, poppa . . . Mr Carp . . .

CARP [*nodding*]: What's new in the world?

FRANK [*dropping newspapers to the table, but keeping one for himself*]: Read 'em and weep. March first tomorrow – spring on the way. Flowers soon budding, birds twittering – south wind . . . Cannons, bombs, and airplane raids! Where's Joe? Did you give him the fiddle yet?

MR BONAPARTE: No, not in yet. Siggie and Anna sleep. Hungry?

FRANK [*beginning to undress – putting his coat on the back of a chair*]: No, I'm tired. I'll see you in the morning, before I leave.

CARP: Going away again?

FRANK: South. Tex-tiles. There's hell down there in tex-tiles. [*He sits on the other side of the room and looks at a paper.*]

CARP: I don't begin to understand it – tex-tiles! What's it his business if the workers in tex-tiles don't make good wages!

MR BONAPARTE: Frank, he fight-a for eat, for good life. Why not!

CARP: Foolish!

MR BONAPARTE: What ever you got ina your nature to do isa not foolish!

CARP [*flipping over the newspaper*]: For instance – look: playing baseball isn't foolish?

MR BONAPARTE: No, if you like-a to do.

CARP: Look! Four or five pages – baseball – tennisball – it gives you an idea what a civilization! You ever seen a baseball game?

MR BONAPARTE: No.

38

CARP [*wagging his head*]: Hit a ball, catch a ball . . . believe me, my friend – nonsense!

FRANK: Poppa, where did you say Joe was?

MR BONAPARTE: Don't know –

FRANK: Poppa, you better brace yourself in your chair!

MR BONAPARTE: What?

[FRANK *places the paper before Mr Bonaparte. He reads aloud.*]

FRANK: Looka this, Joe's had a fight. 'Flash: Chocolate Drop fails to K.O. new cock-eyed wonder.' Take a look at the picture.

CARP: What?

MR BONAPARTE: What?

FRANK: It's my little brother, Joey, or I don't know a scab from a picket!

MR BONAPARTE: Had a fight? That is foolish – not possible.

FRANK [*pointing with his finger*]: There's his name – Bonaparte.

MR BONAPARTE [*puzzled*]: Musta be some other boy.

[FRANK *suddenly flips over the newspaper. The others immediately see the reason:* JOE *stands in the entrance, in the shadows.*]

JOE [*in the shadows*]: Gee, you're up late . . .

MR BONAPARTE: We waita for you.

[JOE *slowly moves into the light. His face is bruised and over one eye is a piece of adhesive tape.*]

JOE [*seeing their looks*]: I had a fight – a boy in the park –

MR BONAPARTE: He hit you?

JOE: I hit him.

MR BONAPARTE: You hurt?

JOE: No.

[MR BONAPARTE *casts a furtive look in the direction of the other men.*]

MR BONAPARTE: Whata you fight him for?

JOE: Didn't like what he said to me.

MR BONAPARTE: What he said?

JOE [*evasively*]: It's a long story and I'm tired.

MR BONAPARTE [*trying to break a pause of embarrassment*]: I was say to Mr Carp tomorrow is your birthday. How you like to be so old?

JOE: I forgot about that! I mean I forgot for the last few hours. Where do you think I was? Do you want the truth?

FRANK: Truth is cheap. We bought it for two cents.

[*He turns over the paper and shows Joe his own face.* JOE *looks at the picture, likes it. General silence.*]

JOE [*finally, belligerently*]: Well, what are you going to do about it?

MR BONAPARTE [*still puzzled*]: Abouta what?

JOE [*challengingly*]: Tomorrow's my birthday!

FRANK: What's that got to do with being a gladiator?

JOE [*turning to Frank, with sudden vehemence*]: Mind your business! You don't know me – I see you once a year; what do you know about me?

FRANK [*smiling*]: You're a dumb kid!

MR BONAPARTE [*starting to his feet*]: Hey, waita one-a minute. What'sa for this excite-a-ment?

JOE [*hotly*]: I don't want to be criticized! Nobody takes me serious here! I want to do what I want. I proved it tonight I'm good – I went out to earn some money and I earned! I had a professional fight tonight – maybe I'll have some more.

CARP: You honest to God had a fight?

JOE [*glaring at Carp*]: Why not?

FRANK [*to Joe*]: No one's criticizin'.

MR BONAPARTE: That's right.

JOE [*half-sheepishly*]: I don't know why I got so sore . . .

FRANK: You're expecting opposition all the time –

MR BONAPARTE: Sit down, Joe – resta you'self.

JOE: Don't want to sit. Every birthday I ever had I sat around. Now'sa time for standing. Poppa, I have to tell you – I don't like myself, past, present, and future. Do you know there are men who have wonderful things from life? Do you think they're better than me? Do you think I like this feeling of no possessions? Of learning about the world from Carp's encyclopedia? Frank don't know what it means – he travels around, sees the world! [*Turning to Frank*]

You don't know what it means to sit around here and watch the months go ticking by! Do you think that's a life for a boy my age? Tomorrow's my birthday! I change my life!

MR BONAPARTE: Justa like that?

JOE: Just like that!

FRANK: And what do you do with music?

JOE: Who says I'm married to music? I take a vacation – the notes won't run away!

FRANK: You're a mysterious kid. Where did you learn the fighting game?

JOE: These past two years, all over the city – in the gyms –

MR BONAPARTE: Hey, Joe, you sounda like crazy! You no gotta nature for fight. You're musician. Whata you say, heh? Whata you do?

JOE: Let's call it a day.

MR BONAPARTE: Isa no true what I say? –

JOE: That's all for tonight. [*His lips tightened, he abruptly exits.*]

MR BONAPARTE [*calling after him*]: Take a gooda sleep, Joe.

FRANK [*smiling*]: It looks like the gold bug has visited our house.

CARP [*sadly*]: Fortunes! I used to hear it in my youth – the streets of America is paved with gold. Say, you forgot to give him the present.

MR BONAPARTE [*slowly, puzzled*]: I don'ta know . . . he say he gonna fight. . . .

Slow fadeout

SCENE 3

Two months later; Moody's office as seen before.

[MOODY *is pacing back and forth in one of his fuming moods. Those present include* LORNA, *stretched out on the couch, blowing cigarette smoke into the air;* TOKIO *sitting quietly on the window sill; and*

ROXY GOTTLIEB, *comfortably spread out in the desk chair, wearing a big white panama hat which he seldom removes.*]

ROXY: They don't like him. They seen him in five fights already. He's a clever boy, that Bonaparte, and speedy – but he's first-class lousy in the shipping department! I bought a piece of him, so I got a right to say it: a mosquito gives out better! Did you read what he wrote in his column, that Drake? He writes he's a regular 'brain trust'.

LORNA: What's wrong with that?

ROXY: I'll tell you in a capsule: the people who'll pay to watch a 'brain trust' you could fit in a telephone booth! Roxy Gottlieb is telling you!

MOODY: Roxy's right. Joe pulls his punches. Two months already and he don't throw his hands right and he don't throw them enough.

LORNA: Tom, what do you want the boy to do? You surely know by now he's not a slugger. His main asset is his science – he's a student.

ROXY [*loftily*]: Excuse me, Miss Moon. In the prizefight ring the cash customer don't look for stoodents. Einstein lives in a college – a wonderful man in *his* line! Also, while I think of it, a woman's place is in the hay, not in the office!

MOODY [*indignantly*]: Where do you come off to make a remark like that?

LORNA [*standing up*]: At the moment a woman's place is in the bar – see you later.

[*She looks at the others with a peculiar smile and exits.* MOODY *stares at Roxy who realizes he has said the wrong thing.*]

MOODY: I'm worried about that boy!

TOKIO: I'd trust him Tom. Joe knows his own needs, as he says. Don't ask him to change his style. A style is best when it's individual, when it comes out of the inner personality and the lay of the muscles and the set of the bones. That boy stands a chance to make the best lightweight since Benny Simon.

ROXY: On *your* nose!

TOKIO: He's got one of the best defences I ever seen. And speedy as the wind.

MOODY: But he won't fight!

ROXY: A momma doll gives out better!

TOKIO: He's a peculiar duck – I want him thinking he's the best thing in shoe leather.

MOODY: He thinks so now.

TOKIO: I don't like to contradict you, Tom, but he don't. It's seventy-five-per-cent front. If you want the goods delivered you have to treat him delicate, gentle – like a girl.

ROXY: Like a girl? Why didn't you say so before?

MOODY: No, Roxy, not you – you just treat him like a human being.

TOKIO: I think we can begin the build-up now.

MOODY: A road tour?

TOKIO: I'd like to take him around the Middle West, about fifteen bouts.

ROXY [*answering a look from* MOODY]: I didn't say no. But will he cooperate?

TOKIO: As soon as I find the password.

MOODY: What's the password to make this kid go in and slug – that's the problem. [*There is a knock at the door.* MOODY *calls*] Yes?
   [*The door opens and* MR BONAPARTE *stands there hesitantly.*]

MR BONAPARTE [*timidly*]: My name is Joe Bonaparte's father. I come-a to see my son's new friends.

MOODY [*expansively*]: Come in, sit down, Mr Bonaparte.

ROXY [*sitting comfortably*]: Take a seat.

MR BONAPARTE: Am I interrupt?

MOODY: Not at all.

ROXY: What's the matter with your boy?

TOKIO [*to Mr Bonaparte*]: This is Mr Moody and Mr Gottlieb.

MR BONAPARTE [*sitting*]: Good afternoon.

MOODY: We were just discussing your son.

MR BONAPARTE: I please to hear. I like find out froma you how's this boxer business for Joe. Whata good in it for him.

MOODY: Your Joe's a very clever fighter.

ROXY: Can you take it? We want to make your boy famous – a millionaire, but he won't let us – won't cooperate. How do you like it?

MR BONAPARTE: Why? Whatta he do?

ROXY [going over and facing the old man in a lecturing position]: I'll ask you. What does he do? What does he do that's right? Nothing! We offer him on a gold platter! Wine, women, and song, to make a figure of speech. We offer him magnitudes! . . .

MR BONAPARTE [waiting]: Yes –?

MOODY: But he won't fight.

MR BONAPARTE [puzzled]: He'sa fighta for you, no?

ROXY: You're right – no! Your boy's got unexplored possibilities – unexplored! But you can't make a purse out of somebody's ear.

MOODY [trying to counteract Roxy's volubility]: My colleague is trying to say that Joe keeps holding back in the ring.

MR BONAPARTE: Holda back?

TOKIO: He nurses his self –

MOODY: He keeps holding back –

TOKIO: His defence is brilliant –

MOODY: Gorgeous – !

ROXY: But where's the offence? You take but you can't give. Figure it out – where would you be in a traffic jam? You know how to reverse – but to shift in second or high? – nothing!

MR BONAPARTE [quietly to Roxy]: Hey, you talka too much – nobody contradicta you.

ROXY [after a momentary setback]: 'Everybody'sa contradicta me!' Even you, and I never met you before. [With a reproachful glance he retires to the desk where he sits and sulks.]

MR BONAPARTE [singling out Tokio as a man to whom he can speak]: Who are you?

TOKIO: Your son's trainer. . . .

MR BONAPARTE: You interest to helpa my boy?

TOKIO [*respectfully*]: Very much. . . .

MR BONAPARTE: Me too. Maybe not so as plan by these-a gentleman here. I don't say price fight'sa no good for Joe. Joe like-a to be fame, not feel ashame. . . .

TOKIO: Is Joe afraid of his hands?

MR BONAPARTE: I don't know. You tella me what'sa what . . . I don't know price fight. His hand coulda get hurt?

MOODY: Every fighter hurts his hands. Sometimes they break –

TOKIO: They heal up in no time.

ROXY [*flaring out*]: What's so special about hands? I suppose your kid plays piano!

MR BONAPARTE: Coulda get hurt! Coulda break!

ROXY: So what?

MR BONAPARTE [*up on his feet*]: Hey, you! I don't like-a you! You no interest in my boy! [*Proudly*] My boy'sa besta violin in New York!

MOODY [*suddenly sickened*]: What . . .?

MR BONAPARTE: Yes, play the violin!

MOODY: That's it! . . .

ROXY [*anguished by this stupidity*]: If I had hair I'd tear it out! Five hundred fiddlers stand on Broadway and 48th Street, on the corner, every day, rain or shine, hot or cold. And your boy dares –! [*Turning to Moody*] How do you like it? [*He waves his hands in despair and retires to the desk, where he sits in fuming disgusted silence.*]

MOODY [*repressing a feeling of triumph*]: Your boy's afraid of his hands because he fiddles?

MR BONAPARTE: Yes, musta be!

TOKIO: Why did you come and tell us this?

MR BONAPARTE: Because I like-a to help my boy. I like-a for him to try himself out. Maybe thisa better business for him. Maybe not. He mus' try to find out, to see whata he want . . . I don't know. Don't help Joe to tell him I come here. Don't say it. [*He slowly walks to the door.*]

MOODY: That means you won't stand in his way?

MR BONAPARTE: My boy coulda break his hand? Gentleman, I'ma not so happy as you ... no! [*He slowly exits.*]

MOODY [*joyously*]: I'm beginning to see the light! Joe's mind ain't made up that the fist is mightier than the fiddle.

ROXY [*bouncing up and down*]: I'll make up his mind. For the money that's involved I'd make Niagara Falls turn around and go back to Canada.

TOKIO: Don't try to bully him into anything.

ROXY: In Roxy Gottlieb he met his match.

MOODY [*explosively*]: What the hell's the matter with you, Roxy! Sit down a minute! [ROXY *sits.*] As I see it, the job is to handle him gently, to make him see how much we prize him – to kill his doubts with goodness.

ROXY: I got it: the password is honey! ...

MOODY: Right! The Middle West tour is on! Tokio goes along to build up a real offensive. I take care of the newspapers here. Chris', I thought it was something serious! I'm getting to feel like 1928 again. Call it intuition: I feel like the Resurrection. [*He gets up and begins to stroll about.*] Once we're out of the tunnel, with thirty bouts behind us –

ROXY: If you hear a noise, it's my mouth watering –

[*The telephone rings.* MOODY *answers.*]

MOODY: Hello? ... Yeah ... I think he'll win – [*Hangs up.*] Who do you think that was? [*Imitating*] 'Fuseli is speaking.' Eddie Fuseli!

ROXY: Fuseli! What's he want?

MOODY: Will Joe win against Vincenti Tuesday. Tokio, from now on it's your job.

TOKIO: I got faith in the boy.

MOODY [*to* ROXY]: I have to ask one thing – when Joe comes over from the gym let me do the talking.

TOKIO: And don't mention music!

[LORNA *enters.*]

LORNA: Shh! Here's Joe.

[JOE BONAPARTE *enters the office. Immediately* MOODY *and* ROXY *put on their softest kid gloves. Their methods of salesmanship will shortly become so apparent that both* JOE *and* LORNA *become suspicious.*]

MOODY [*slowly circling around*]: Glad to see you, Joe. Joe, you remember in reference to what we were speaking about yesterday? Well ... we had several friends on the long-distance phone. We're booking fifteen out of town bouts for you. Tough ones, too.

ROXY: Tonight I'm calling my Chicago connexions.

MOODY: We talked it over with Tokio and he says – well, tell him what you said, Tokio – tell him the truth.

TOKIO: I think you got a wonderful future.

MOODY [*to Tokio*]: Name the names, Tokio.

TOKIO: Well, I said Benny Simon – as good as Simon, I said.

MOODY: Tokio's gonna work with you – help you develop a right –

ROXY: And a left! What's a right without a left?

MOODY: Tokio thinks that when he brings you back you'll be a contender for Number One.

JOE [*a little defensively*]: Really? ...

MOODY: But *you* have to help *us* help *you*.

ROXY: Could Webster say it better?

MOODY [*softly singing a siren song, his arms around Joe's shoulder*]: This job needs gorgeous concentration. All your time and thoughts. No side-lines, no side-interests –

JOE [*defensively*]: I don't go out with girls.

MOODY: You're in the fighting game. It's like being a priest – your work comes first. What would you rather do than fight?

JOE [*defensively*]: I don't know what you mean.

MOODY [*carefully picking his words*]: Some boys, for instance, like to save their looks. They'd practically throw the fight to keep their nose intact.

JOE [*smiling wryly*]: My looks don't interest me.

[LORNA *is listening with rapt attention.*]

MOODY [*still singing the siren song*]: Then what's holding you back,

Joe? You can tell me, Joe. We've set up housekeeping together, Joe, and I want you to tell me if you can't cook a steak – it don't matter. We're married anyway. . . .

JOE [*uneasily*]: Who's being put to bed?

MOODY: What do you mean?

JOE: I don't like this seduction scene. [*To Tokio*] What are they after?

TOKIO: They think you're afraid of your hands.

MOODY: Are you?

JOE: Half . . .

TOKIO: Why?

ROXY [*bouncing up*]: Tell the truth!

JOE: What truth?

MOODY [*holding back Roxy with a look*]: Are you afraid your hands'll bust, Joe? [JOE *remains silent.*] What's a busted hand to a *fighter*? You can't go in and do your best if you're scared of your mitts . . . can you? You tell me. . . .

JOE: No. . . .

MOODY: Whyn't you give up outside ideas, Joe?

ROXY [*suddenly, in a loud voice to Tokio*]: You shoulda seen that bunch of musicians on 48th Street before. Fiddlers, drummers, cornetists – not a dime in a car-load. Bums in the park! Oh, excuse me, Tom, I was just telling Tokio –

[JOE *is now aware that the others know of the violin. Now he is completely closed to them.* MOODY *sees this. He says to Roxy:*]

MOODY [*wrathfully*]: What would you like to say, my feathered friend?

ROXY [*simulating bewilderment*]: What's the matter? What happened? [*Receiving no answer, he looks around several times and adds, with a shrug*] I think I'll run across the street and pick up an eight-cylinder lunch.

MOODY: Sprinkle it with arsenic. Do that for me, for me, sweet-heart!

ROXY [*hurt*]: That's a fine remark from a friend. [*He haughtily exits.*]

JOE: What do you want, Mr Moody?

MOODY: At the moment, nothing. I'm puffed out. See you tomorrow over the gym.

JOE: Maybe I won't be there. I might give up fighting as a bad job. I'm not over-convinced it's what I want. I can do other things. . . .

TOKIO: I'll see you tomorrow at the gym, Joe.

[JOE *looks at both the men, says nothing, exits.*]

That Mr Gottlieb is a case. See you later.

MOODY [*not looking up*]: Okay.

[TOKIO *exits.* LORNA *and* MOODY *are alone. She blows cigarette smoke to the ceiling.* MOODY *puts his feet up on the desk and leans back wearily. Snorting through his nostrils*] The password is honey!

LORNA: What was that all about?

[*The telephone rings.*]

MOODY [*of the ringing bell*]: If that's for me, tear it up. I ain't in, not even for God.

LORNA [*answering*]: Hello? . . . [*Putting her hand on the mouthpiece*] It's Mrs God – your wife.

[MOODY *makes a grimace of distaste but picks up the phone and puts on a sweet voice.*]

MOODY: Yes, Monica darling. . . . Yeah . . . you and your support. You're gonna fifty-buck me to death! . . . Monica, if I had fifty bucks I'd buy myself a big juicy coffin – what? – so throw me in jail. [*He hangs up the phone.*] Bitch! That'll be time number three. She means it too.

LORNA: What was that scene with Bonaparte?

MOODY: Sweetheart, the jig is up! Believe it or not, Bonaparte's a violinist. Maybe he was on the radio. I don't know what the hell he was. His old man came here and told us. His mitts are on his mind. You can't do a thing with a nut like that.

LORNA: Won't he give up the violin?

MOODY: You heard him stalling. This is the end, Lorna. It's our last

49

chance for a decent life, for getting married – we have to make that kid fight! He's *more* than a meal ticket – he's everything we want and need from life!

[LORNA *goes over and slaps him on the back.*]

LORNA: Pick up your chin, little man.

MOODY: Don't Brisbane me, Lorna. I'm licked. I'm tired. Find me a mouse-hole to crawl in. . . .

LORNA: Why don't you ask me when you want something? You got the brains of a flea. Do you want Bonaparte to fight?

MOODY: Do I wanna see tomorrow?

LORNA: I'll make him fight.

MOODY: How?

LORNA: How? . . . I'm 'a tramp from Newark', Tom. . . . I know a dozen ways. . . .

Slow fadeout

SCENE 4

A few nights later.

[JOE *and* LORNA *sit on a bench in the park. It is night. There is carousel music in the distance. Cars ride by in front of the boy and girl in the late spring night. Out of sight a traffic light changes from red to green and back again throughout the scene and casts its colours on the faces of the boy and girl.*]

LORNA: Success and fame! Or just a lousy living. You're lucky you won't have to worry about these things. . . .

JOE: Won't I?

LORNA: Unless Tom Moody's a liar.

JOE: You like him, don't you?

LORNA [*after a pause*]: I like him.

JOE: I like how you dress. The girls look nice in the summer time.

Did you ever stand at the Fifth Avenue Library and watch those girls go by?

LORNA: No, I never did. [*Switching the subject*] That's the carousel, that music. Did you ever ride on one of those?

JOE: That's for kids.

LORNA: Weren't you ever a kid, for God's sake?

JOE: Not a happy kid.

LORNA: Why?

JOE: Well, I always felt different. Even my name was special – Bonaparte – and my eyes ...

LORNA: I wouldn't have taken that too serious ...

[*There is a silent pause. JOE looks straight ahead.*]

JOE: Gee, all those cars ...

LORNA: Lots of horses trot around here. The rich know how to live. You'll be rich ...

JOE: My brother Frank is an organizer for the C.I.O.

LORNA: What's that?

JOE: If you worked in a factory you'd know. Did you ever work?

LORNA [*with a smile*]: No, when I came out of the cocoon I was a butterfly and butterflies don't work.

JOE: All those cars ... whizz, whizz. [*Now turning less casual*] Where's Mr Moody tonight?

LORNA: He goes up to see his kid on Tuesday nights. It's a sick kid, a girl. His wife leaves it at her mother's house.

JOE: That leaves you free, don't it?

LORNA: What are you hinting at?

JOE: I'm thinking about you and Mr Moody.

LORNA: Why think about it? I don't. Why should you?

JOE: If you belonged to me I wouldn't think about it.

LORNA: Haven't you got a girl?

JOE: No.

LORNA: Why not?

JOE [*evasively*]: Oh ...

LORNA: Tokio says you're going far in the fighting game.

JOE: Music means more to me. May I tell you something?

LORNA: Of course.

JOE: If you laugh I'll never speak to you again.

LORNA: I'm not the laughing type.

JOE: With music I'm never alone when I'm alone – Playing music ... that's like saying, 'I am man. I belong here. How do you do, World – good evening!' When I play music nothing is closed to me. I'm not afraid of people and what they say. There's no war in music. It's not like the streets. Does this sound funny?

LORNA: No.

JOE: But when you leave your room ... down in the street ... it's war! Music can't help me there. Understand?

LORNA: Yes.

JOE: People have hurt my feelings for years. I never forget. You can't get even with people by playing the fiddle. If music shot bullets I'd like it better – artists and people like that are freaks today. The world moves fast and they sit around like forgotten dopes.

LORNA: You're loaded with fireworks. Why don't you fight?

JOE: You have to be what you are –!

LORNA: Fight! see what happens –

JOE: Or end up in the bughouse!

LORNA: God's teeth! Who says you have to be one thing?

JOE: My nature isn't fighting!

LORNA: Don't Tokio know what he's talking about? Don't Tom? Joe, listen: be a fighter! Show the world! If you made your fame and fortune – and you can – you'd be anything you want. Do it! Bang your way to the lightweight crown. Get a bank account. Hire a great doctor with a beard – get your eyes fixed –

JOE: What's the matter with my eyes?

LORNA: Excuse me, I stand corrected. [*After a pause*] You get mad all the time.

JOE: That's from thinking about myself.

LORNA: How old are you, Joe?

JOE: Twenty-one and a half, and the months are going fast.

LORNA: You're very smart for twenty-one and a half 'and the months are going fast'.

JOE: Why not? I read every page of the Encyclopaedia Britannica. My father's friend, Mr Carp, has it. A shrimp with glasses had to do something.

LORNA: I'd like to meet your father. Your mother dead?

JOE: Yes.

LORNA: So is mine.

JOE: Where do you come from? The city is full of girls who look as if they never had parents.

LORNA: I'm a girl from over the river. My father is still alive – shucking oysters and bumming drinks somewhere in the wilds of Jersey. I'll tell you a secret: I don't like you.

JOE [surprised]: Why?

LORNA: You're too sufficient by yourself . . . too inside yourself.

JOE: You like it or you don't.

LORNA: You're on an island –

JOE: Robinson Crusoe . . .

LORNA: That's right – 'me, myself, and I'. Why not come out and see the world?

JOE: Does it seem that way?

LORNA: Can't you see yourself?

JOE: No . . .

LORNA: Take a bird's-eye view; you don't know what's right or wrong. You don't know what to pick, but you won't admit it.

JOE: Do you?

LORNA: Leave me out. This is the anatomy of Joe Bonaparte.

JOE: You're dancing on my nose, huh?

LORNA: Shall I stop?

JOE: No.

LORNA: You're a miserable creature. You want your arm in *gel* up to the elbow. You'll take fame so people won't laugh or scorn your face. You'd give your soul for those things. But every time you turn your back your little soul kicks you in the teeth. It don't give in so easy.

JOE: And what does your soul do in its perfumed vanity case?

LORNA: Forget about me.

JOE: Don't you want –?

LORNA [*suddenly nasty*]: I told you to forget it!

JOE [*quietly*]: Moody sent you after me – a decoy! You made a mistake, Lorna, for two reasons. I make up my own mind to fight. Point two, he doesn't know you don't love him –

LORNA: You're a fresh kid.

JOE: In fact he doesn't know anything about you at all.

LORNA [*challengingly*]: But you do?

JOE: This is the anatomy of Lorna Moon: she's a lost baby. She doesn't know what's right or wrong. She's a miserable creature who never knew what to pick. But she'd never admit it. And I'll tell you why you picked Moody!

LORNA: You don't know what you're talking about.

JOE: Go home, Lorna. If you stay, I'll know something about you . . .

LORNA: You don't know anything.

JOE: Now's your chance – go home!

LORNA: Tom loves me.

JOE [*after a long silence, looking ahead*]: I'm going to buy a car.

LORNA: They make wonderful cars today. Even the lizzies –

JOE: Gary Cooper's got the kind I want. I saw it in the paper, but it costs too much – fourteen thousand. If I found one second-hand –

LORNA: And if you had the cash –

JOE: I'll get it –

LORNA: Sure, if you'd go in and really fight!

JOE [*in a sudden burst*]: Tell your Mr Moody I'll dazzle the eyes out of his head!

LORNA: You mean it?

JOE [*looking out ahead*]: Those cars are poison in my blood. When you sit in a car and speed you're looking down at the world. Speed, speed, everything is speed – nobody gets me!

54

LORNA: You mean in the ring?

JOE: In or out, nobody gets me! Gee, I like to stroke that gas!

LORNA: You sound like Jack the Ripper.

JOE [*standing up suddenly*]: I'll walk you back to your house – your hotel, I mean. [LORNA *stands.* JOE *continues*] Do you have the same room?

LORNA [*with sneaking admiration*]: You're a fresh kid!

JOE: When you're lying in his arms tonight, tell him, for me, that the next World's Champ is feeding in his stable.

LORNA: Did you really read those Britannia books?

JOE: From A to Z.

LORNA: And you're only twenty-one?

JOE: And a half.

LORNA: Something's wrong somewhere.

JOE: I know. . . .

[*They slowly walk out as*]

Fadeout

SCENE 5

The next week.

[*It is near midnight in the dining-room of the Bonaparte home. An open suitcase rests on the table.* SIGGIE *is pouring samples of wine for Lorna Moon. He himself drinks appreciatively. To one side sits* MR BONAPARTE *silently, thoughtfully, watchfully – pretending to read the newspaper.*]

SIGGIE: I was fit to be knocked down with a feather when I heard it. I couldn't believe it until I seen him fight over at the Keystone last week. You never know what somebody's got in him – like the man with germs – suddenly he's down in bed with a crisis!

[JOE *enters with an armful of clothes which he begins to pack in the* suitcase.]

LORNA: Joe's road tour will do him lots of good.

[ANNA *enters and takes off an apron. Silence, in which* SIGGIE *and* LORNA *sip their wine.*]

ANNA: How do you like that wine, Miss Moon? My father makes better wine than any Eyetalian in New York. My father knows everything – don't you, poppa?

[*With a faint smile,* MR BONAPARTE *shrugs his shoulders.*]

SIGGIE: We're thinking of sending the old man to a leper colony . . .

ANNA: Don't my husband say funny things? Tell her what you told the janitor Tuesday, Siggie.

SIGGIE: Never mind, never mind.

ANNA: You know how I met Siggie? He was a United Cigar Store clerk and I walked in for a pack of Camels and the first thing you know he said something funny. It was raw, so I can't say it. He had me laughing from the first. Seven years and I haven't stopped laughing yet. [*She laughs loudly, pleasurably.*] This will be the first time Joe ever went travelling. Was you ever out of New York, Miss Moon?

LORNA: Oh, many times.

ANNA: That's nice. Far?

LORNA: California, Detroit, Chicago. I was an airplane hostess for two months.

ANNA: That's nice – it's a real adventure. I'd like to fly.

SIGGIE: Stay on the ground! Fly! What for? Who do you know up there? Eagles?

ANNA: It must be a wonderful way to see life.

LORNA [*drinking*]: I've seen life in all its aspects.

[MR BONAPARTE *stands up with a smile.* LORNA'S *eyes follow him as he exits.*]

[*To Joe*] I think your father left because he don't like me.

JOE: He likes you.

ANNA: My father likes everybody. He's a very deep man. My father has more friends than any man alive. But best of all he likes his horse, Dolly, who drives the fruit wagon. My father can't sit still on Sunday afternoon – he has to go see what that horse is doing. [*Her eyes catch sight of the suitcase.*] Joe, you don't know how to pack. [*She starts over to assist him.*]

SIGGIE [*querulously*]: Rest the feet awhile, Duchess.

ANNA [*explaining her move*]: He don't know how to pack. [*Beginning to rearrange the suitcase*]

[MR BONAPARTE *returns and hands Joe a sweater.*]

MR BONAPARTE: You forget your good sweater.

JOE: Thanks.

[MR BONAPARTE *sits.* JOE *looks at him sideways.*]

ANNA: When you get out to Chicago, buy yourself some new underwear, Joe. I hear everything's cheaper in Chicago. Is that right, Miss Moon?

LORNA [*after taking another drink*]: Chicago? I don't know. I was there only one night – I got news that night my mother died. As a matter of fact, she killed herself.

ANNA: That's very sad.

LORNA: No, my father's an old drunk son-of-a-bitch. Did you ask me about my father?

MR BONAPARTE [*who has been listening intently*]: Yes ...

LORNA: Twice a week he kicked my mother's face in. If I let myself go I'd be a drunkard in a year.

ANNA: My father never said one bad word to my mother in her whole lifetime. And she was a big nuisance right up till the day she died. She was more like me, more on the stout side. Take care of your health, Joe, when you're out there. What's better than health?

LORNA [*turning to Mr Bonaparte, with whom she is self-conscious*]: The question is, do you like me or do you not?

MR BONAPARTE [*with a faint smile*]: Yes ...

LORNA: Your family is very cute – Now do you like me?

MR BONAPARTE: Yes ...

LORNA: Why do you look at me that way?

MR BONAPARTE: I don't look special. You gonna travel on those train with my son?

LORNA: God's teeth, no! I'm a friend of his manager's, that's all. And a friend of Joe's, too.

MR BONAPARTE: You are in favour for my son to prizefight?

[JOE *looks at his father sideways and exits.*]

LORNA: Certainly. Aren't you?

MR BONAPARTE: Joe has a dream many year to be superior violin. Was it boyhood thing? Was it real? Or is this real now? Those are-a my question, Miss Moon. Maybe you are friend to my son. Then I aska you, look out for him. Study him. Help him find what'sa right. Tell me, Miss Moon, when you find out. Help Joe find truthful success. Will you do it for me?

LORNA: I'll be glad to keep my eye on him.

[JOE *enters with slippers, which he puts in bag.*]

ANNA [*to Joe*]: You could stand some new shirts, too.

SIGGIE: Listen, pop, I'm a natural man and I don't like wise guys. Joe went in the boxing game 'cause he's ashamed to be poor. That's his way to enter a little enterprise. All other remarks are so much alfalfa!

[JOE *locks the bag.*]

ANNA [*taking the wine glass from Siggie's hand*]: Drunk as a horse fly!

JOE: It's getting late and the train won't wait.

SIGGIE [*standing up*]: My god is success. Need I say more? I'm prouda you, Joe. Come home a champ. Make enough dough to buy your sister's boy friend a new cab. Yes, boys and girls, I'm looking in that old crystal ball and I see strange and wonderful events! Yazoo!

ANNA [*giggling*]: Drunk as a horse fly!

JOE [*to Siggie*]: You can't drive us down to the station in this condition.

SIGGIE: What condition?

ANNA: You're drunk, stupid.

SIGGIE: Shut the face, foolish! Just because I don't hold in my nerves she thinks I'm drunk. If you hold in your nerves you get ulcers.

[*To Joe*] Get your 'chapow' and let's go. Or don't you want me to drive you down?

JOE: No.

SIGGIE: I should worry – my cab's in the garage anyway! [*Suddenly he sits.*]

JOE: We'd better start . . .

LORNA [*to Mr Bonaparte*]: I'd like to have another talk with you some time.

MR BONAPARTE: Come any time in the evening. You are a very lovely girl. [MR CARP *stands in the doorway.*] Here is Mr Carp to say good-bye.

SIGGIE: Come in, my little prince.

CARP [*coming in and shaking hands with Joe*]: I wish you good luck in every undertaking.

JOE [*uneasily, because his father is looking at him*]: Thanks.

MR BONAPARTE [*introducing Carp*]: Miss Moon, my neighbour, Mr Carp.

CARP: A pleasure to meet you.

LORNA: Hello.

[MR BONAPARTE *brings the violin case from its hiding place in the buffet.*]

MR BONAPARTE: Joe, I buy you this some time ago. Don't give cause I don't know whatta you gonna do. Take him with you now. Play for yourself. It gonna remember you your old days of musical life.

[JOE *puts down the suitcase and picks up the violin. He plucks the strings, he tightens one of them. In spite of the tension his face turns soft and tender.*]

LORNA [*watching intently*]: We better not miss the train – Tokio's waiting.

MR BONAPARTE [*of violin*]: Take him with you, Joe.

JOE: It's beautiful. . . .

MR BONAPARTE: Practise on the road.

[JOE *abruptly turns and with the violin exits. The others listen, each standing in his place, as rich violin music comes from the other room.* JOE *returns. There is silence as he places the violin on the table in front of his father.*]

JOE [*in a low voice*]: Return it, poppa.

ANNA [*hugging Joe*]: Have a good trip, Joey.

CARP: Eat in good restaurants. . . .

[*There is silence: the* FATHER *and* SON *look at each other. The others in the room sense the drama between the two. Finally:*]

JOE: I have to do this, poppa.

MR BONAPARTE [*to Joe*]: Be careful fora your hands.

JOE: Poppa, give me the word –

MR BONAPARTE: What word?

JOE: Give me the word to go ahead. You're looking at yesterday – I see tomorrow. Maybe you think I ought to spend my whole life here – you and Carp blowing off steam.

MR BONAPARTE [*holding himself back*]: Oh, Joe, shut your mouth!

JOE: Give me the word to go ahead!

MR BONAPARTE: Be careful fora your hands!

JOE: I want you to give me the word!

MR BONAPARTE [*crying out*]: No! No word! You gonna fight? All right! Okay! But I don't gonna give no word! No!

JOE: That's how you feel?

MR BONAPARTE: That'sa how I feel!

[MR BONAPARTE'S *voice breaks and there is nothing for father and son to do but to clutch each other in a hasty embrace. Finally,* MR BONAPARTE *disentangles himself and turns away.* JOE *abruptly grabs up his suitcase and exits.* LORNA *follows, stopping at the door to look back at Mr Bonaparte. In the ensuing silence* ANNA *looks at her father and shakes her head.* SIGGIE *suddenly lumbers to his feet and sounds off like a chime.*]

SIGGIE: Gong gong gong gong!

ANNA: Gee, poppa . . .

SIGGIE: Come to bed, Anna. . . . Anna-banana . . . [SIGGIE *exits.*]

ANNA: Gee, poppa . . . [*She touches her father sympathetically.*]

MR BONAPARTE [*without turning*]: Gone to bed, Anna....

[ANNA *slowly exits.* MR BONAPARTE *now slowly comes back to the table and looks down at the violin.*]

CARP [*seating himself slowly*]: Come, my friend ... we will have a nice talk on a cultural topic. [*Looking at the violin*] You'll work around a number of years before you make it up, the price of that fiddle...

[MR BONAPARTE *stands looking down at the violin.*]

CARP [*sadly*]: Yes, my friend, what is man? As Schopenhauer says, and in the last analysis ...

Slow fadeout

ACT TWO

SCENE I

Six months later.

> [*Present in the corner of a gymnasium are* ROXY, MOODY, LORNA, *and* TOKIO. *They are looking off right, watching* JOE BONAPARTE *work out with a partner. From off right come the sounds of typical gym activities: the thud of boxing gloves, the rat-a-tat of the punching bag, and from time to time the general bell which is a signal for rest periods. Tacked on the tin walls are an ad for Everlast boxing equipment, boxing 'card' placards, a soiled American flag, some faded exit signs.*
> *The group watches silently for several seconds after the lights fade in. A* BOXER, *wiping his perspiring body with a towel, passes from left to right and looks back at Lorna's legs. As* ROXY *watches, his head moves to and fro in the rhythm of Joe's sparring off-stage.* ROXY *nods his head in admiration.*]

ROXY: Tokio. I gotta give the devil his dues: in the past six months you done a noble job!

TOKIO [*calling off*]: With the left! A long left, Joe! . . .

LORNA [*looking off*]: Joe's a very good-looking boy. I never quite noticed it before.

> [*The general bell sounds: the boxing din off-stage stops.*]

MOODY [*rubbing his hands enthusiastically*]: 'Let it rain, let it pour! It ain't gonna rain where we're headed for!'

ROXY: I'm tickled to death to see the canary bird's left his gloves.

TOKIO: He's the king of all he surveys.

MOODY: Boy, oh, boy, how he surprised them in the Bronx last night! . . . But one thing I can't explain – that knockout he took in Philly five weeks ago.

62

TOKIO: That night he was off his feed, Tom. Where do you see speed like that? That's style, real style – you can't tag him. And he's giving it with both hands.

MOODY: You don't have to sell me his virtues – I'm sold. Nevertheless, he got tagged in Philly.

TOKIO: Here's what happened there: we run into some man when we're leaving the hotel. Joe goes pale. I ask him what it is. 'Nothing,' he says. But I see for myself – a man with long hair and a violin case. When we turn the corner, he says, 'He's after me,' he says. As if it's cops and robbers!

[*The general bell sounds; the fighting din begins again.*]

ROXY: A kidnapper?

LORNA: Don't be a fool. He was reminded . . .

ROXY: Speak when spoken to, Miss Moon!

MOODY [*moodily*]: And when he got in the ring that night, he kept his hands in his pockets?

TOKIO: Yeah. I didn't mention this before – it's not important.

MOODY: But it's still a danger –

TOKIO: No. No.

MOODY: But anyway, we better get him away from his home. We can't afford no more possible bad showings at this stage of the game. No more apparitions, like suddenly a fiddle flies across the room on wings!

[*The group again intently watches Joe off-stage.*]

MOODY: Oh! Did you see that? He's packing a real Sunday punch in that right. [*Calling off*] Hit 'im, Joe, hit 'im! [*As an indistinct answer comes back*] Ha ha, looka that, hahaha. . . . [*Now turning to Tokio*] What's your idea of a match with Lombardo?

TOKIO: Can you get it?

MOODY: Maybe.

TOKIO: Get it.

MOODY: Sure?

TOKIO: It's an easy win, on points at least.

[*During the last few lines a thin dark man has entered. His dark hair is*

greyed at the temples, an inarticulate look in his face. He is EDDIE
FUSELI, *a renowned gambler and gunman.*]

EDDIE FUSELI [*approaching the group*]: Hello.

ROXY [*nervously*]: Hello, Eddie.

MOODY [*turning*]: I haven't seen you for a dog's age, Fuseli.

EDDIE [*pointing off left*]: You got this certain boy – Bonaparte. I like
his looks. American born?

ROXY: Right from here.

EDDIE [*watching Joe off*]: Like a cat, never off his position. He appeals
to me. [*To Moody*] They call you the Brown Fox. What's your
opinion of this boy?

MOODY [*coolly, on guard*]: Possibilities . . .

EDDIE [*to Tokio*]: What's your idea?

TOKIO: Tom said it.

EDDIE: Could he get on top?

MOODY [*as above*]: I can't see that far ahead. I don't read palms.

EDDIE: Could I buy a piece?

MOODY: No.

EDDIE [*coolly*]: Could I?

MOODY: No!

EDDIE [*with a certain tenderness*]: I like a good fighter. I like to see you
after, Tom. [*Of Lorna*] This your girl?

LORNA [*pertly*]: I'm my mother's girl.

EDDIE [*with a small mirthless laugh*]: Ha ha – that's a hot one.

[*He coolly drifts out of the scene on his cat's feet. The general bell
sounds. The din ceases.*]

LORNA: What exhaust pipe did he crawl out of?

ROXY: I remember this Eddie Fuseli when he came back from the
war with a gun. He's still got the gun and he still gives me goose
pimples!

MOODY: That Fuseli's a black mark on my book. Every once
in a while he shoots across my quiet existence like a Roman
candle!

LORNA: Sell or don't sell. But better be careful, that guy's tough.

[*A* FIGHTER, *robed, hooded with towel, passes across: A* GAMBLING TYPE *passes in the opposite direction. Both look at Lorna's legs.*]

MOODY: Give a rat like that a finger and you lose a hand before you know it!

TOKIO: Did you know Joe bought a car this morning?

ROXY: What kinda car?

TOKIO: A Deusenberg.

MOODY: One of those fancy speed wagons?

TOKIO [*agreeing*]: It cost him five grand, second-hand.

MOODY [*flaring up*]: Am I a step-child around here? I'm glad you tell me now, if only outa courtesy!

ROXY [*indignantly*]: Whatta you keep a thing like that incognito for?

MOODY: He drives like a maniac! That time we drove to Long Beach! I almost lost my scalp! We can't let him drive around like that! Boy, he's getting a bushel of bad habits! We gotta be careful.

[*The general bell sounds again; the fighting din stops.*]

MOODY: Here's the truth: our boy can be the champ in three easy lessons – Lombardo, Fulton, the Chocolate Drop. But we gotta be careful!

LORNA: Here he comes.

[JOE *enters in bathrobe, taking off his headgear, which* TOKIO *takes from him.*]

MOODY [*completely changing his tone*]: You looked very good in there, Joe. You're going swell and I like it. I'd work more with that long left if I were you.

JOE: Yes, I was speaking to Tokio about that. I feel my form's improving. I like to work. I'm getting somewhere – I feel it better every day.

LORNA: Happy?

JOE [*looking at her intently*]: Every day's Saturday!

ROXY [*officiously*]: Say, what's this I hear you bought a Deusenberg?

JOE: What's your objection – I might have some fun?

ROXY: I got my wampum on you. I like to know your habits. Ain't I permitted?

[JOE *is about to retort hotly when* MOODY *gently takes his arm in an attempt to soothe him.*]

MOODY: Wait a minute, Joe. After all we have your welfare at heart. And after all a Deusenberg can go one fifty per –

[EDDIE FUSELI *appears above, unseen by the others. He listens.*]

JOE: Who'd want to drive that fast?

MOODY: And since we're vitally interested in your future –

JOE [*shaking off Moody's arm and saying what is really on his mind*]: I you're vitally interested in my future, prove it! Get me some fights – fights with contenders, not with dumb-bunny club fighters. Get me some main bouts in the metropolitan area! –

MOODY [*losing his temper*]: For a kid who got kayoed five weeks ago, your mouth is pretty big!

[*The general bell sounds; the din begins.*]

JOE: That won't happen again! And how about some mention in the Press? Twenty-six bouts – no one knows I'm alive. This isn't vacation for me – it's a profession! I'm staying more than a week. Match me up against real talent. You can't go too fast for me. Don't worry about autos!

MOODY: We can go too fast! You're not so good!

JOE [*with a boyish grin*]: Look at the records!

[JOE *abruptly exits.* TOKIO *follows him, first giving the others a glance.*]

MOODY: Boy, oh, boy, that kid's changing!

ROXY: He goes past my head like a cold wind from the river!

LORNA: But you're gettin' what you want – the contender for the crown!

MOODY: I wish I was sure.

ROXY: Frankenstein!

[EDDIE FUSELI *saunters down to the others.*]

EDDIE: I thought it over, Tom. I like to get a piece of that boy.

MOODY [*angrily*]: I thought it over, too – not for sale. In fact I had a visitation from Jehovah. He came down on the calm waters and He said, 'Let there be unity in the ownership.'

66

EDDIE [*with a dead face*]: I had a visit, too. He come down in the bar and He ate a pretzel. And He says, 'Eddie Fuseli, I like you to buy a piece!'

MOODY [*trying to delay the inevitable*]: Why not see me in my office tomorrow?

EDDIE: It's a cheap office. I get depressed in that office.

MOODY [*finally*]: I can't make any guarantees about the boy.

EDDIE: How do you mean it, Tom?

MOODY: I don't know what the hell he'll do in the next six months.

ROXY: Eddie, it's like flap-jacks – up and down – you don't know which side next!

EDDIE [*with his small mirthless laugh*]: Ha ha, that's a good one. You oughta be on the radio.

MOODY: No, it's a fact –

ROXY: We had enough headaches already! He's got a father, but how!

EDDIE: Don't want him to fight?

ROXY: His father sits on the kid's head like a bird's nest!

    [ROXY *puts his hand on Eddie's arm*.]

EDDIE: Take your hand off. [ROXY *hastily withdraws*.] Let the boy decide. . . .

MOODY: If you buy in?

EDDIE: Let the boy decide.

MOODY: Sure! But if he says no –

    [*Before* MOODY *can finish* JOE *enters.* EDDIE *whirls around and faces Joe, getting his cue from the others. Curiously,* EDDIE *is almost embarrassed before Joe. The bell sounds; the din stops.*]

MOODY: Joe, this is Eddie Fuseli. He's a man around town –

EDDIE [*facing Joe, his back to the others*]: With good connexions –

MOODY: He wantsa buy a piece of you –

EDDIE [*whirling around*]: I will tell him myself. [*Turning back to Joe, with quiet intense dignity*] I'm Eyetalian too – Eyetalian born, but an American citizen. I like to buy a piece of you. I don't care for no profit. I could turn it back to – *you* could take my share. But I like

a good fighter; I like a good boy who could win the crown. It's the
in-ter-est of my life. It would be a proud thing for me when
Bonaparte could win the crown like I think he can.

MOODY [*confidently*]: It's up to you, Joe, if he buys in.

EDDIE [*wooingly*]: Some managers can't give you what you need –

MOODY: Don't say that!

EDDIE: *Some* managers can't! I'll see you get good bouts ... also
Press notices ... I know how. You're a boy who needs that. You
decide ...

[*There is a pause;* JOE'S *eyes flit from Lorna to the others and back to
Eddie.*]

JOE: Not my half.

EDDIE: Not your half.

JOE: As long as Mr Fuseli doesn't mix in my private life ... cut it
up any way you like. Excuse me, I got a date with Miss Deusenberg.

[*The others silently watch* JOE *exit.*]

EDDIE: A date with who?

MOODY [*snorting*]: Miss Deusenberg!

ROXY: An automobile. It gives you an idea what a boy – 'Miss
Deusenberg'!

EDDIE: How do you like it, Tom? Big bills or little bills?

MOODY: Don't think you're buying in for an apple and an
egg.

EDDIE: Take big bills – they're new, they feel good. See you in that
office tomorrow.

[*The bell clangs off stage.* EDDIE *starts off, but abruptly turns and
faces Roxy whom he inwardly terrifies.*]

EDDIE: It's a trick you don't know, Roxy: when a bird sits on your
head and interferes with the championship, you shoot him off. All
kinds of birds. You be surprised how fast they fall on the ground.
Which is my intention in this syndicate. [*He smiles thinly and then
moves out of the scene like a cat.*]

MOODY: I don't like that!

ROXY: I'm not so happy myself at the present time. How do you like it with our boy for gratitude? He leaves us here standing in our brevities!

LORNA: What makes you think you're worthy of gratitude?

MOODY [to Lorna]: For Pete's sake, pipe down! Are you with us or against us?

ROXY [haughtily to Moody]: Take my advice, Tom. Marry her and the first year give her a baby. Then she'll sit in the corner and get fat and sleepy, and not have such a big mouth! Uncle Roxy's telling you!

LORNA [to Roxy]: Couldn't you keep quiet about the father to that gunman? Go home and let your wife give *you* a baby!

ROXY: A woman shouldn't interfere –

MOODY: Peace, for Chri' sake, peace! Lorna, we're in a bad spot with Joe. He's getting hard to manage and this is the time when everything's gotta be right. I'm seeing Lombardo's manager tomorrow! Now that gunman's on my tail. You have to help me. You and I wanna do it like the story books, 'happy ever after'? Then help me.

LORNA: How?

MOODY: Go after the boy. Keep him away from his folks. Get him away from the buggies –

LORNA: How?

MOODY [impatiently]: You know how.

ROXY: Now you're talking.

LORNA [pointing to Roxy]: You mean the way I see it on his face?

MOODY: For crying out loud! Where do you come off to make a remark like that?

LORNA: You expect me to sleep with that boy?

MOODY: I could tear your ears off for a remark like that!

ROXY [discreetly]: I think I'll go grab a corn-beef sandwich. [He exits.]

MOODY [after silence]: Are you mad?

LORNA [tight-lipped]: No.

MOODY [seductively]: I'm not a bad guy, Lorna. I don't mean any-

69

thing bad. . . . All right, I'm crude – sometimes I'm worried and I'm crude.

[*The bell clangs; the boxing din stops.*]

But what the hell, my heart's in the right place. . . . [*Coming behind her and putting his arm around her as she looks ahead*] Lorna, don't we both want that sun to come up and shine on us? Don't we? Before you know it the summer'll be here. Then it's the winter again, and it's another year again . . . and we're not married yet. See? . . . See what I mean? . . .

LORNA [*quietly*]: Yes. . . .

MOODY [*beaming, but with uncertainty*]: That sounds like the girl I used to know.

LORNA: I see what you mean. . . .

MOODY [*worried underneath*]: You're not still mad?

LORNA [*briefly*]: I'm not mad. [*But she abruptly cuts out of the scene, leaving* MOODY *standing there.*]

MOODY [*shaking his head*]: Boy, I still don't know anything about women! . . .

Medium fadeout

SCENE 2

A few nights later.

[LORNA *and* JOE *sit on the same park bench.*]

JOE: Some nights I wake up – my heart's beating a mile a minute! Before I open my eyes I know what it is – the feeling that someone's standing at my bed. Then I open my eyes . . . it's gone – ran away!

LORNA: Maybe it's that old fiddle of yours.

JOE: Lorna, maybe it's you. . . .

LORNA: Don't you ever think of it any more – music?

JOE: What're you trying to remind me of? A kid with a Buster

Brown collar and a violin case tucked under his arm? Does that sound appetizing to you?

LORNA: Not when you say it that way. You said it different once. . . .

JOE: What's on your mind, Lorna?

LORNA: What's on yours?

JOE [*simply*]: You . . . You're real for me – the way music was real.

LORNA: You've got your car, your career – what do you want with me?

JOE: I develop the ability to knock down anyone my weight. But what point have I made? Don't you think I know that? I went off to the wars 'cause someone called me a name – because I wanted to be two other guys. Now it's happening. . . . I'm not sure I like it.

LORNA: Moody's against that car of yours.

JOE: I'm against Moody, so we're even.

LORNA: Why don't you like him?

JOE: He's a manager! He treats me like a possession! I'm just a little silver mine for him – he bangs me around with a shovel!

LORNA: He's helped you –

JOE: No, Tokio's helped me. Why don't you give him up? It's terrible to have just a Tuesday-night girl. Why don't you belong to me every night of the week? Why don't you teach me love? . . . Or am I being a fool?

LORNA: You're not a fool, Joe.

JOE: I want you to be my family, my life – Why don't you do it, Lorna, why?

LORNA: He loves me.

JOE: I love you!

LORNA [*treading delicately*]: Well . . . Anyway, the early bird got the worm. Anyway, I can't give him anguish. I . . . I know what it's like. You shouldn't kick Moody around. He's poor compared to you. You're alive, you've got yourself – I can't feel sorry for you!

JOE: But you don't love him!

LORNA: I'm not much interested in myself. But the thing I like best about you . . . you still feel like a flop. It's mysterious, Joe. It makes me put my hand out. [*She gives him her hand and he grasps it.*]

JOE: I feel very close to you, Lorna.

LORNA: I know. . . .

JOE: And you feel close to me. But you're afraid –

LORNA: Of what?

JOE: To take a chance! Lorna darling, you won't let me wake you up! I feel it all the time – you're half dead, and you don't know it!

LORNA [*half-smiling*]: Maybe I do. . . .

JOE: Don't smile – don't be hard-boiled!

LORNA [*sincerely*]: I'm not.

JOE: Don't you trust me?

LORNA [*evasively*]: Why start what we can't finish?

JOE [*fiercely*]: Oh, Lorna, deep as my voice will reach – *listen!* Why can't you leave him? Why?

LORNA: Don't pull my dress off – I hear you.

JOE: Why?

LORNA: Because he needs me and you don't –

JOE: That's not true!

LORNA: Because he's a desperate guy who always starts out with two strikes against him. Because he's a kid at forty-two and you're a man at twenty-two.

JOE: You're sorry for him?

LORNA: What's wrong with that?

JOE: But what do *you* get?

LORNA: I told you before I don't care.

JOE: I don't believe it!

LORNA: I can't help that!

JOE: What did he ever do for you?

LORNA [*with sudden verve*]: Would you like to know? He loved me in a world of enemies, of stags and bulls! . . . and I loved him for that. He picked me up in Friskin's hotel on 39th Street. I was nine

72

weeks behind in rent. I hadn't hit the gutter yet, but I was near. He washed my face and combed my hair. He stiffened the space between my shoulder blades. Misery reached out to misery –

JOE: And now you're dead.

LORNA [*lashing out*]: I don't know what the hell you're talking about!

JOE: Yes, you do. . . .

LORNA [*withdrawing*]: Ho hum . . .

[*There is silence. The soft park music plays in the distance. The traffic lights change.* LORNA *is trying to appear impassive.* JOE *begins to whistle softly. Finally* LORNA *picks up his last note and continues; he stops. He picks up her note, and after he whistles a few phrases she picks him up again. This whistling duet continues for almost a minute Then the traffic lights change.*]

LORNA [*beginning in a low voice*]: You make me feel too human, Joe. All I want is peace and quiet, not love. I'm a tired old lady, Joe, and I don't mind being what you call 'half dead'. In fact, it's what I like. [*Her voice mounting higher*] The twice I was in love I took an awful beating and I don't want it again! [*Now half-crying*] I want you to stop it! Don't devil me, Joe. I beg you, don't devil me . . . let me alone. . . . [*She cries softly.* JOE *reaches out and takes her hand; he gives her a handkerchief which she uses.*]

LORNA [*finally*]: That's the third time I cried in my life. . . .

JOE: Now I know you love me.

LORNA [*bitterly*]: Well . . .

JOE: I'll tell Moody.

LORNA: Not yet. Maybe he'd kill you if he knew.

JOE: Maybe.

LORNA: Then Fuseli'd kill him. . . . I guess I'd be left to kill myself. I'll tell him. . . .

JOE: When?

LORNA: Not tonight.

JOE: Swiftly, do it swiftly –

LORNA: Not tonight.

73

JOE: Everything's easy if you do it swiftly.

LORNA: He went up there tonight with six hundred bucks to bribe her into divorce.

JOE: Oh . . .

LORNA [*sadly*]: He's a good guy, neat all over – sweet. I'll tell him tomorrow. I'd like a drink.

JOE: Let's drive over the Washington Bridge.

LORNA [*standing*]: No, I'd like a drink.

JOE [*standing to face her*]: Lorna, when I talk to you . . . something moves in my heart. Gee, it's the beginning of a wonderful life! A man and his girl! A warm living girl who shares your room. . . .

LORNA: Take me home with you.

JOE: Yes.

LORNA: But how do I know you love me?

JOE: Lorna . . .

LORNA: How do I know it's true? You'll get to be the champ. They'll all want you, all the girls! But I don't care! I've been undersea a long time! When they'd put their hands on me I used to say, 'This isn't it! This isn't what I mean!' It's been a mysterious world for me! But, Joe, I think you're it! I don't know why, I think you're it! Take me home with you.

JOE: Lorna!

LORNA: Poor Tom . . .

JOE: Poor Lorna!

[*The rest is embrace and kiss and clutching each other.*]

Slow fadeout

SCENE 3

The next day: the office.

    [LORNA *and* MOODY *are present. She has a hangover and is restless.*]

MOODY: Boy, you certainly double-scotched yourself last night. What's the idea, you making a career of drinking in your old age? Headache?

LORNA: No.

MOODY: I won't let you walk alone in the park any more, if you do that.

LORNA [*nasty in spite of her best intentions*]: Well, if you stayed away from your wife for a change . . .

MOODY: It's pretty late to bring that up, isn't it? Tuesday nights –

LORNA: I can't help it – I feel like a tramp. I've felt like a tramp for years.

MOODY: She was pretty friendly last night.

LORNA: Yeah? Did you sleep with her?

MOODY: What the hell's the matter with you, Lorna? [*He goes to her. She shrugs away from him.*]

LORNA: Keep off the grass!
[MOODY *gives her a quizzical look, goes back to his desk, and from there gives her another quizzical look.*]

MOODY: Why do you drink like that?

LORNA [*pointing to her chest*]: Right here – there's a hard lump and I drink to dissolve it. Do you mind?

MOODY: I don't mind – as long as you keep your health.

LORNA: Aw, Christ! – you and your health talks!

MOODY: You're looking for a fight, dolly-girl!

LORNA: And you'll give it?

MOODY [*with a grin*]: No, I'm feeling too good.

LORNA [*sitting wearily*]: Who left you a fortune?

MOODY: Better. Monica's seen the light. The truth is she's begun to run around with a retired brewer and now *she* wants the divorce.

LORNA: Good, now she can begin paying *you*.

MOODY: She goes to Reno in a few months.

LORNA [*moodily*]: I feel like a tramp. . . .

MOODY: That's what I'm telling you – In a few months we'll be married! [*He laughs with pleasure.*]

LORNA: You still want to marry me? Don't I feel like an old shoe to you?

MOODY [*coming to her*]: Honest, you're so dumb!

LORNA [*touched by his boyishness*]: You're so sweet. . . .

MOODY: And flash! – I signed Lombardo today! They meet six weeks from tonight.

LORNA: Goody. . .

MOODY [*disappointed by her flippant reaction, but continuing*]: I'm still not sure what he'll show with Lombardo. But my present worry is this: help me get that kid straight. Did you speak to him about the driving last night?

LORNA: I didn't see him. . . .

MOODY: It's very important. A Lombardo win clinches everything. In the fall we ride up to the Chocolate's door and dump him in the gutter! After that . . . I don't like to exaggerate – but the kid's primed! And you and I – Lorna baby, we're set. [*Happily*] What do you think of that?

LORNA [*evasively*]: You draw beautiful pictures.

[*A knock sounds on the door.*]

MOODY: Come in.

[SIGGIE *enters, dressed in cab driver's garb.*]

SIGGIE: Hello, Miss Moon.

LORNA: Hello. You know Mr Moody.

SIGGIE [*to Moody*]: Hello.

MOODY: What can we do for you?

SIGGIE: For me you can't do nothing. I'm sore. I'm here against my better instinct. [*Taking a roll of money from his pocket and slapping it on the desk*] He didn't want it – no part of it! My father-in-law don't want it. Joe sent it up – two hundred bucks – enough to choke a horse – but he don't want it!

MOODY: Why?

LORNA: That's nice he remembers his folks.

SIGGIE: Listen, I got a father-in-law nothing's nice to him but feeding his horse and giving a laugh and slicing philosophical salami across the table! He's sore because Joe don't come home half the time. As a matter of fact, ain't he suppose to come to sleep no more? The old man's worried.

MOODY: That's not my concern.

SIGGIE: I can't see what it's such a sorry. A boy gets in the higher brackets – what's the worry? He's got enough clothes now to leave three suits home in the closet. [*Turning to Lorna*] It won't hurt if he sends me a few passes – tell him I said so.

LORNA: How's the wife?

SIGGIE: The Duchess? Still laughing.

LORNA: When you getting that cab?

SIGGIE: Do me a favour, Miss Moon – tell him I could use this wad for the first instalment.

LORNA: I'll tell him. Tell Mr Bonaparte I saw Joe last night. He's fine.

MOODY: I'll see you get some passes.

SIGGIE: Thanks, thanks to both of you. Adios. [*He exits.*]

LORNA: He and his wife are crazy for each other. Married ... they throw each other around, but they're like love birds. Marriage is something special. ... I guess you have to deserve it.

MOODY: I thought you didn't see Joe last night.

LORNA: I didn't, but why worry his father?

MOODY: The hell with his father.

LORNA: The hell with you!

MOODY [*after a brooding pause*]: I'll tell you something, Lorna. I'm not overjoyed the way Joe looks at you.

LORNA: How's he look?

MOODY: As if he saw the whole island of Manhattan in your face, and I don't like it.

LORNA: You thought of that too late.

MOODY: Too late for what?

LORNA: To bawl me out.

MOODY: Who's bawling you out?

LORNA: You were about to. Or warn me. I don't need warnings.

77

[*Coasting away from the argument*] If you saw Joe's father you'd like him.

MOODY: I saw him.

LORNA: If you knew him you'd like him.

MOODY: Who wantsa like him? What do I need him for? I don't like him and I don't like his son! It's a business – Joe does his work, I do mine. Like this telephone – I pay the bill and I use it!

LORNA: He's human. . . .

MOODY: What're we fighting about?

LORNA: We're fighting about love. I'm trying to tell you how cynical I am. Tell the truth, love doesn't last –

MOODY [*suddenly quietly serious*]: Everything I said about *Joe* – the opposite goes for you. Love lasts . . . if you want it to. . . . I want it to last. I need it to last. What the hell's all this struggle to make a living for if not for a woman and a home? I don't kid myself. I know what I need. I need you, Lorna.

LORNA: It has to end. . . .

MOODY: What has to end?

LORNA: Everything.

MOODY: What're you talking about?

LORNA: I oughta burn. I'm leaving you. . . .

MOODY [*with a sick smile*]: That's what you think.

LORNA [*not looking at him*]: I mean it.

MOODY [*as above*]: I mean it too.

LORNA [*after looking at him for a moment*]: You can't take a joke?

MOODY [*not knowing where he stands*]: It all depends. . . . I don't like a joke that pushes the blood down in my feet.

LORNA [*coming to him and putting her arms around his neck*]: That's true, you're pale.

MOODY: Who's the man?

LORNA [*heartsick, and unable to tell him the truth*]: There's no man, Tom . . . even if there was, I couldn't leave you. [*She looks at him, unable to say more.*]

MOODY [*after a pause*]: How about some lunch? I'll buy it. . . .

LORNA [*wearily*]: Where would I put it, Tom?

MOODY [*impulsively*]: In your hat! [*And suddenly he embraces her roughly and kisses her fully and she allows it.* JOE *walks into the office,* EDDIE FUSELI *behind him. They break apart.*]

JOE: The first time I walked in here that was going on. It's one long duet around here.

MOODY: Hello.

EDDIE [*sardonically*]: Hello, Partner ... [LORNA *is silent and avoids Joe's looks.*]

JOE: How about that fight with Lombardo?

MOODY: Six weeks from tonight.

JOE: He's gonna be surprised.

MOODY [*coolly*]: No one doubts it.

JOE [*sharply*]: I didn't say it was doubted!

MOODY: Boy, everyone's off his feed today. It started with the elevator boy – next it's Lorna – now it's you! What are *you* sore about?

LORNA [*trying to turn the conversation; to Joe*]: Siggie was here looking for you. Your father's worried –

JOE: Not as much as my 'manager' worries me.

MOODY: I don't need you to tell me how to run my business. I'll book the matches –

JOE: That doesn't worry me.

MOODY: But you and your speeding worries me! First it's music, then it's motors. Christ, next it'll be girls and booze!

JOE: It's girls already.

LORNA: Joe –

JOE [*bitterly*]: Certainly! By the dozens!

EDDIE: Haha – that's a hot one. Don't ask me which is worst – women or spiders.

LORNA: Siggie left this money – your father won't take it. Siggie says buy him a cab –

[JOE *takes the money.*]

EDDIE: Your relative? I'll get him a cab. [*To Moody*] How about a flock of bouts for Bonaparte over the summer?

MOODY [*bitterly*]: All he wants – practice fights – to make him a better 'artiste'.

EDDIE: That is what we like.

[JOE *is looking at Lorna*.]

MOODY: 'We?' Where do *I* come in?

EDDIE: You push the buttons, the *right* buttons. I wanna see Bonaparte with the crown.

MOODY [*sarcastically*]: Your concern touches me deep in my heart!

EDDIE: What's the matter, Tom? You getting tired?

MOODY [*coolly*]: I get tired, don't you?

EDDIE: Don't get tired, Tom . . . not in a crucial time.

MOODY: Get him to give up that Deusenberg.

EDDIE [*after looking at Joe*]: That's his fun. . . .

MOODY: His fun might cost your crown.

JOE [*suddenly, to Lorna*]: Why did you kiss him?

MOODY [*to Joe*]: It's about time you shut your mouth and minded your own goddamn business. Also, that you took some orders.

JOE [*suddenly savage*]: Who are you, God?

MOODY: Yes! I'm your maker, you cock-eyed gutter rat! Outa sawdust and spit I made you! I own you – without me you're a blank! Your insolence is gorgeous, but this is the end! I'm a son of a gun! What're you so superior about?

EDDIE: Don't talk so quick, Tom. You don't know . . .

MOODY: I wouldn't take the crap of this last six eight months from the President himself! Cut me up in little pieces, baby – but not me!

EDDIE [*quietly*]: You could get cut up in little pieces.

MOODY [*retiring in disgust*]: Sisst!

EDDIE: You hear me?

MOODY [*from his desk*]: You wanna manage this boy? Help yourself – do it! I'll sell my piece for half of what it's worth. You wanna buy?

EDDIE: You are a funny man.

MOODY: Gimme twenty thousand and lemme out. Ten, I'll take ten.

I got my girl. I don't need crowns or jewels. I take my girl and we go sit by the river and it's everything.

JOE: What girl?

MOODY: I'm not on speaking terms with you! [*To Eddie*] Well?

EDDIE: It would be funny if your arms got broke.

JOE: Wait a minute! Lorna loves me and I love her.

MOODY [*after looking from Joe to Lorna and back*]: Crazy as a bat! [*He laughs.*]

JOE [*frigidly*]: Is it so impossible?

MOODY: About as possible as hell freezes over. [*He and* JOE *simultaneously turn to Lorna.*]

JOE: Tell him . . .

LORNA [*looking Joe in the face*]: I love Tom. Tell him what?

[JOE *looks at her intently. Silence.* JOE *then turns and quietly exits from the office.* MOODY *shakes his head with a grin.*]

MOODY: Eddie, I take everything back. I was a fool to get sore – that boy's a real nutsy-Fagan!

[*He offers his hand.* EDDIE *looks at it and then viciously slaps it down.*]

EDDIE [*repressing a trembling voice*]: I don't like no one to laugh at that boy. You call a boy like that a rat? An educated boy? What is your idea to call him cock-eyed? When you do it in front of me, I say, 'Tom don't like himself' . . . for Bonaparte is a good friend to me . . . you're a clever manager for him. That's the only reason I take your slop. Do your business, Tom. [*To Lorna*] And that goes for you, too! No tricks, Miss Moon!

[*He slowly exits.* MOODY *stands there thoughtfully.* LORNA *moves to the couch.*]

MOODY: I'm a son of a gun!

LORNA: I feel like I'm shot from a cannon.

MOODY: Why?

LORNA: I'm sorry for him.

MOODY: Why? Because he's a queer?

LORNA: I'm not talking of Fuseli.

[*Suddenly* LORNA'S *eyes flood with tears.* MOODY *takes her hand, half-sensing the truth.*]

MOODY: What's wrong, Lorna? You can tell me. . . .

LORNA: I feel like the wrath of God.

MOODY: You like that boy, don't you?

LORNA: I love him, Tom.

Slow fadeout

SCENE 4

Six weeks later.

A dressing-room before the Lombardo fight. There are a couple of rubbing tables in the room. There are some lockers and a few hooks on which hang pieces of clothing. A door to the left leads to the showers; a door to the right leads to the arena.

[*As the lights fade in,* MR BONAPARTE *and* SIGGIE *are sitting to one side, on a long wooden bench.* TOKIO *is fussing around in a locker. A fighter,* PEPPER WHITE, *hands already bandaged, is being rubbed down by his trainer-manager,* MICKEY. *Throughout the scene is heard the distant roar of the crowd and the clanging of the bell.*]

MR BONAPARTE [*after a silence of intense listening*]: What is that noise?

SIGGIE: That's the roar of the crowd.

MR BONAPARTE: A thousand people?

SIGGIE: Six thousand.

PEPPER WHITE [*turning his head as he lies on his belly*]: Nine thousand.

SIGGIE: That's right, nine. You're sitting under nine thousand people. Suppose they fell down on your head? Did you ever think of that?

[*The outside door opens;* EDDIE FUSELI *enters. The distant bell clangs.* EDDIE *looks around suspiciously, then asks Tokio:*]

EDDIE: Where's Bonaparte?

TOKIO: Still with the newspapermen.

EDDIE [*unpleasantly surprised*]: He's what?

TOKIO: Tom took him upstairs – some sports writers.

EDDIE: A half-hour before a fight? What is Moody trying to do?

TOKIO: Tom's the boss.

EDDIE: Looka, Tokio – in the future you are gonna take your orders from me! [*Pointing to Siggie and Mr Bonaparte*] Who is this?

TOKIO: Joe's relatives.

DDIE [*going over to them*]: Is this his father?

MR BONAPARTE [*sombrely*]: Yes, thisa his father.

SIGGIE: And this is his brother-in-law. Joe sent passes up the house. We just got here. I thought it was in Coney Island – it's lucky I looked at the tickets. Believe it or not, the old man never seen a fight in his life! Is it human?

EDDIE [*coldly*]: Shut your mouth a minute! This is The Arena – Bonaparte is fighting a good man tonight –

SIGGIE: Ahh, that Lombardo's a bag of oats!

EDDIE: When Bonaparte goes in there I like him to have one thing on his mind – fighting! I hope you understand me. An' I don't like to find you here when I return! I hope you understand that. . . . [*After a full glance at them* EDDIE *gracefully exits.*]

SIGGIE: That's a positive personality!

TOKIO: That's Eddie Fuseli.

SIGGIE: Momma-mia! No wonder I smelled gun-powder! [*Turning to Mr Bonaparte*] Pop, that's a paradox in human behaviour: he shoots you for a nickel – then for fifty bucks he sends you flowers!

TOKIO [*referring to the distant bell*]: That's the next bout.

SIGGIE [*to Mr Bonaparte*]: Come on, we don't wanna miss the whole show.

MR BONAPARTE: I waita for Joe.

SIGGIE: You heard what Fuseli said –

MR BONAPARTE [*with sombre stubbornness*]: I gonna wait!

SIGGIE: Listen, pop, you –

MR BONAPARTE [*with sudden force*]: *I say I gonna wait!*

SIGGIE [*handing Mr Bonaparte a ticket*]: Ticket. [*Shrugging*] Good-bye, you're letting flies in!

[SIGGIE *exits jauntily.* MR BONAPARTE *silently watches* TOKIO *work over the fighter's materials. A* SECOND *comes in, puts a pail under the table where* TOKIO *hovers, and exits.* PEPPER WHITE, *his head turned, watches Mr Bonaparte as he hums a song.*]

PEPPER:

Oh, Sweet Dardanella, I love your harem eyes,

Oh, Sweet Dardanella, I'm a lucky fellow to get such a prize. . . .
[*To Mr Bonaparte*] So you're Bonaparte's little boy, Buddy? Why didn't you say so before? Come over here and shake my hand. [MR BONAPARTE *does so.*]

PEPPER: Tell Bonaparte I like to fight him.

MR BONAPARTE: Why?

PEPPER: I like to beat him up.

MR BONAPARTE [*naïvely, not amused*]: Why? You don't like him?

PEPPER: Don't kid me, Buddy!

[*A* CALL BOY *looks in at the door.*]

CALL BOY: Pepper White! Ready, Pepper White!

[CALL BOY *exits.* PEPPER WHITE *slips off the table and begins to change his shoes.*]

PEPPER *to Mr Bonaparte*]: When I get back I'll explain you all the ins and outs.

[*A* SECOND *enters, takes a pail from Mickey and exits.* LORNA *enters.*]

PEPPER [*indignantly*]: Who told girls to come in here?!

LORNA: Modest? Close your eyes. Is Moody . . . ? [*Suddenly seeing* MR BONAPARTE] Hello, Mr Bonaparte!

MR BONAPARTE[*glad to see a familiar face*]: Hello, hello, Missa Moon! Howa you feel?

LORNA: What brings you to this part of the world?

MR BONAPARTE [*sombrely*]: I come-a to see Joe. . . .

LORNA: Why, what's wrong?

MR BONAPARTE [*with a slow shrug*]: He don't come-a to see me. . . .

LORNA: Does he know you're here?

MR BONAPARTE: No.

[LORNA *looks at him sympathetically.*]

LORNA [*finally*]: It's a three-ring circus, isn't it?

MR BONAPARTE: How you mean?

LORNA: Oh, I mean you ... and him ... and other people ...

MR BONAPARTE: I gonna see how he fight.

LORNA: I owe you a report. I wish I had good news for you, but I haven't.

MR BONAPARTE: Yes, I know ... he gotta wild wolf inside – eat him up!

LORNA: You could build a city with his ambition to be somebody.

MR BONAPARTE [*sadly, shaking his head*]: No ... burn down!

[*Now the outside door is thrust open – the distant bell clangs.* JOE *enters, behind him* MOODY *and* ROXY. JOE *stops in his tracks when he sees Lorna and his father together – the last two persons in the world he wants to see now. His hands are already bandaged, a bathrobe is thrown around his shoulders.*]

JOE: Hello, poppa. ...

MR BONAPARTE: Hello, Joe. ...

JOE [*turning to Tokio*]: Throw out the girls – this isn't a hotel bedroom!

MOODY: That's no way to talk!

JOE [*coolly*]: I talk as I please!

MOODY [*angrily*]: The future Mrs Moody –

JOE: I don't want her here!

LORNA: He's right, Tom. Why fight about it? [*She exits.*]

JOE [*to Moody*]: Also, I don't want to see writers again before a fight; it makes me nervous!

ROXY [*softly, for a wonder*]: They're very important, Joe –

JOE: *I'm* important! My mind must be clear before I fight. I have to think before I go in. Don't you know that yet?

ROXY [*suddenly*]: Yeah, we know – you're a stoodent – you gotta look in your notes.

JOE: What's funny about that? I do, *I do!!*

ROXY [*retreating*]: So I said you do!

[PEPPER WHITE *comes forward, about to exit.*]

PEPPER [*to Moody*]: How 'bout a bout with Napoleon?

MOODY: On your way, louse!

PEPPER [*with a grin*]: Pickin' setups?

[JOE *suddenly turns and starts for Pepper.* TOKIO *quickly steps in between the two boys.*]

TOKIO: Save it for the ring!

[*The two fighters glare at each other.* JOE *slowly turns and starts back for the table.*]

PEPPER: You think he'll be the champ? Where'd you ever read about a cock-eyed champ?

[JOE *spins around, speeds across the room –* PEPPER *is on the floor!* MICKEY *now starts for* JOE. TOKIO *starts for* MICKEY. PEPPER *gets up off the floor and finds himself occupied with* MOODY. *For a moment the fight is general.* EDDIE FUSELI *enters. All see him. The fighting magically stops on the second.*]

EDDIE: What'sa matter? Cowboys and Indians? [*To Pepper*] Out!

[MICKEY *and* PEPPER *sullenly exit.*]

EDDIE [*to Moody*]: I'm lookin' for you! You're a manager and a half! You and your fat friend! [*meaning Roxy*] You think this boy is a toy?

JOE: Eddie's the only one here who understands me.

MOODY: Who the hell wantsa understand you! I got one wish – for Lombardo to give you the business! The quicker he taps you off tonight, the better! You gotta be took down a dozen pegs! I'm versus you! Completely versus!

EDDIE [*quietly, to Moody*]: Moody, your brains is in your feet! This is how to handle a coming champ, to give him the jitters before a bout? Go out and take some air! ...

[*Seeing Eddie's quiet deadliness,* MOODY *swallows his wrath and exits;* ROXY *follows with pursed lips.*]

EDDIE: Lay down, Joe – take it easy. [JOE *sits on a table.*] Who hurt you, Joe? Someone hurt your feelings?

JOE: Everything's all right.

EDDIE: Tokio, I put fifty bucks on Bonaparte's nose for you. It's my appreciation to you. . . .

TOKIO: Thanks.

EDDIE [*of Mr Bonaparte*]: Whatta you want me to do with him?

JOE: Leave him here.

EDDIE: Tell me if you want something. . . .

JOE: Nothing.

EDDIE: Forget that Miss Moon. Stop lookin' down her dress. Go out there and kill Lombardo! Send him out to Woodlawn! Tear his skull off! . . . as I know Bonaparte can do it! [EDDIE *gives Mr Bonaparte a sharp look and exits. There is silence intensified by the distant clang of the bell and the muted roar of the crowd.* TOKIO *looks over at Mr Bonaparte who has been silently seated on the bench all this time.*]

JOE [*not quite knowing what to say*]: How is Anna, poppa?

MR BONAPARTE: Fine.

JOE: Siggie watching the fights?

MR BONAPARTE: Yes . . .

JOE: You look fine. . . .

MR BONAPARTE: Yes, feela good. . . .

JOE: Why did you send that money back? [*There is no answer.*] Why did you come here? . . . You sit there like my conscience. . . .

MR BONAPARTE: Why you say so?

JOE: Poppa, I have to fight, no matter what you say or think! This is my profession! I'm out for fame and fortune, not to be different or artistic! I don't intend to be ashamed of my life!

MR BONAPARTE [*standing up*]: Yeah, I understanda you. . . .

JOE: Go out and watch the fights.

MR BONAPARTE [*sombrely*]: Yeah . . . you fight. Now I know . . . is'a too late for music. The men musta be free an' happy for music . . . not like-a you. Now I see whatta you are . . . I give-a you every word to fight . . . I sorry for you. . . .

[*Silence. The distant roar of the crowd climbs up and falls down; the bell clangs again.*]

TOKIO [*gently*]: I'll have to ask you to leave, Mr Bonaparte. ...

MR BONAPARTE [*holding back his tears*]: Joe ... I hope-a you win every fight.

[*MR BONAPARTE slowly exits. As he opens and closes the door the roar of the crowd swells up for an instant.*]

TOKIO: Lay down, Joe. There's five minutes left to tune you up.

JOE [*in a low voice*]: That's right, tune me up. ...

[*JOE stretches out on his stomach and TOKIO's busy hands start up the back of his legs.*]

TOKIO [*working with steady briskness*]: I never worried less about a boy ... in my life. You're a real sweetheart. ...

[*Suddenly JOE begins to cry in his arms. TOKIO looks down, momentarily hesitates in his work – then slowly goes ahead with his massaging hands. The BOY continues to shake with silent sobs. Again the bell clangs in the distance.*]

TOKIO [*in a soft caressing voice*]: You're getting good, honey. Maybe I never told you that before. I seen it happen before. [*Continuing the massaging*] It seems to happen sudden – a fighter gets good. He gets easy and graceful. He learns how to save himself – no energy wasted ... he slips and slides – he travels with the punch. ... Oh, sure I like the way you're shaping up. [*TOKIO continues massaging. JOE is silent. His sobbing stops. After a moment TOKIO continues.*] What was you saying about Lombardo's trick? I understood you to say he's a bull's-eye for a straight shot from the inside. I think you're right, Joe, but that kind of boy is liable to meet you straight-on in a clinch and give you the back of his head under the chin. Watch out for that.

JOE: He needs a straight punch. ... [*JOE suddenly sits up on the table, his legs dangling.*] Now I'm alone. They're all against me – Moody, the girl ... you're my family now, Tokio – you and Eddie! I'll show them all – nobody stands in my way! My father's had his hand on me for years. No more. No more for her either – she had

her chance! When a bullet sings through the air it has no past –
only future – like me! Nobody, nothing stands in my way!

[*In a sudden spurt of feeling* JOE *starts sparring around lightly in a
shadow-boxing routine.* TOKIO *smiles with satisfaction. Now the
roar of the crowd reaches a frenzied shriek and hangs there. The
bell clangs rapidly several times. The roar of the crowd settles down
again.*]

TOKIO: That sounds like the kill.

[JOE *draws his bathrobe around him and prances on his toes.*]

JOE: I'm a new boy tonight! I could take two Lombardos! [*Vigorously
shaking out his bandaged hands above his head*] Hallelujah! We're on
the Millionaire Express tonight! Nobody gets me!

[*The door is thrust open and a* CALL BOY *shouts.*]

CALL BOY: Bonaparte, ready. Bonaparte, ready.

[PEPPER WHITE *and* MICKEY *enter as the* CALL BOY *speeds away.*
PEPPER *is flushed with victory.*]

PEPPER [*to Joe*]: Tell me when you want it; you can have it the way I
just give it to Pulaski!

[JOE *looks Pepper in the face, flexes his hands several times and
suddenly breaks out in laughter, to* PEPPER'S *astonishment.* JOE *and*
TOKIO *exit.* PEPPER *throws off his robe and displays his body.*]

PEPPER: Look me over – not a mark. How do you like that for class!
I'm in a hurry to grab a cab to Flushing.

MICKEY [*impassively*]: Keep away from her.

PEPPER: I don't even hear you.

MICKEY: Keep away from her!

PEPPER: I go for her like a bee and the flower.

MICKEY [*in a droning prophetic voice*]: The flower is married. Her
husband is an excitable Armenian from the Orient. There will be
hell to pay! Keep away from her!

[*Now in the distance is heard the indistinct high voice of the announcer.*]

PEPPER: You oughta get me a fight with that cock-eye Napoleon –
insteada sticking your nose where it don't belong! I could slaughter
him in next to nothing.

MICKEY [*impassively*]: If you could make his weight and slaughter him, you'd be the next world's champ. But you can't make his weight, you can't slaughter him, and you can't be the champ. Why the hell don't you take a shower?

[*The bell clangs – in the arena,* JOE'S *fight is on.*]

PEPPER [*plaintively, beginning to dress at his locker*]: If my girl don't like me without a shower, I'll tell her a thing or two.

MICKEY: If her husband don't tell you first.

[*The roar of the crowd swells up as the door opens and* MR BONAPARTE *enters. He is unusually agitated. He looks at Pepper and Mickey and sits on a bench. The roar of the crowd mounts higher than before, then drops.*]

PEPPER [*to Mr Bonaparte*]: What's the matter with you?

MR BONAPARTE [*shaking his head*]: Don't like to see . . .

PEPPER [*delighted*]: Why? Your boy gettin' smeared?

MR BONAPARTE: They fighta for money, no?

MICKEY: No, they're fighting for a noble cause –

MR BONAPARTE: If they wasa fight for cause or for woman, woulda not be so bad.

PEPPER [*still dressing behind the locker*]: I fight for money and I like it. I don't fight for under a thousand bucks. Do I, Mickey?

MICKEY: Nope.

PEPPER [*boasting naïvely*]: I didn't fight for under a thousand for five years. Did I, Mickey?

MICKEY [*impassively*]: Nope.

PEPPER: I get a thousand bucks tonight, don't I?

MICKEY: Nope.

PEPPER [*up like a shot*]: How much? How much tonight?

MICKEY: Twelve hundred bucks.

PEPPER: What? Mickey, I oughta bust you in the nose. How many times do I have to say I don't fight for under one thousand bucks! [*To Mr Bonaparte*] Now you see what I'm up against with this manager!

MICKEY [*impassively*]: Okay, you'll get a thousand.

PEPPER: I better, Buddy! That's all I say – I better! [*To Mr Bonaparte*] I tell him I want to fight your kid and he don't lift a finger.

[*The roar of the crowd crescendos and drops down again.*]

MICKEY: You don't rate no fight with Bonaparte. [*To Mr Bonaparte, of Pepper*] He's an old man, a fossil!

MR BONAPARTE: Who?

MICKEY: Him – he's twenty-nine.

MR BONAPARTE: Old?

MICKEY: In this business, twenty-nine is ancient.

PEPPER: My girl don't think so.

MICKEY: Keep away from her.

[*The roar of the crowd mounts up to a devilish shriek.*]

PEPPER: Wow, is your boy getting schlocked!

MR BONAPARTE: My boy isa win.

PEPPER: Yeah, and that's why you ran away?

MR BONAPARTE: Whatta the difference who's-a win? Is terrible to see!

PEPPER [*grinning*]: If I wasn't in a hurry, I'd wait around to help pick up your little Joey's head off the floor. [*He draws on a sports shirt.*]

MICKEY [*to Pepper*]: What are you wearing a polo shirt on a winter night for?

PEPPER: For crying out loud, I just bought it! ... So long, Mr Bonaparte.

MR BONAPARTE: I aska you please – whatta happen to a boy's hands when he fight a longa time?

PEPPER [*holding up his fists*]: Take a look at mine – I got a good pair. See those knuckles? Flat!

MR BONAPARTE: Broke?

PEPPER: Not broke, flat! – pushed down!

MR BONAPARTE: Hurt?

PEPPER: You get used to it.

MR BONAPARTE: Can you use them?

PEPPER: Go down the hall and look at Pulaski.

MR BONAPARTE: Can you open thees-a hands?

PEPPER: What for?

MR BONAPARTE [*gently touching the fists*]: So strong, so hard . . .

PEPPER: You said it, Buddy. So long, Buddy. [*To Mickey*] Take my stuff.

MICKEY: Sam'll take it after. Keep away from her!

[PEPPER *looks at Mickey with a sardonic grin and exits followed by* MICKEY.]

MR BONAPARTE [*to himself*]: So strong . . . so useless . . .

[*The roar of the crowd mounts up and calls for a kill.* MR BONAPARTE *trembles. For a moment he sits quietly on the bench. Then he goes to the door of the shower room and looks around at the boxing paraphernalia. In the distance the bell begins to clang repeatedly.* MR BONAPARTE *stares in the direction of the arena. He goes to the exit door. The crowd is cheering and howling.* MR BONAPARTE *hesitates a moment at the door and then rapidly walks back to the bench, where he sits. Head cocked, he listens for a moment. The roar of the crowd is heated, demanding, and hateful. Suddenly* MR BONAPARTE *jumps to his feet. He is in a murderous mood. He shakes his clenched fist in the direction of the noise – he roars aloud. The roar of the crowd dies down. The door opens, Pepper's second,* SAM, *enters, softly whistling to himself. Deftly he begins to sling together Pepper's paraphernalia.*]

MR BONAPARTE: What'sa happen in the fight?

SAM: Knockout.

MR BONAPARTE: Who?

SAM: Lombardo's stiff.

[MR BONAPARTE *slowly sits. Softly whistling,* SAM *exits with the paraphernalia. The outside door is flung open. In come* JOE, TOKIO, MOODY, *and* ROXY, *who is elated beyond sanity.* JOE'S *eyes glitter; his face is hard and flushed. He has won by a knockout.*]

ROXY [*almost dancing*]: My boy! My darling boy! My dear darling boy!

[*Silently* JOE *sits on the edge of the table, ignoring his father after a glance. His robe drops from his shoulders.* ROXY *turns to Moody.*]

ROXY: How do you like it, Tom? He knocks him out in two rounds!

MOODY [*stiffly, to Joe*]: It's good business to call the sports writers in –

ROXY: That's right, give a statement!

[MOODY *gives Joe a rapid glance and hurriedly exits.*]

ROXY: I'm collecting a bet on you. All my faith and patience is rewarded. [*As he opens the door he almost knocks over Eddie Fuseli.*] Haha! How do you like it, Eddie? Haha! [*He exits.* EDDIE FUSELI *closes the door and stands with his back to it.* TOKIO *moves up to Joe and begins to remove a glove.*]

TOKIO [*gently*]: You're a real sweetheart. . . .

[TOKIO *removes the sweaty glove and begins to fumble with the lace of the other one.* JOE *carefully moves his glove out of Tokio's reach, resting it on his opposite arm.*]

JOE [*almost proudly*]: Better cut it off. . . .

[MR BONAPARTE *is watching tensely.* EDDIE *watches from the door.*]

TOKIO: . . . Broke? . . .

JOE [*holding the hand out proudly*]: Yes, it's broke. . . .

[TOKIO *slowly reaches for a knife. He begins carefully to cut the glove.*]

JOE: Hallelujah!! It's the beginning of the world!

[MR BONAPARTE, *lips compressed, slowly turns his head away.* EDDIE *watches with inner excitement and pleasure: Joe has become a fighter.* TOKIO *continues with his work.* JOE *begins to laugh loudly, victoriously, exultantly – with a deep thrill of satisfaction.*]

Slow fadeout

ACT THREE

SCENE I

MOODY'S *office, six months later.*

[*Present are* MOODY, *acting the persuasive salesman with two sports writers,* DRAKE *and* LEWIS; ROXY GOTTLIEB *being helpful in his usual manner;* TOKIO, *to one side, completely quiet ... and* JOE BONAPARTE. BONAPARTE *sits on the desk and diffidently swings his legs as he eats a sandwich. His success has added a certain bellicosity to his attitude; it has changed his clothing to silk shirts and custom-made suits.*]

MOODY: He's got his own style. He won't rush –

ROXY: Nobody claims our boy's Niagara Falls.

DRAKE [*a newspaperman for twenty years*]: Except himself!

MOODY: You newspaper boys are right.

DRAKE: We newspaper boys are always right!

MOODY: He won't take chances tomorrow night if he can help it. He'll study his man, pick out flaws – then shoot at them.

JOE [*casually*]: It won't matter a helluva lot if I win late in the bout or near the opening. The main thing with Bonaparte is to win.

DRAKE [*dryly*]: Well, what does Bonaparte expect to do tomorrow night?

JOE [*as dryly*]: Win.

MOODY: Why shouldn't we have a win from the Chocolate Drop? Look at our record! –

LEWIS [*good-natured and slow*]: We just wanna get an impression –

MOODY: Seventeen knockouts? Fulton, Lombardo, Guffey Talbot –?

JOE: Phil Weiner ...

MOODY: Weiner?

ROXY: That's no powderpuff hitter!

LEWIS: In this fight tomorrow night, can you name the round?

94

JOE: Which round would you like?

DRAKE: You're either a genius or an idiot!

MOODY: Joe don't mean – ·

DRAKE [*sharply*]: Let him talk for himself.

JOE [*getting off the desk*]: Listen, Drake, I'm not the boy I used to be – the honeymoon's over. I don't blush and stammer these days. Bonaparte goes in and slugs with the best. In the bargain his brain is *better* than the best. That's the truth; why deny it?

DRAKE: The last time you met Chocolate you never even touched him!

JOE: It's almost two years since I 'never even touched him'. Now I know how!

MOODY: What Joe means to say –

DRAKE: He's the genuine and only modest cock-eyed wonder!

JOE: What good is modesty? I'm a fighter! The whole essence of prizefighting is immodesty! 'I'm better than you are – I'll prove it by breaking your face in!' What do you expect? A conscience and a meek smile? I don't believe that bull the meek'll inherit the earth!

DRAKE: Oh, so it's the earth you want!

JOE: I know what I want – that's my business! But I don't want your guff!

DRAKE: I have two sons of my own – I like boys. But I'm a son-of-a-bitch if I can stomach your conceit.

MOODY [*trying to save the situation*]: They serve a helluva rum Collins across the street –

DRAKE: Bonaparte, I'll watch for Waterloo with more than interest!

MOODY: Why don't we run across for a drink? How 'bout some drinks?

DRAKE: Tom, you can buy me twenty drinks and I still won't change my mind about him. [*He exits.*]

LEWIS [*smiling*]: You're all right, Bonaparte.

JOE: Thanks . . .

LEWIS [*clinching a cigarette at the desk*]: How's that big blonde of yours, Tom?

95

MOODY: Fine.

LEWIS: How does she feel about the wedding bells? Sunday is it? [*This is news to Joe, and Moody knows it is.*]

MOODY [*nervously*]: Happy, the way I am. Yeah, Sunday.

ROXY: How about the drinks? We'll drink to everybody's health!

LEWIS [*to Joe*]: Good luck tomorrow.

JOE: Thanks ... [*They exit, MOODY throwing a resentful look at Joe. JOE and TOKIO are left. In the silence JOE goes back to the remains of his lunch.*]

TOKIO: That Drake is a case.

JOE [*pushing the food away*]: They don't make cheesecake the way they used to when I was a boy. Or maybe I don't like it any more. When are they getting married?

TOKIO: Moody? Sunday.

JOE: Those writers hate me.

TOKIO: You give them too much lip.

JOE [*looking down at his clenched fists*]: I'd rather give than take it. That's one reason I became a fighter. When did Moody get his divorce?

TOKIO: Few weeks ago. ... [*Cannily*] Why don't you forget Lorna?

JOE [*as if not understanding*]: What?

TOKIO: I'll say it again ... why not forget her? [*No answer comes.*] Joe, you're loaded with love. Find something to give it to. Your heart ain't in fighting ... your *hate* is. But a man with hate and nothing else ... he's half a man ... and half a man ... is no man. Find something to love, or someone. Am I stepping on your toes?

JOE [*coldly*]: I won't be unhappy if you mind your business.

TOKIO: Okay ... [*TOKIO goes to the door, stops there.*] Watch your dinner tonight. No girls either.

JOE: Excuse me for saying that –

TOKIO [*with a faint smile*]: Okay.

[*TOKIO opens the door and LORNA MOON enters. TOKIO smiles at her and exits. She carries a pack of newspapers under her arm. JOE and she do not know what to say to each other – they wish they had not*]

96

met here. LORNA *crosses and puts the newspapers on the desk. She begins to bang through the desk drawers, looking for the scissors.*]

JOE: I hear you're making the leap tomorrow. . . .

LORNA: Sunday. . . .

JOE: Sunday.

[*Intense silence.*]

LORNA [*to say anything*]: I'm looking for the scissors. . . .

JOE: Who're you cutting today?

LORNA [*bringing out the shears*]: Items on Bonaparte, for the Press book.

[*She turns and begins to unfold and clip a sheet of newspaper.* JOE *is at a loss for words.*]

JOE [*finally*]: Congratulations . . .

LORNA [*without turning*]: Thanks . . .

[*In a sudden irresistible surge* JOE *tears the papers out of Lorna's hands and hurls them behind the desk. The two stand facing each other.*]

JOE: When I speak to you, look at me!

LORNA: What would you like to say?

[*They stand face to face, straining. Finally:*]

JOE: Marry anyone you like!

LORNA: Thanks for permission!

JOE: Queen Lorna, the tramp of Newark!

LORNA: You haven't spoken to me for months. Why break your silence?

JOE: You're a historical character for me – dead and buried!

LORNA: Then everything's simple; go about your business.

JOE: Moody's right for you – perfect – the mating of zero and zero!

LORNA: I'm not sorry to marry Tom –

JOE [*scornfully*]: That's from the etiquette book – page twelve: 'When you marry a man say you like it!'

LORNA: I know I could do worse when I look at you. When did you look in the mirror last? Getting to be a killer! You're getting to be like Fuseli! You're not the boy I cared about, not you. You murdered that boy with the generous face – God knows where you hid the body! I don't know you.

JOE: I suppose I never kissed your mouth –

LORNA: What do you want from me? Revenge? Sorry – we're all out of revenge today!

JOE: I wouldn't look at you twice if they hung you naked from a Christmas tree!

[*At this moment* EDDIE FUSELI *enters with a pair of packages. He looks intently at Lorna, then crosses and puts the packages on the desk. He and Joe are dressed almost identically.* LORNA *exits without a word.* EDDIE *is aware of what has happened but begins to talk casually about the packages.*]

EDDIE: This one's your new headgear. This is shirts from Jacobs Brothers. He says the neck bands are gonna shrink, so I had him make sixteens – they'll fit you after one washing. [*Holding up a shirt*] You like that colour?

JOE: Thanks.

EDDIE: Your brother-in-law drove me over. Picked him up on 49th. Don't you ever see them no more?

JOE [*sharply*]: What for?

EDDIE: What'sa matter?

JOE: Why? You see a crowd around here, Eddie?

EDDIE: No.

JOE: That's right, you don't! But I do! I see a crowd of Eddies all around me, suffocating me, burying me in good times and silk shirts!

EDDIE [*dialling the telephone*]: You wanna go to the Scandals tonight? I got tickets. [*Into the telephone*] Charley? Fuseli is speaking. . . . I'm giving four to five on Bonaparte tomorrow. . . . Four G's worth . . . Yes. [*Hanging up the phone*] It's gonna be a good fight tomorrow.

JOE [*belligerently*]: How do you know?

EDDIE: I know Bonaparte. I got eighteen thousand spread out on him tomorrow night.

JOE: Suppose Bonaparte loses?

EDDIE: I look at the proposition from all sides – I know he'll win.

JOE: What the hell do you think I am? A machine? Maybe I'm lonely, maybe –

EDDIE: You wanna walk in a parade? Everybody's lonely. Get the money and you're not so lonely.

JOE: I want some personal life.

EDDIE: I give Bonaparte a good personal life. I got loyalty to his cause. . . .

JOE: You use me like a gun! Your loyalty's to keep me oiled and polished!

EDDIE: A year ago Bonaparte was a rookie with a two-pants suit. Now he wears the best, eats the best, sleeps the best. He walks down the street respected – the golden boy! They howl their heads off when Bonaparte steps in the ring . . . and I done it for him!

JOE: There are other things. . . .

EDDIE: There's no other things! Don't think so much – it could make you very sick! You're in this up to your neck. You owe me a lot – I don't like you to forget. You better be on your toes when you step in that ring tomorrow night. [EDDIE *turns and begins to dial the telephone.*]

JOE: Your loyalty makes me shiver. [JOE *starts for the door.*]

EDDIE: Take the shirts.

JOE: What do I want them for? I can only wear one at a time. . . .

EDDIE [*Speaking into phone*]: Meyer? . . . Fuseli is speaking. . . . I'm giving four to five on Bonaparte tomorrow. . . . Two? . . . Yeah. . . .

[*About to exit,* JOE *stands at the door and watches Eddie as he calmly begins to dial the phone again.*]

Medium fadeout

SCENE 2

The next night.

> *[The lights fade in on an empty stage. We are in the same dressing-room as seen in Act Two. Far in the distance is heard the same roar of the crowd. The distant bell clangs menacingly. The room is shadows and patches of light. The silence here has its own ugly dead quality.*
>
> *LORNA MOON enters. She looks around nervously; she lights a cigarette; this reminds her to rouge her lips; she puffs the cigarette. The distant bell clangs again. EDDIE FUSELI enters, pale and tense. He sees Lorna and stops short in his tracks. There is an intense silence as they look at each other.]*

LORNA: How's the fight?

EDDIE: I like to talk to you.

LORNA: Is Joe still on his feet?

EDDIE: Take a month in the country, Miss Moon.

LORNA: Why?

EDDIE [*repressing a murderous mood*]: Give the boy . . . or move away.

LORNA: I get married tomorrow. . . .

EDDIE: You heard my request – give him or go!

LORNA: Don't Moody count?

EDDIE: If not for Bonaparte they'd find you in a barrel long ago – in the river or a bush!

LORNA: I'm not afraid of you. . . .

> *[The distant bell clangs.]*

EDDIE [*after turning his head and listening*]: That's the beginning of the eighth. Bonaparte's unsettled – fighting like a drunken sailor. He can't win no more, unless he knocks the Chocolate out. . . .

LORNA [*at a complete loss*]: Don't look at me . . . what'd you . . . I . . .

EDDIE: Get outa town!

> *[The roar of the crowd mounts to a demand for a kill.]*
>
> *[Listening intently]: He's like a bum tonight . . . and a bum done it! You! [The roar grows fuller.] I can't watch him get slaughtered. . . .*

LORNA: I couldn't watch it myself. . . .

[*The bell clangs loudly several times. The roar of the crowd hangs high in the air.*]

What's happening now?

EDDIE: Someone's getting murdered. . . .

LORNA: It's me. . . .

EDDIE [*quietly, intensely*]: That's right . . . if he lost . . . the trees are ready for your coffin.

[*The roar of the crowd tones down.*]

You can go now. I don't wanna make a scandal around his name. . . . I'll find you when I want you. Don't be here when they carry him in.

LORNA [*at a complete loss*]: Where do you want me to go?

EDDIE [*suddenly releasing his wrath*]: Get outa my sight! You turned down the sweetest boy who ever walked in shoes! You turned him down, the golden boy, that king among the juven-niles! He gave you his hand – you spit in his face! You led him on like Gertie's whoore! You sold him down the river! And now you got the nerve to stand here, to wait and see him bleeding from the mouth! –

LORNA: Fuseli, for God's sake –

EDDIE: Get outa my sight!

LORNA: Fuseli, please –

EDDIE: Outa my sight, you nickel whoore!

[*Completely enraged and out of control,* EDDIE *half-brings his gun out from under his left armpit.* JOE *appears in the doorway. Behind him are* ROXY, MOODY, *and a* SECOND.]

JOE: Eddie! [EDDIE *whirls around. The others enter the room. In the ensuing silence,* MOODY, *sensing what has happened, crosses to Lorna.*]

LORNA [*quietly*]: What happened?

ROXY: What happened? [*He darts forward and picks up Joe's arm in the sign of victory. The arm drops back limply.*] The monarch of the masses!

EDDIE [*to the Second*]: Keep everybody out. Only the newspaper boys.

[*The* SECOND *exits and closes the door.* JOE *sits on a table. Physically he is a very tired boy. There is a high puff under one eye; the other is completely closed. His body is stained with angry splotches.*]

TOKIO [*gently*]: I have to hand it to you, Joe. . . .

ROXY [*explaining to the frigid Eddie, elaborately*]: The beginning of the eighth: first the bell! Next the Chocolate Drop comes out like a waltz clog, confident. Oh, he was so confident! Haha! The next thing I know the Chocolate's on the floor, the referee lifts our arm, we got on our bathrobe, and we're here in the dressing-room! How do you like it?

EDDIE [*narrowly*]: I like it.

TOKIO [*taking off Joe's gloves*]: I'll have you feelin' better in a minute. [*After which he cuts the tapes.*]

JOE: I feel all right.

EDDIE [*to Tokio*]: Gimme his gloves.

MOODY [*wary of Joe*]: That's a bad lump under your eye.

JOE: Not as bad as the Chocolate Drop got when he hit the floor!

ROXY: Darling, how you gave it to him! Not to my enemies!

JOE: 'Twas a straight right – with no trimmings or apologies! Aside from fouling me in the second and fifth –

MOODY: I called them on it –

ROXY: I seen the bastard –

JOE: That second time I nearly went through the floor. I gave him the fury of a lifetime in that final punch!

[EDDIE *has taken the soggy boxing gloves for his own property.* TOKIO *is daubing the bruise under Joe's eye.*]

And did you hear them cheer! [*Bitterly, as if reading a news report*] Flash! As thousands cheer, that veritable whirlwind Bonaparte – that veritable cock-eyed wonder, Bonaparte – he comes from behind in the eighth stanza to slaughter the Chocolate Drop and clinch a bout with the champ! Well, how do you like me, boys? Am I good or am I good?

ROXY: Believe *me*!

TOKIO [*attempting to settle Joe*]: You won the right for a crack at the title. You won it fair and clean. Now lay down. . . .

JOE [*in a vehement outburst*]: I'd like to go outside my weight and beat up the whole damn world!

MOODY [*coldly*]: Well, the world's your oyster now!

TOKIO [*insistently*]: Take it easy. Lemme fix that eye, Joe –

[*Now a bustling little Irishman,* DRISCOLL, *hustles into the room.*]

DRISCOLL: Who's got the happy boy's gloves?

EDDIE: Here . . . why?

[DRISCOLL *rapidly takes the gloves, 'breaks', and examines them.*]

TOKIO: What's the matter, Drisc?

JOE: What's wrong?

DRISCOLL [*handing the gloves back to Eddie*]: Chocolate's a sick boy. Your hands are clean.

[DRISCOLL *hustles for the door.* JOE *is up and to him.*]

JOE: What happened?

DRISCOLL [*bustling*]: It looks like the Pride of Baltimore is out for good. Change your clothes.

JOE: How do you mean?

DRISCOLL: Just like I said – out! [DRISCOLL *pats Joe's shoulder, hustles out, closing the door in Joe's face.* JOE *slowly sits on the nearest bench. Immediately* TOKIO *comes to him, as tender as a mother.*]

TOKIO: You didn't foul him – you're a clean fighter. You're so honest in the ring it's stupid. If something's happened, it's an accident.

[*The others stand around stunned, not knowing what to do or say.*]

MOODY [*very worried*]: That's right, there's nothing to worry about.

ROXY [*ditto*]: That's right. . . .

JOE: Gee . . .

[JOE *stands up, slowly crosses the room and sits on the table, head in his hands, his back to the others. No one knows what to say.*]

EDDIE [*to Moody*]: Go out there and size up the situation. [MOODY, *glad of the opportunity to leave the room, turns to the door which is suddenly violently thrust open.* BARKER, *the Chocolate Drop's manager, pushes Moody into the room with him, leaving the door open. From outside a small group of curious people look in.* BARKER, *bereft of his senses, grabs Moody by the coat lapel.*]

BARKER: Do you know it? Do you know it?

MOODY: Now wait a minute, Barker –

[BARKER *runs over to Joe and screams*]:

BARKER: You murdered my boy! He's dead! You killed him!

TOKIO [*getting between Joe and Barker*]: Just a minute!

BARKER [*literally wringing his hands*]: He's dead! Chocolate's dead!

TOKIO: We're very sorry about it. Now pull yourself together.

[EDDIE *crosses the room and slams the door shut as* BARKER *points an accusing finger at Joe and screams*:]

BARKER: This dirty little wop killed my boy!

EDDIE [*coming to Barker*]: Go back in your room.

BARKER: Yes he did!! [EDDIE'S *answer is to shove Barker roughly toward the door, weeping*] Yes, he did!!

EDDIE: Get out before I slug your teeth apart!

JOE [*jumping to his feet*]: Eddie, for God sakes, don't hit him! Let him alone! [EDDIE *immediately desists.* BARKER *stands there, a weeping idiot.*]

MOODY: Accidents can happen.

BARKER: I know . . . I know. . . .

MOODY: Chocolate fouled us twice.

BARKER: I know, I know. . . . [BARKER *stammers, gulps, and tries to say something more. Suddenly he dashes out of the room. There is a long silent pause during which* JOE *sits down again.*]

EDDIE: We'll have to wait for an investigation.

TOKIO [*to Joe*]: Don't blame yourself for nothing. . . .

JOE: That poor guy . . . with those sleepy little eyes. . . .

ROXY [*solemnly*]: It's in the hands of God, a thing like that. [LEWIS, *the sports writer, tries to enter the room.*]

EDDIE [*herding him out*]: Stay outside. [*To Moody*] See what's happening? [MOODY *immediately leaves.*] Everybody out – leave Bonaparte to calm hisself. I'll watch the door.

TOKIO: Don't worry, Joe. [*He exits, followed by* ROXY. EDDIE *turns and looks at Lorna.*]

EDDIE: You too, Miss Moon – this ain't no cocktail lounge.

LORNA: I'll stay here. [EDDIE *looks at her sharply, shifts his glance from her to Joe and back again; he exits.*] Joe . . .

JOE: Gee, that poor boy. . . .

LORNA [*holding herself off*]: But it wasn't your fault.

JOE: That's right – it wasn't my fault!

LORNA: You didn't mean it!

JOE: That's right – I didn't mean it! I wouldn't want to do that, would I? Everybody knows I wouldn't want to kill a man. Lorna, you know it!

LORNA: Of course!

JOE: But I *did* it! That's the thing – I *did* it! What will my father say when he hears I murdered a man? Lorna, I see what I did. I murdered myself, too! I've been running around in circles. Now I'm smashed! That's the truth. Yes, I was a real sparrow, and I wanted to be a fake eagle! But now I'm hung up by my finger tips – I'm no good – my feet are off the earth!

LORNA [*in a sudden burst, going to Joe*]: Joe, I love you! We love each other. Need each other!

JOE: Lorna darling, I see what's happened!

LORNA: You wanted to conquer the world –

JOE: Yes –

LORNA: But it's not the kings and dictators who do it – it's that kid in the park –

JOE: Yes, that boy who might have said, 'I have myself; I am what I want to be!'

LORNA: And now, tonight, here, this minute – finding yourself again – that's what makes you a champ. Don't you see that?

JOE: Yes, Lorna – yes!

LORNA: It isn't too late to tell the world good evening again!

JOE: With what? These fists?

LORNA: Give up the fighting business!

JOE: Tonight!

LORNA: Yes, and go back to your music –

JOE: But my hands are ruined. I'll never play again! What's left, Lorna? Half a man, nothing, useless. . . .

LORNA: No, *we're* left! Two together! We have each other! Somewhere there must be happy boys and girls who can teach us the way of life! We'll find some city where poverty's no shame – where music is no crime! – where there's no war in the streets – where a man is glad to be himself, to live and make his woman herself!

JOE: No more fighting, but where do we go?

LORNA: Tonight? Joe, we ride in your car. We speed through the night, across the park, over the Triboro Bridge –

JOE [*taking Lorna's arms in his trembling hands*]: Ride! That's it, we ride – clear my head. We'll drive through the night. When you mow down the night with headlights, nobody gets you! You're on top of the world then – nobody laughs! That's it – speed! We're off the earth – unconnected! We don't have to think!! That's what speed's for, an easy way to live! Lorna darling, we'll burn up the night! [*He turns and as he begins to throw his street clothes out of his locker*]

Medium fadeout

SCENE 3

Late the same night.

[*In the Bonaparte home sit* EDDIE FUSELI, MOODY, ROXY, *and* SIGGIE, *drinking homemade wine, already half-drunk.* MR BONAPARTE *stands on the other side of the room, looking out of the window.* FRANK *sits near him, a bandage around his head.* MOODY *is at the telephone as the lights fade in.*]

MOODY [*impatiently*]: . . . 'lo? Hello! . . .

SIGGIE: I'll tell you why we need another drink. . . .

ROXY: No, I'll tell you. . . .

MOODY [*turning*]: Quiet! For Pete's sake! I can't hear myself think! [*Turning to the phone*] Hello? . . . This is Moody. Any calls for me? Messages? . . . No sign of Miss Moon? . . . Thanks. Call me if she comes in – the number I gave you before. [*Hanging up and returning to his wine glass; to Mr Bonaparte*] I thought you said Joe was coming up here!

MR BONAPARTE: I say maybe. . . .

MOODY [*sitting*]: I'll wait another fifteen minutes. [*He drinks.*]

SIGGIE: Here's why we need another drink; it's a night of success! Joe's in those lofty brackets from now on! We're gonna move to a better neighbourhood, have a buncha kids! [*To Mr Bonaparte*] Hey, pop, I wish we had a mortgage so we could pay it off! To the next champ of the world!

[SIGGIE *lifts his glass; the others join him.*]

ROXY: Bonaparte.

EDDIE: Don't you drink, Mr Bonaparte?

SIGGIE: You, too, Frank – it's all in the family. [MR BONAPARTE *shrugs and comes down, accepting a glass.*]

ROXY: It's in the nature of a celebration!

MR BONAPARTE: My son'sa kill a man tonight – what'sa celebrate? What'so gonna be, heh?

SIGGIE: Ahh, don't worry – they can't do him nothing for that! An accident!

EDDIE [*coldly, to Mr Bonaparte*]: Listen, it's old news. It's been out on the front page two-three hours.

MR BONAPARTE: Poor colour boy . . .

MOODY: Nobody's fault. Everybody's sorry – we give the mother a few bucks. But we got the next champ! Bottoms up.

[*All drink,* FRANK *included.*]

ROXY [*to Mr Bonaparte*]: You see how a boy can make a success nowa-days?

MR BONAPARTE: Yeah ... I see.

EDDIE [*resenting Mr Bonaparte's attitude*]: Do we bother you? If I didn't think Joe was here I don't come up. I don't like nobody to gimme a boycott!

MR BONAPARTE [*going back to the window*]: Helpa you'self to more wine.

SIGGIE [*to Eddie*]: Leave him alone – he don't feel social tonight.

MOODY: Don't worry, Mr Bonaparte. Looka me – take a lesson from me – I'm not worried. I'm getting married tomorrow – *this afternoon!* – I don't know where my girl is, but I'm not worried! What for? We're all in clover up to our necks!

SIGGIE: Shh ... don't wake up my wife.

[MOODY *suddenly sits heavily; jealousy begins to gnaw at him despite his optimism.* ROXY *takes another drink.* EDDIE *asks Frank, apropos of his bandaged head*]:

EDDIE: What's that 'Spirit of '76' outfit for?

SIGGIE [*grinning to Eddie*]: Didn't you hear what he said before? They gave it to him in a strike –

EDDIE [*to Frank*]: You got a good build – you could be a fighter.

FRANK: I fight. ...

EDDIE: Yeah? For what?

FRANK: A lotta things I believe in. ...

[EDDIE *looks at Frank and appreciates his quality.*]

EDDIE: Whatta you get for it?

ROXY [*laughing*]: Can't you see? A busted head!

FRANK: I'm not fooled by a lotta things Joe's fooled by. I don't get autos and custom-made suits. But I get what Joe don't.

EDDIE: What don't he get?

[MR BONAPARTE *comes in and listens intently*.]

FRANK [*modestly*]: The pleasure of acting as you think! The satisfaction of staying where you belong, being what you are ... at harmony with millions of others!

ROXY [*pricking up his ears*]: Harmony? That's music! the family's starting up music again!

FRANK [*smiling*]: That's right, that's music – [*Now* MOODY *emphatically stamps his glass down on the table and stands.*]

MOODY: What's the use waiting around! They won't be back. [*Bitterly*] Lorna's got a helluva lotta nerve, riding around in Long Island with him! Without even asking me!

SIGGIE: Long Island's famous for the best eating ducks.

EDDIE [*to Moody*]: You got the champ – you can't have everything.

MOODY: What's that supposed to mean?

EDDIE [*coldly*]: That girl belongs to Bonaparte. They're together now, in some roadhouse ... and they ain't eating duck!

MOODY [*finally, unsteadily*]: You don't know what you're talking about!

EDDIE: Moody, what do you figger your interest is worth in Bonaparte?

MOODY: Why?

EDDIE [*without turning*]: Roxy ... are you listening?

ROXY: Yeah. ...

EDDIE: 'Cause after tonight I'd like to handle Bonaparte myself.

MOODY: ... Your gall is gorgeous! But I got a contract. ...

ROXY: Eddie, have a heart – I'm holding a little twenty per cent. ...
[*Out of sheer rage* MOODY *drinks more wine;* ROXY *follows his example.*]

FRANK [*to Eddie*]: How much does Joe own of himself?

EDDIE: Thirty per cent. After tonight I own the rest.

MOODY: Oh, no! No, sir-ee!

EDDIE: You're drunk tonight! Tomorrow!

MR BONAPARTE [*coming forward*]: Maybe Joe don't gonna fight no more, after tonight. ...

EDDIE: Listen, you creep! Why don't you change your tune for a minute!

ROXY [*to Mr Bonaparte*]: What're YOU worried about?

MR BONAPARTE: My boy usta coulda be great for all men. Whatta he got now, heh? Pardon me fora nota to feel so confident in Joe'sa future! Pardon me fora to be anxious. ...

EDDIE [*standing up*]: I don't like this talk!

SIGGIE: Sit down, pop – you're rocking the boat! Shh! Shh! [*He slips out of the room.*]

ROXY: Does anyone here know what he's talking about?

FRANK: He's trying to say he's worried for Joe.

ROXY: But why? Why? Don't he realize his kid's worth a fortune from tonight on? [*After giving Eddie a quick glance*] Ain't he got brains enough to see two feet ahead? Tell him in Italian – he don't understand our language – this is a festive occasion! To Bonaparte, the Monarch of the Masses! [*The telephone rings.*]

MOODY [*triumphantly, to Eddie*]: That's my hotel! You see, you were all wrong! That's Lorna! [*Speaking into the telephone*] Hello? ... No.... [*Turning to Mr Bonaparte*] It's for you.

[MOODY *extends the telephone in Mr Bonaparte's direction, but the latter stands in his place, unable to move. After a few seconds* FRANK *sees this and briskly moves to the telephone, taking it from Moody. In the meantime* MOODY *has begun to address Eddie with drunken eloquence. Wavering on his feet.*]

There's a constitution in this country, Eddie Fuseli. Every man here enjoys life, liberty, and the pursuit of happiness!

FRANK [*speaking into the telephone*]: Yes? ... No, this is his son....

[MR BONAPARTE *watches Frank mutely as he listens at the telephone.*]

MOODY: There's laws in this country, Fuseli! – *contracts*! We live in a civilized world –!

FRANK [*loudly, to the others*]: Keep quiet! [*Resumes listening.*] Yes ... yes ...

ROXY [*to Eddie*]: And there's a God in heaven – don't forget it!

FRANK [*on the telephone*]: Say it again ... [*He listens.*] Yes.

MOODY [*to Eddie*]: You're a killer! A man tries to do his best – but you're a killer! [FRANK *lowers the telephone and comes down to the others.*]

FRANK: *You're all killers!* [MR BONAPARTE *advances a step toward Frank.*]

MR BONAPARTE: Frank ... is it ... ?

FRANK: I don't know how to tell you, poppa. . . .

MR BONAPARTE [*hopefully*]: Yes? . . .

FRANK: We'll have to go there –

EDDIE: Go where?

FRANK: Both of them . . . they were killed in a crash –

EDDIE: Who! What!

FRANK: They're waiting for identification – Long Island, Babylon.

EDDIE [*moving to Frank*]: What are you handing me?! [EDDIE, *suddenly knowing the truth, stops in his tracks. The telephone operator signals for the telephone to be replaced. The mechanical clicks call* FRANK *to attention; he slowly replaces the instrument.*]

MOODY: I don't believe that! Do you hear me? I don't believe it –

FRANK: What waste! . . .

MOODY: It's a goddam lie!!

MR BONAPARTE: What have-a you expect? . . .

MOODY [*suddenly weeping*]: Lorna! . . .

MR BONAPARTE [*standing, his head high*]: Joe. . . Come, we bring-a him home . . . where he belong. . . .

Slow fadeout

AWAKE AND SING!

FOR MY FATHER AND MOTHER

Awake and sing, ye that dwell in dust.
ISAIAH, 26:19

THE CHARACTERS OF THE PLAY

All of the characters in Awake and Sing! *share a fundamental activity: a struggle for life amidst petty conditions.*

BESSIE BERGER, *as she herself states, is not only the mother in this home but also the father. She is constantly arranging and taking care of her family. She loves life, likes to laugh, has great resourcefulness, and enjoys living from day to day. A high degree of energy accounts for her quick exasperation at ineptitude. She is a shrewd judge of realistic qualities in people in the sense of being able to gauge quickly their effectiveness. In her eyes all of the people in the house are equal. She is naïve and quick in emotional response. She is afraid of utter poverty. She is proper according to her own standards, which are fairly close to those of most middle-class families. She knows that when one lives in the jungle one must look out for the wild life.*

MYRON, *her husband, is a born follower. He would like to be a leader. He would like to make a million dollars. He is not sad or ever depressed. Life is an even sweet event to him, but the 'old days' were sweeter yet. He has a dignified sense of himself. He likes people. He likes everything. But he is heartbroken without being aware of it.*

HENNIE *is a girl who has had few friends, male or female. She is proud of her body. She won't ask favours. She travels alone. She is fatalistic about being trapped, but will escape if possible. She is self-reliant in the best sense. Till the day she dies she will be faithful to a loved man. She inherits her mother's sense of humour and energy.*

RALPH *is a boy with a clean spirit. He wants to know, wants to learn. He is ardent, he is romantic, he is sensitive. He is naïve too. He is trying to find why so much dirt must be cleared away before it is possible to 'get to first base'.*

JACOB, too, is trying to find a right path for himself and the others. He is aware of justice, of dignity. He is an observer of the others, compares their activities with his real and ideal sense of life. This produces a reflective nature. In this home he is a constant boarder. He is a sentimental idealist with no power to turn ideal to action.

With physical facts – such as housework – he putters. But as a barber he demonstrates the flair of an artist. He is an old Jew with living eyes in a tired face.

UNCLE MORTY is a successful American businessman with five good senses. Something sinister comes out of the fact that the lives of others seldom touch him deeply. He holds to his own line of life. When he is generous, he wants others to be aware of it. He is pleased by attention – a rich relative to the Berger family. He is a shrewd judge of material values. He will die unmarried. Two and two make four, never five with him. He can blink in the sun for hours, a fat tomcat. Tickle him, he laughs. He lives in a penthouse with a real Japanese butler to serve him. He sleeps with dress models, but not from his own showrooms. He plays cards for hours on end. He smokes expensive cigars. He sees every Mickey Mouse cartoon that appears. He is a 32-degree Mason. He is really deeply intolerant finally.

MOE AXELROD lost a leg in the war. He seldom forgets that fact. He has killed two men in extra-martial activity. He is mordant, bitter. Life has taught him a disbelief in everything, but he will fight his way through. He seldom shows his feelings: fights against his own sensitivity. He has been everywhere and seen everything. All he wants is Hennie. He is very proud. He scorns the inability of others to make their way in life, but he likes people for whatever good qualities they possess. His passionate outbursts come from a strong but contained emotional mechanism.

SAM FEINSCHREIBER wants to find a home. He is a lonely man, a foreigner in a strange land, hypersensitive about this fact, conditioned by the humiliation of not making his way alone. He has a sense of others laughing at him. At night he gets up and sits alone in the dark. He hears acutely all the small sounds of life. He might have been a poet in another time and place.

He approaches his wife as if he were offering her a delicate flower. Life is a high chill wind weaving itself around his head.

SCHLOSSER, *the janitor, is an overworked German whose wife ran away with another man and left him with a young daughter who in turn ran away and joined a burlesque show as chorus girl. The man suffers rheumatic pains. He has lost his identity twenty years before.*

ACT ONE

Time: The present; the family finishing supper.
Place: An apartment in the Bronx, New York City.
Exposed on the stage are the dining-room and adjoining front room of the
Berger apartment. These two rooms are typically furnished. There is a
curtain between them. A small door off the front room leads to Jacob's room.
When his door is open one sees a picture of Sacco and Vanzetti on the wall
and several shelves of books. Stage left of this door presents the entrance to the
foyer hall of the apartment. The two other bedrooms of the apartment are off
this hall, but not necessarily shown.
Stage left of the dining-room presents a swinging door which opens on the
kitchen.

RALPH: Where's advancement down the place? Work like crazy!
Think they see it? You'd drop dead first.

MYRON: Never mind, son, merit goes unrewarded. Teddy Roosevelt
used to say –

HENNIE: It rewarded you – thirty years a haberdashery clerk!
[JACOB *laughs.*]

RALPH: All I want's a chance to get to first base!

HENNIE: That's all?

RALPH: Stuck down in that joint on Fourth Avenue – a stock clerk in
a silk house! Just look at Eddie. I'm as good as he is – pulling in
two-fifty a week for forty-eight minutes a day. A headliner, his
name in all the papers.

JACOB: That's what you want, Ralphie? Your name in the papers?

RALPH: I wanna make up my own mind about things . . . be something! Didn't I want to take up tap dancing, too?

BESSIE: So take lessons. Who stopped you?

RALPH: On what?

BESSIE: On what? Save money.

RALPH: Sure, five dollars a week for expenses and the rest in the house. I can't save even for shoe laces.

BESSIE: You mean we shouldn't have food in the house, but you'll make a jig on the street corner?

RALPH: I mean something.

BESSIE: You also mean something when you studied on the drum, Mr Smartie!

RALPH: I don't know. . . . Every other day to sit around with the blues and mud in your mouth.

MYRON: That's how it is – life is like that – a cake-walk.

RALPH: What's it get you?

HENNIE: A four-car funeral.

RALPH: What's it for?

JACOB: What's it for? If this life leads to a revolution it's a good life. Otherwise it's for nothing.

BESSIE: Never mind, Pop! Pass me the salt.

RALPH: It's crazy – all my life I want a pair of black and white shoes and can't get them. It's crazy!

BESSIE: In a minute I'll get up from the table. I can't take a bite in my mouth no more.

MYRON [restraining her]: Now, Momma, just don't excite yourself –

BESSIE: I'm so nervous I can't hold a knife in my hand.

MYRON: Is that a way to talk, Ralphie? Don't Momma work hard enough all day?

[BESSIE allows herself to be reseated.]

BESSIE: On my feet twenty-four hours?

MYRON: On her feet –

RALPH [jumps up]: What do I do – go to night-clubs with Greta Garbo? Then when I come home can't even have my own room? Sleep on a day-bed in the front room! [Choked, he exits to front room.]

BESSIE: He's starting up that stuff again. [Shouts to him] When Hennie marries you'll have her room – I should only live to see the day.

HENNIE: Me, too.

[*They settle down to serious eating.*]

MYRON: This morning the sink was full of ants. Where they come from I just don't know. I thought it was coffee grounds ... and then they began moving.

BESSIE: You gave the dog eat?

JACOB: I gave the dog eat.

[HENNIE *drops a knife and picks it up again.*]

BESSIE: You got dropsy tonight.

HENNIE: Company's coming.

MYRON: You can buy a ticket for fifty cents and win fortunes. A man came in the store – it's the Irish Sweepstakes.

BESSIE: What?

MYRON: Like a raffle, only different. A man came in –

BESSIE: Who spends fifty-cent pieces for Irish raffles? They threw out a family on Dawson Street today. All the furniture on the sidewalk. A fine old woman with grey hair.

JACOB: Come eat, Ralph.

MYRON: A butcher on Beck Street won eighty thousand dollars.

BESSIE: Eighty thousand dollars! You'll excuse my expression, you're bughouse!

MYRON: I seen it in the paper – on one ticket – 765 Beck Street.

BESSIE: Impossible!

MYRON: He did ... yes he did. He says he'll take his old mother to Europe ... an Austrian –

HENNIE: Europe ...

MYRON: Six per cent on eighty thousand – forty-eight hundred a year.

BESSIE: I'll give you money. Buy a ticket in Hennie's name. Say, you can't tell – lightning never struck us yet. If they win on Beck Street we could win on Longwood Avenue.

JACOB [*ironically*]: If it rained pearls – who would work?

BESSIE: Another county heard from.

[RALPH *enters and silently seats himself.*]

MYRON: I forgot, Beauty – Sam Feinschreiber sent you a present. Since I brought him for supper he just can't stop talking about you.

HENNIE: What's that 'mockie' bothering about? Who needs him?

MYRON: He's a very lonely boy.

HENNIE: So I'll sit down and burst out crying ''cause he's lonely'.

BESSIE [opening candy]: He'd marry you one two three.

HENNIE: Too bad about him.

BESSIE [naïvely delighted]: Chocolate peanuts.

HENNIE: Loft's week-end special, two for thirty-nine.

BESSIE: You could think about it. It wouldn't hurt.

HENNIE [laughing]: To quote Moe Axelrod, 'Don't make me laugh.'

BESSIE: Never mind laughing. It's time you already had in your head a serious thought. A girl twenty-six don't grow younger. When I was your age it was already a big family with responsibilities.

HENNIE [laughing]: Maybe that's what ails you, Mom.

BESSIE: Don't you feel well?

HENNIE: 'Cause I'm laughing? I feel fine. It's just funny – that poor guy sending me presents 'cause he loves me.

BESSIE: I think it's very, very nice.

HENNIE: Sure . . . swell!

BESSIE: Mrs Marcus's Rose is engaged to a Brooklyn boy, a dentist. He came in his car today. A little dope should get such a boy.
   [Finished with the meal, BESSIE, MYRON, and JACOB rise. Both HENNIE and RALPH sit silently at the table, he eating. Suddenly she rises.]

HENNIE: Tell you what, Mom. I saved for a new dress, but I'll take you and Pop to the Franklin. Don't need a dress. From now on I'm planning to stay in nights. Hold everything!

BESSIE: What's the matter – a bedbug bit you suddenly?

HENNIE: It's a good bill – Belle Baker. Maybe she'll sing 'Eli, Eli'.

BESSIE: We was going to a movie.

HENNIE: Forget it. Let's go.

MYRON: I see in the paper [*as he picks his teeth*] Sophie Tucker took off twenty-six pounds. Fearful business with Japan.

HENNIE: Write a book, Pop! Come on, we'll go early for good seats.

MYRON: Moe said you had a date with him for tonight.

BESSIE: Axelrod?

HENNIE: I told him no, but he don't believe it. I'll tell him no for the next hundred years, too.

MYRON: Don't break appointments, Beauty, and hurt people's feelings.

[BESSIE *exits*.]

HENNIE: His hands got free wheeling. [*She exits*.]

MYRON: I don't know . . . people ain't the same. N-O- The whole world's changing right under our eyes. Presto! No manners. Like the great Italian lover in the movies. What was his name? The Sheik. . . . No one remembers? [*Exits, shaking his head*.]

RALPH [*unmoving at the table*]: Jake . . .

JACOB: Noo?

RALPH: I can't stand it.

JACOB: There's an expression – 'strong as iron you must be'.

RALPH: It's a cock-eyed world.

JACOB: Boys like you could fix it some day. Look on the world, not on yourself so much. Every country with starving millions, no? In Germany and Poland a Jew couldn't walk in the street. Everybody hates, nobody loves.

RALPH: I don't get all that.

JACOB: For years, I watched you grow up. Wait! You'll graduate from my university.

[*The others enter, dressed*.]

MYRON [*lighting*]: Good cigars now for a nickel.

BESSIE [*to Jacob*]: After take Tootsie on the roof. [*To Ralph*] What'll you do?

RALPH: Don't know.

BESSIE: You'll see the boys around the block?

RALPH: I'll stay home every night!

MYRON: Momma don't mean for you –

RALPH: I'm flying to Hollywood by plane, that's what I'm doing.
[*Doorbell rings.* MYRON *answers it.*]

BESSIE: I don't like my boy to be seen with those tramps on the corner.

MYRON [*without*]: Schlosser's here, Momma, with the garbage can.

BESSIE: Come in here, Schlosser. [*Sotto voce*] Wait, I'll give him a piece of my mind.

[MYRON *ushers in* SCHLOSSER *who carries a garbage can in each hand.*]

What's the matter the dumbwaiter's broken again?

SCHLOSSER: Mr Wimmer sends new ropes next week. I got a sore arm.

BESSIE: He should live so long your Mr Wimmer. For seven years already he's sending new ropes. No dumbwaiter, no hot water, no steam – In a respectable house, they don't allow such conditions.

SCHLOSSER: In a decent house dogs are not running to make dirty the hallway.

BESSIE: Tootsie's making dirty? Our Tootsie's making dirty in the hall?

SCHLOSSER [*to Jacob*]: I tell you yesterday again. You must not leave her –

BESSIE [*indignantly*]: Excuse me! Please don't yell on an old man. He's got more brains in his finger than you got – I don't know where. Did you ever see – he should talk to you an old man?

MYRON: Awful.

BESSIE: From now on we don't walk up the stairs no more. You keep it so clean we'll fly in the windows.

SCHLOSSER: I speak to Mr Wimmer.

BESSIE: Speak! Speak! Tootsie walks behind me like a lady any time, any place. So good-bye ... good-bye, Mr Schlosser.

SCHLOSSER: I tell you dot – I verk verry hard here. My arms is . . . [*Exits in confusion.*]

BESSIE: Tootsie should lay all day in the kitchen maybe. Give him back if he yells on you. What's funny?

JACOB [*laughing*]: Nothing.

BESSIE: Come. [*Exits.*]

JACOB: Hennie, take care. . . .

HENNIE: Sure.

JACOB: Bye-bye.

[HENNIE *exits.* MYRON *pops head back in door.*]

MYRON: Valentino! That's the one! [*He exits.*]

RALPH: I never in my life even had a birthday party. Every time I went and cried in the toilet when my birthday came.

JACOB [*seeing Ralph remove his tie*]: You're going to bed?

RALPH: No, I'm putting on a clean shirt.

JACOB: Why?

RALPH: I got a girl. . . . Don't laugh!

JACOB: Who laughs? Since when?

RALPH: Three weeks. She lives in Yorkville with an aunt and uncle. A bunch of relatives, but no parents.

JACOB: An orphan girl – tch, tch.

RALPH: But she's got me! Boy, I'm telling you I could sing! Jake, she's like stars. She's so beautiful you look at her and cry! She's like French words! We went to the park the other night. Heard the last band concert.

JACOB: Music . . .

RALPH [*stuffing shirt in trousers*]: It got cold and I gave her my coat to wear. We just walked along like that, see, without a word, see. I never was so happy in all my life. It got late . . . we just sat there. She looked at me – you know what I mean, how a girl looks at you – right in the eyes? 'I love you,' she says, 'Ralph.' I took her home. . . . I wanted to cry. That's how I felt!

JACOB: It's a beautiful feeling.

RALPH: You said a mouthful!

JACOB: Her name is –

RALPH: Blanche.

JACOB: A fine name. Bring her sometimes here.

RALPH: She's scared to meet Mom.

JACOB: Why?

RALPH: You know Mom's not letting my sixteen bucks out of the house if she can help it. She'd take one look at Blanche and insult her in a minute – a kid who's got nothing.

JACOB: Boychick!

RALPH: What's the diff?

JACOB: It's no difference – a plain bourgeois prejudice – but when they find out a poor girl – it ain't so kosher.

RALPH: They don't have to know I've got a girl.

JACOB: What's in the end?

RALPH: Out I go! I don't mean maybe!

JACOB: And then what?

RALPH: Life begins.

JACOB: What life?

RALPH: Life with my girl. Boy, I could sing when I think about it! Her and me together – that's a new life!

JACOB: Don't make a mistake! A new death!

RALPH: What's the idea?

JACOB: Me, I'm the idea! Once I had in *my* heart a dream, a vision, but came marriage and then you forget. Children come and you forget because –

RALPH: Don't worry, Jake.

JACOB: Remember, a woman insults a man's soul like no other thing in the whole world!

RALPH: Why get so excited? No one –

JACOB: Boychick, wake up! Be something! Make your life something good. For the love of an old man who sees in your young days his new life, for such love take the world in your two hands and make it like new. Go out and fight so life shouldn't be printed on dollar bills. A woman waits.

RALPH: Say, I'm no fool!

JACOB: From my heart I hope not. In the meantime –
[*Bell rings.*]

RALPH: See who it is, will you? [*Stands off.*] Don't want Mom to catch me with a clean shirt.

JACOB [*calls*]: Come in. [*Sotto voce*] Moe Axelrod.
[MOE *enters.*]

MOE: Hello girls, how's your whiskers? [*To Ralph*] All dolled up. What's it, the weekly visit to the cat house?

RALPH: Please mind your business.

MOE: Okay, sweetheart.

RALPH [*taking a hidden dollar from a book*]: If Mom asks where I went –

JACOB: I know. Enjoy yourself.

RALPH: Bye-bye. [*He exits.*]

JACOB: Bye-bye.

MOE: Who's home?

JACOB: Me.

MOE: Good. I'll stick around a few minutes. Where's Hennie?

JACOB: She went with Bessie and Myron to a show.

MOE: She what?!

JACOB: You had a date?

MOE [*hiding his feelings*]: Here – I brought you some halavah.

JACOB: Halavah? Thanks, I'll eat a piece after.

MOE: So Ralph's got a dame? Hot stuff – a kid can't even play a card game.

JACOB: Moe, you're a no-good, a bum of the first water. To your dying day you won't change.

MOE: Where'd you get that stuff, a no-good?

JACOB: But I like you.

MOE: Didn't I go fight in France for democracy? Didn't I get my goddam leg shot off in that war the day before the armistice? Uncle Sam give me the Order of the Purple Heart, didn't he? What'd you mean, a no-good?

JACOB: Excuse me.

MOE: If you got an orange I'll eat an orange.

JACOB: No orange. An apple.

MOE: No oranges, huh? – what a dump!

JACOB: Bessie hears you once talking like this she'll knock your head off.

MOE: Hennie went with, huh? She wantsa see me squirm, only I don't squirm for dames.

JACOB: You came to see her?

MOE: What for? I got a present for our boy friend, Myron. He'll drop dead when I tell him his gentle horse galloped in fifteen to one. He'll die.

JACOB: It really won? The first time I remember.

MOE: Where'd they go?

JACOB: A vaudeville by the Franklin.

MOE: What's special tonight?

JACOB: Someone tells a few jokes ... and they forget the street is filled with starving beggars.

MOE: What'll they do – start a war?

JACOB: I don't know.

MOE: You oughta know. What the hell you got all the books for?

JACOB: It needs a new world.

MOE: That's why they had the big war – to make a new world, they said – safe for democracy. Sure every big general laying up in a Paris hotel with a half-dozen broads pinned on his moustache. Democracy! I learned a lesson.

JACOB: An imperial war. You know what this means?

MOE: Sure, I know everything!

JACOB: By money men the interests must be protected. Who gave you such a rotten haircut? Please [*fishing in his vest pocket*], give me for a cent a cigarette. I didn't have since yesterday –

MOE [*giving one*]: Don't make me laugh. [*A cent passes back and forth between them*, MOE *finally throwing it over his shoulder.*] Don't look so tired all the time. You're a wow – always sore about something.

JACOB: And you?

MOE: You got one thing – you can play pinochle. I'll take you over in a game. Then you'll have something to be sore on.

JACOB: Who'll wash dishes?

[MOE *takes deck from buffet drawer.*]

MOE: Do 'em after. Ten cents a deal.

JACOB: Who's got ten cents?

MOE: I got ten cents. I'll lend it to you.

JACOB: Commence.

MOE [*shaking cards*]: The first time I had my hands on a pack in two days. Lemme shake up these cards. I'll make 'em talk.

[JACOB *goes to his room where he puts on a Caruso record.*]

JACOB: You should live so long.

MOE: Ever see oranges grow? I know a certain place – One summer I laid under a tree and let them fall right in my mouth.

JACOB [*off, the music is playing; the card game begins*]: From *L'Africana* . . . a big explorer comes on a new land – 'O Paradiso'. From act four this piece. Caruso stands on the ship and looks on a Utopia. You hear? 'O paradise! Oh paradise on earth! Oh blue sky, oh fragrant air –'

MOE: Ask him does he see any oranges?

[BESSIE, MYRON, *and* HENNIE *enter.*]

JACOB: You came back so soon?

BESSIE: Hennie got sick on the way.

MYRON: Hello, Moe. . . .

[MOE *puts cards back in pocket.*]

BESSIE: Take off the phonograph, Pop. [*To Hennie*] Lay down . . . I'll call the doctor. You should see how she got sick on Prospect Avenue. Two weeks already she don't feel right.

MYRON: Moe . . . ?

BESSIE: Go to bed, Hennie.

HENNIE: I'll sit here.

BESSIE: Such a girl I never saw! Now you'll be stubborn?

MYRON: It's for your own good, Beauty. Influenza –

HENNIE: I'll sit here.

BESSIE: You ever seen a girl should say no to everything. She can't stand on her feet, so –

HENNIE: Don't yell in my ears, I hear. Nothing's wrong. I ate tuna fish for lunch.

MYRON: Canned goods. . . .

BESSIE: Last week you also ate tuna fish?

HENNIE: Yeah, I'm funny for tuna fish. Go to the show – have a good time.

BESSIE: I don't understand what I did to God He blessed me with such children. From the whole world –

MOE [*coming to aid of Hennie*]: For Chris' sake, don't kibitz so much!

BESSIE: You don't like it?

MOE [*aping*]: No, I don't like it.

BESSIE: That's too bad, Axelrod. Maybe it's better by your cigar-store friends. Here we're different people.

MOE: Don't gimme that cigar-store line, Bessie. I walked up five flights –

BESSIE: To take out Hennie. But my daughter ain't in your class, Axelrod.

MOE: To see Myron.

MYRON: Did he, did he, Moe?

MOE: Did he what?

MYRON: 'Sky Rocket'?

BESSIE: You bet on a horse!

MOE: Paid twelve and a half to one.

MYRON: There! You hear that, Momma? Our horse came in. You see, it happens, and twelve and a half to one. Just look at that!

MOE: What the hell, a sure thing. I told you.

BESSIE: If Moe said a sure thing, you couldn't bet a few dollars instead of fifty cents?

JACOB [*laughs*]: 'Aie, aie, aie.'

MOE [*at his wallet*]: I'm carrying six hundred 'plunks' in big denominations.

BESSIE: A banker!

MOE: Uncle Sam sends me a ninety a month.

BESSIE: So you save it?

MOE: Run it up, Run-it-up-Axelrod, that's me.

BESSIE: The police should know how.

MOE [*shutting her up*]: All right, all right – Change twenty, sweetheart.

MYRON: Can you make change?

BESSIE: Don't be crazy.

MOE: I'll meet a guy in Goldman's restaurant. I'll meet 'im and come back with change.

MYRON [*figuring on paper*]: You can give it to me tomorrow in the store.

BESSIE [*acquisitive*]: He'll come back, he'll come back!

MOE: Lucky I bet some bucks myself. [*In derision to Hennie*] Let's step out tomorrow night, Par-a-dise. [*Thumbs his nose at her, laughs mordantly, and exits.*]

MYRON: Oh, that's big percentage. If I picked a winner every day . . .

BESSIE: Poppa, did you take Tootsie on the roof?

JACOB: All right.

MYRON: Just look at that – a cake walk. We can make –

BESSIE: It's enough talk. I got a splitting headache. Hennie, go in bed. I'll call Dr Cantor.

HENNIE: I'll sit here . . . and don't call that old Ignatz 'cause I won't see him.

MYRON: If you get sick Momma can't nurse you. You don't want to go to a hospital.

JACOB: She don't look sick, Bessie, it's a fact.

BESSIE: She's got fever. I see in her eyes, so he tells me no. Myron, call Dr Cantor. [MYRON *picks up phone, but* HENNIE *grabs it from him.*]

HENNIE: I don't want any doctor, I ain't sick. Leave me alone.

MYRON: Beauty, it's for your own sake.

HENNIE: Day in and day out pestering. Why are you always right and no one else can say a word?

BESSIE: When you have your own children –

HENNIE: I'm not sick! Hear what I say? I'm not sick! Nothing's the matter with me! I don't want a doctor.

[BESSIE *is watching her with slow progressive understanding.*]

BESSIE: What's the matter?

HENNIE: Nothing, I told you!

BESSIE: You told me, but – [*A long pause of examination follows.*]

HENNIE: See much?

BESSIE: Myron, put down the ... the ... [*He slowly puts the phone down.*] Tell me what happened. ...

HENNIE: Brooklyn Bridge fell down.

BESSIE [*approaching*]: I'm asking a question. ...

MYRON: What's happened, Momma?

BESSIE: Listen to me!

HENNIE: What the hell are you talking?

BESSIE: Poppa – take Tootsie on the roof.

HENNIE [*holding Jacob back*]: If he wants he can stay here.

MYRON: What's wrong, Momma?

BESSIE [*her voice quivering slightly*]: Myron, your fine Beauty's in trouble. Our society lady ...

MYRON: Trouble? I don't under – is it – ?

BESSIE: Look in her face.

[*He looks, understands, and slowly sits in a chair, utterly crushed.*] Who's the man?

HENNIE: The Prince of Wales.

BESSIE: My gall is busting in me. In two seconds –

HENNIE [*in a violent outburst*]: Shut up! Shut up! I'll jump out the window in a minute! Shut up! [*Finally she gains control of herself, says in a low, hard voice*] You don't know him.

JACOB: Bessie ...

BESSIE: He's a Bronx boy?

HENNIE: From out of town.

BESSIE: What do you mean?

HENNIE: From out of town!!

BESSIE: A long time you know him? You were sleeping by a girl from the office Saturday nights? You slept good, my lovely lady. You'll go to him . . . he'll marry you.

HENNIE: That's what you say.

BESSIE: That's what I say! He'll do it, take MY word he'll do it!

HENNIE: Where? [*To Jacob*] Give her the letter. [*Jacob does so.*]

BESSIE: What? [*Reads*] 'Dear sir: In reply to your request of the 14th inst., we can state that no Mr Ben Grossman has ever been connected with our organization. . . .' You don't know where he is?

HENNIE: No.

BESSIE [*walks back and forth*]: Stop crying like a baby, Myron.

MYRON: It's like a play on the stage. . . .

BESSIE: To a mother you couldn't say something before. I'm old-fashioned – like your friends I'm not smart – I don't eat chop suey and run around Coney Island with tramps. [*She walks reflectively to buffet, picks up a box of candy, puts it down, says to Myron*] Tomorrow night bring Sam Feinschreiber for supper.

HENNIE: I won't do it.

BESSIE: You'll do it, my fine beauty, you'll do it!

HENNIE: I'm not marrying a poor foreigner like him. Can't even speak an English word. Not me! I'll go to my grave without a husband.

BESSIE: You don't say! We'll find you somewhere a millionaire with a pleasure boat. He's going to night school, Sam. For a boy only three years in the country he speaks very nice. In three years he put enough in the bank, a good living.

JACOB: This is serious?

BESSIE: What then? I'm talking for my health? He'll come tomorrow night for supper. By Saturday they're engaged.

JACOB: Such a thing you can't do.

BESSIE: Who asked your advice?

JACOB: Such a thing –

BESSIE: Never mind!

JACOB: The lowest from the low!

BESSIE: Don't talk! I'm warning you! A man who don't believe in God – with crazy ideas –

JACOB: So bad I never imagined you could be.

BESSIE: Maybe if you don't talk so much it wouldn't happen like this. You with your ideas – I'm a mother. I raise a family they should have respect.

JACOB: Respect? [*Spits.*] Respect! For the neighbours' opinion! You insult me, Bessie!

BESSIE: Go in your room, Papa. Every job he ever had he lost because he's got a big mouth. He opens his mouth and the whole Bronx could fall in. Everybody said it –

MYRON: Momma, they'll hear you down the dumbwaiter.

BESSIE: A good barber not to hold a job a week. Maybe you never heard charity starts at home. You never heard it, Pop?

JACOB: All you know, I heard, and more yet. But Ralph you don't make like you. Before you do it, I'll die first. He'll find a girl. He'll go in a fresh world with her. This is a house? Marx said it – abolish such families.

BESSIE: Go in your room, Papa.

JACOB: Ralph you don't make like you!

BESSIE: Go lay in your room with Caruso and the books together.

JACOB: All right!

BESSIE: Go in the room!

JACOB: Some day I'll come out I'll – [*Unable to continue, he turns, looks at Hennie, goes to his door and there says with an attempt at humour*] Bessie, some day you'll talk to me so fresh . . . I'll leave the house for good! [*He exits.*]

BESSIE [*crying*]: You ever in your life seen it? He should dare! He should just dare say in the house another word. Your gall could bust from such a man.

[*Bell rings,* MYRON *goes.*]

Go to sleep now. It won't hurt.

HENNIE: Yeah? [MOE *enters, a box in his hand.* MYRON *follows and sits down.*]

MOE [*looks around first – putting box on table*]: Cake. [*About to give Myron the money, he turns instead to Bessie.*] Six fifty, four bits change ... come on, hand over half a buck. [*She does so. Of Myron*] Who bit him?

BESSIE: We're soon losing our Hennie, Moe.

MOE: Why? What's the matter?

BESSIE: She made her engagement.

MOE: Zat so?

BESSIE: Today it happened ... he asked her.

MOE: Did he? Who? Who's the corpse?

BESSIE: It's a secret.

MOE: In the bag, huh?

HENNIE: Yeah ...

BESSIE: When a mother gives away an only daughter it's no joke. Wait, when you'll get married you'll know. ...

MOE [*bitterly*]: Don't make me laugh – when I get married! What I think a women? Take 'em all, cut 'em in little pieces like a herring in Greek salad. A guy in France had the right idea – dropped his wife in a bathtub fulla acid. [*Whistles.*] Sss, down the pipe! Pfft – not even a corset button left!

MYRON: Corsets don't have buttons.

MOE [*to Hennie*]: What's the great idea? Gone big time, Paradise? Christ, it's suicide! Sure, kids you'll have, gold teeth, get fat, big in the tangerines –

HENNIE: Shut your face!

MOE: Who's it – some dope pullin' down twenty bucks a week? Cut your throat, sweetheart. Save time.

BESSIE: Never mind your two cents, Axelrod.

MOE: I say what I think – that's me!

HENNIE: That's you – a lousy fourflusher who'd steal the glasses off a blind man.

MOE: Get hot!

HENNIE: My God, do I need it – to listen to this mutt shoot his mouth off?

137

MYRON: Please ...

MOE: Now wait a minute, sweetheart, wait a minute. I don't have to take that from you.

BESSIE: Don't yell at her!

HENNIE: For two cents I'd spit in your eye.

MOE [*throwing coin to table*]: Here's two bits.

[HENNIE *looks at him and then starts across the room.*]

BESSIE: Where are you going?

HENNIE [*crying*]: For my beauty nap, Mussolini. Wake me up when it's apple-blossom time in Normandy. [*Exits.*]

MOE: Pretty, pretty – a sweet gal, your Hennie. See the look in her eyes?

BESSIE: She don't feel well. ...

MYRON: Canned goods. ...

BESSIE: So don't start with her.

MOE: Like a battleship she's got it. Not like other dames – shove 'em and they lay. Not her. I got a yen for her and I don't mean a Chinee coin.

BESSIE: Listen, Axelrod, in my house you don't talk this way. Either have respect or get out.

MOE: When I think about it ... maybe I'd marry her myself.

BESSIE [*suddenly aware of Moe*]: You could – What do you mean, Moe?

MOE: You ain't sunburnt – you heard me.

BESSIE: Why don't you, Moe? An old friend of the family like you. It would be a blessing on all of us.

MOE: You said she's engaged.

BESSIE: But maybe she don't know her own mind. Say, it's –

MOE: I need a wife like a hole in the head. ... What's to know about women, I know. Even if I asked her. She won't do it! A guy with one leg – it gives her the heebie-jeebies. I know what she's looking for. An arrow-collar guy, a hero, but with a wad of jack. Only the two don't go together. But I got what it takes ... plenty, and more where it comes from. ...

[*Breaks off, snorts, and rubs his knee. A pause. In his room* JACOB *puts on Caruso singing the lament from* The Pearl Fishers.]

BESSIE: It's right – she wants a millionaire with a mansion on Riverside Drive. So go fight City Hall. Cake?

MOE: Cake.

BESSIE: I'll make tea. But one thing – she's got a fine boy with a business brain. Caruso! [*Exits into the front room and stands in the dark, at the window.*]

MOE: No wet smack ... a fine girl. ... She'll burn that guy out in a month. [MOE *retrieves the quarter and spins it on the table.*]

MYRON: I remember that song ... beautiful. Nora Bayes sang it at the old Proctor's Twenty-third Street – 'When It's Apple Blossom Time in Normandy'. ...

MOE: She wantsa see me crawl – my head on a plate she wants! A snowball in hell's got a better chance. [*Out of sheer fury he spins the quarter in his fingers.*]

MYRON [*as his eyes slowly fill with tears*]: Beautiful ...

MOE: Match you for a quarter. Match you for any goddam thing you got. [*Spins the coin viciously.*] What the hell kind of house is this it ain't got an orange!!

Slow curtain

ACT TWO

SCENE I

One year later, a Sunday afternoon. The front room.

> [JACOB *is giving his son* MORDECAI (UNCLE MORTY) *a haircut, newspapers spread around the base of the chair.* MOE *is reading a newspaper, leg propped on a chair.* RALPH, *in another chair, is spasmodically reading a paper.* UNCLE MORTY *reads coloured jokes. Silence, then* BESSIE *enters.*]

BESSIE: Dinner's in half an hour, Morty.

MORTY [*still reading jokes*]: I got time.

BESSIE: A duck. Don't get hair on the rug, Pop. [*Goes to window and pulls down shade.*] What's the matter the shade's up to the ceiling?

JACOB [*pulling it up again*]: Since when do I give a haircut in the dark? [*He mimics her tone.*]

BESSIE: When you're finished, pull it down. I like my house to look respectable. Ralphie, bring up two bottles seltzer from Weiss.

RALPH: I'm reading the paper.

BESSIE: Uncle Morty likes a little seltzer.

RALPH: I'm expecting a phone call.

BESSIE: Noo, if it comes you'll be back. What's the matter? [*Gives him money from apron pocket.*] Take down the old bottles.

RALPH [*to Jacob*]: Get that call if it comes. Say I'll be right back.
> [JACOB *nods assent.*]

MORTY [*giving change from waistcoat*]: Get grandpa some cigarettes.

RALPH: Okay. [*Exits.*]

JACOB: What's new in the paper, Moe?

MOE: Still jumping off the high buildings like flies – the big shots who lost all their coconuts. Pfft!

JACOB: Suicides?

MOE: Plenty can't take it – good in the break, but can't take the whip in the stretch.

MORTY [*without looking up*]: I saw it happen Monday in my building. My hair stood up how they shovelled him together – like a pancake – a bankrupt manufacturer.

MOE: No brains.

MORTY: Enough ... all over the sidewalk.

JACOB: If someone said five–ten years ago I couldn't make for myself a living, I wouldn't believe –

MORTY: Duck for dinner?

BESSIE: The best Long Island duck.

MORTY: I like goose.

BESSIE: A duck is just like a goose, only better.

MORTY: I like a goose.

BESSIE: The next time you'll be for Sunday dinner I'll make a goose.

MORTY [*sniffs deeply*]: Smells good. I'm a great boy for smells.

BESSIE: Ain't you ashamed? Once in a blue moon he should come to an only sister's house.

MORTY: Bessie, leave me live.

BESSIE: You should be ashamed!

MORTY: Quack quack!

BESSIE: No, better to lay around Mecca Temple playing cards with the Masons.

MORTY [*with good nature*]: Bessie, don't you see Pop's giving me a haircut?

BESSIE: You don't need no haircut. Look, two hairs he took off.

MORTY: Pop likes to give me a haircut. If I said no he don't forget for a year, do you, Pop? An old man's like that.

JACOB: I still do an A-1 job.

MORTY [*winking*]: Pop cuts hair to fit the face, don't you, Pop?

JACOB: For sure, Morty. To each face a different haircut. Custom built, no ready made. A round face needs special –

BESSIE [*cutting him short*]: A graduate from the B.M.T. [*Going*] Don't forget the shade. [*The phone rings. She beats Jacob to it.*] Hello? Who is it, please? . . . Who is it, please? . . . Miss Hirsch? No, he ain't here. . . . No, I couldn't say when. [*Hangs up sharply.*]

JACOB: For Ralph?

BESSIE: A wrong number. [JACOB *looks at her and goes back to his job.*]

JACOB: Excuse me!

BESSIE [*to Morty*]: Ralphie took another cut down the place yesterday.

MORTY: Business is bad. I saw his boss Harry Glicksman Thursday. I bought some velvets . . . they're coming in again.

BESSIE: Do something for Ralphie down there.

MORTY: What can I do? I mentioned it to Glicksman. He told me they squeezed out half the people. . . . [MYRON *enters dressed in apron.*]

BESSIE: What's gonna be the end? Myron's working only three days a week now.

MYRON: It's conditions.

BESSIE: Hennie's married with a baby . . . money just don't come in. I never saw conditions should be so bad.

MORTY: Times'll change.

MOE: The only thing'll change is my underwear.

MORTY: These last few years I got my share of grey hairs. [*Still reading jokes without having looked up once*] Ha, ha, ha – Popeye the sailor ate spinach and knocked out four bums.

MYRON: I'll tell you the way I see it. The country needs a great man now – a regular Teddy Roosevelt.

MOE: What this country needs is a good five-cent earthquake.

JACOB: So long labour lives it should increase private gain –

BESSIE [*to Jacob*]: Listen, Poppa, go talk on the street corner. The government'll give you free board the rest of your life.

MORTY: I'm surprised. Don't I send a five-dollar cheque for Pop every week.

BESSIE: You could afford a couple more and not miss it.

MORTY: Tell me jokes. Business is so rotten I could just as soon lay all day in the Turkish bath.

MYRON: Why'd I come in here? [*Puzzled, he exits.*]

MORTY [*to Moe*]: I hear the bootleggers still do business, Moe.

MOE: Wake up! I kissed bootlegging bye-bye two years back.

MORTY: For a fact? What kind of racket is it now?

MOE: If I told you, you'd know something.

[HENNIE *comes from bedroom.*]

HENNIE: Where's Sam?

BESSIE: Sam? In the kitchen.

HENNIE [*calls*]: Sam. Come take the diaper.

MORTY: How's the Mickey Louse? Ha, ha, ha. . . .

HENNIE: Sleeping.

MORTY: Ah, that's life to a baby. He sleeps – gets it in the mouth – sleeps some more. To raise a family nowadays you must be a damn fool.

BESSIE: Never mind, never mind, a woman who don't raise a family – a girl – should jump overboard. What's she good for? [*To Moe – to change the subject*] Your leg bothers you bad?

MOE: It's okay, sweetheart.

BESSIE [*to Morty*]: It hurts him every time it's cold out. He's got four legs in the closet.

MORTY: Four wooden legs?

MOE: Three.

MORTY: What's the big idea?

MOE: Why not? Uncle Sam gives them out free.

MORTY: Say, maybe if Uncle Sam gave out less legs we could balance the budget.

JACOB: Or not have a war so they wouldn't have to give out legs.

MORTY: Shame on you, Pop. Everybody knows war is necessary.

MOE: Don't make me laugh. Ask me – the first time you pick up a dead one in the trench – then you learn war ain't so damn necessary.

MORTY: Say, you should kick. The rest of your life Uncle Sam pays you ninety a month. Look, not a worry in the world.

MOE: Don't make me laugh. Uncle Sam can take his *seventy* bucks and – [*Finishes with a gesture.*] Nothing good hurts. [*He rubs his stump.*]

HENNIE: Use a crutch, Axelrod. Give the stump a rest.

MOE: Mind your business, Feinschreiber.

BESSIE: It's a sensible idea.

MOE: Who asked you?

BESSIE: Look, he's ashamed.

MOE: So's your Aunt Fanny.

BESSIE [*naïvely*]: Who's got an Aunt Fanny? [*She cleans a rubber plant's leaves with her apron.*]

MORTY: It's a joke!

MOE: I don't want my paper creased before I read it. I want it fresh. Fifty times I said that.

BESSIE: Don't get so excited for a five-cent paper – our star boarder.

MOE: And I don't want no one using my razor either. Get it straight. I'm not buying ten blades a week for the Berger family. [*Furious, he limps out.*]

BESSIE: Maybe I'm using his razor too.

HENNIE: Proud!

BESSIE: You need luck with plants. I didn't clean off the leaves in a month.

MORTY: You keep the house like a pin and I like your cooking. Any time Myron fires you, come to me, Bessie. I'll let the butler go and you'll be my housekeeper. I don't like Japs so much – sneaky.

BESSIE: Say, you can't tell. Maybe any day I'm coming to stay.
    [HENNIE *exits.*]

JACOB: Finished.

MORTY: How much, Ed. Pinaud? [*Disengages self from chair.*]

JACOB: Five cents.

MORTY: Still five cents for a haircut to fit the face?

JACOB: Prices don't change by me. [*Takes a dollar.*] I can't change –

MORTY: Keep it. Buy yourself a Packard. Ha, ha, ha.

JACOB [*taking large envelope from pocket*]: Please, you'll keep this for me. Put it away.

MORTY: What is it?

JACOB: My insurance policy. I don't like it should lay around where something could happen.

MORTY: What could happen?

JACOB: Who knows, robbers, fire ... they took next door. Fifty dollars from O'Reilly.

MORTY: Say, lucky a Berger didn't lose it.

JACOB: Put it downtown in the safe. Bessie don't have to know.

MORTY: It's made out to Bessie?

JACOB: No, to Ralph.

MORTY: To Ralph?

JACOB: He don't know. Some day he'll get three thousand.

MORTY: You got good years ahead.

JACOB: Behind.

[RALPH *enters.*]

RALPH: Cigarettes. Did a call come?

JACOB: A few minutes. She don't let me answer it.

RALPH: Did Mom say I was coming back?

JACOB: No.

[MORTY *is back at new jokes.*]

RALPH: She starting that stuff again? [BESSIE *enters.*] A call come for me?

BESSIE [*waters pot from milk bottle*]: A wrong number.

JACOB: Don't say a lie, Bessie.

RALPH: Blanche said she'd call me at two – was it her?

BESSIE: I said a wrong number.

RALPH: Please, Mom, if it was her tell me.

BESSIE: You call me a liar next. You got no shame – to start a scene in front of Uncle Morty. Once in a blue moon he comes –

RALPH: What's the shame? If my girl calls I wanna know it.

BESSIE: You made enough mish mosh with her until now.

MORTY: I'm surprised, Bessie. For the love of Mike tell him yes or no.

BESSIE: I didn't tell him? No!

MORTY [*to Ralph*] : No!

[RALPH *goes to a window and looks out.*]

BESSIE: Morty, I didn't say before – he runs around steady with a girl.

MORTY: Terrible. Should he run around with a foxie-woxie?

BESSIE: A girl with no parents.

MORTY: An orphan?

BESSIE: I could die from shame. A year already he runs around with her. He brought her once for supper. Believe me, she didn't come again, no!

RALPH: Don't think I didn't ask her.

BESSIE: You hear? You raise them and what's in the end for all your trouble?

JACOB: When you'll lay in a grave, no more trouble. [*Exits.*]

MORTY: Quack, quack!

BESSIE: A girl like that he wants to marry. A skinny consumptive-looking . . . six months already she's not working – taking charity from an aunt. You should see her. In a year she's dead on his hands.

RALPH: You'd cut her throat if you could.

BESSIE: That's right! Before she'd ruin a nice boy's life I would first go to prison. Miss Nobody should step in the picture and I'll stand by with my mouth shut.

RALPH: Miss Nobody! Who am I? Al Jolson?

BESSIE: Fix your tie!

RALPH: I'll take care of my own life.

BESSIE: You'll take care? Excuse my expression, you can't even wipe your nose yet! He'll take care!

MORTY [*to Bessie*]: I'm surprised. Don't worry so much, Bessie. When it's time to settle down he won't marry a poor girl, will you? In the long run common sense is thicker than love. I'm a great boy for live and let live.

BESSIE: Sure, it's easy to say. In the meantime he eats out my heart. You know I'm not strong.

MORTY: I know . . . a pussy cat . . . ha, ha, ha.

BESSIE: You got money and money talks. But without the dollar who sleeps at night?

RALPH: I been working for years, bringing in money here – putting it in your hand like a kid. All right, I can't get my teeth fixed. All right, that a new suit's like trying to buy the Chrysler Building. You never in your life bought me a pair of skates even – things I died for when I was a kid. I don't care about that stuff, see. Only just remember I pay some of the bills around here, just a few . . . and if my girl calls me on the phone I'll talk to her any time I please. [*He exits.* HENNIE *applauds.*]

BESSIE: Don't be so smart, Miss America! [*To Morty*] He didn't have skates! But when he got sick, a twelve-year-old boy, who called a big specialist for the last $25 in the house? Skates!

JACOB [*just in. Adjusts window shade*]: It looks like snow today.

MORTY: It's about time – winter.

BESSIE: Poppa here could talk like Samuel Webster, too, but it's just talk. He should try to buy a two-cent pickle in the Burland Market without money.

MORTY: I'm getting an appetite.

BESSIE: Right away we'll eat. I made chopped liver for you.

MORTY: My specialty!

BESSIE: Ralph should only be a success like you, Morty. I should only live to see the day when he rides up to the door in a big car with a chauffeur and a radio. I could die happy, believe me.

MORTY: Success she says. She should see how we spend thousands of dollars making up a winter line and winter don't come – summer in January. Can you beat it?

JACOB: Don't live, just make success.

MORTY: Chopped liver – ha!

JACOB: Ha! [*Exits.*]

MORTY: When they start arguing, I don't hear. Suddenly I'm deaf. I'm a great boy for the practical side. [*He looks over to* HENNIE *who sits rubbing her hands with lotion.*]

HENNIE: Hands like a raw potato.

MORTY: What's the matter? You don't look so well ... no pep.

HENNIE: I'm swell.

MORTY: You used to be such a pretty girl.

HENNIE: Maybe I got the blues. You can't tell.

MORTY: You could stand a new dress.

HENNIE: That's not all I could stand.

MORTY: Come down to the place tomorrow and pick out a couple from the 'eleven-eighty' line. Only don't sing me the blues.

HENNIE: Thanks. I need some new clothes.

MORTY: I got two thousand pieces of merchandise waiting in the stock room for winter.

HENNIE: I never had anything from life. Sam don't help.

MORTY: He's crazy about the kid.

HENNIE: Crazy is right. Twenty-one a week he brings in – a nigger don't have it so hard. I wore my fingers off on an Underwood for six years. For what? Now I wash baby diapers. Sure, I'm crazy about the kid too. But half the night the kid's up. Try to sleep. You don't know how it is, Uncle Morty.

MORTY: No, I don't know. I was born yesterday. Ha, ha, ha. Some day I'll leave you a little nest egg. You like eggs? Ha?

HENNIE: When? When I'm dead and buried?

MORTY: No, when *I'm* dead and buried. Ha, ha, ha.

HENNIE: You should know what I'm thinking.

MORTY: Ha, ha, ha, I know.

[MYRON *enters.*]

MYRON: I never take a drink. I'm just surprised at myself, I –

MORTY: I got a pain. Maybe I'm hungry.

MYRON: Come inside, Morty. Bessie's got some schnapps.

MORTY: I'll take a drink. Yesterday I missed the Turkish bath.

MYRON: I get so bitter when I take a drink, it just surprises me.

MORTY: Look how fat. Say, you live once. ... Quack, quack.

[*Both exit.* MOE *stands silently in the doorway.*]

SAM [*entering*]: I'll make Leon's bottle now!

HENNIE: No, let him sleep, Sam. Take away the diaper.
[*He does. Exits.*]

MOE [*advancing into the room*]: That your husband?

HENNIE: Don't you know?

MOE: Maybe he's a nurse you hired for the kid – it looks it – how he tends it. A guy comes howling to your old lady every time you look cock-eyed. Does he sleep with you?

HENNIE: Don't be so wise!

MOE [*indicating newspaper*]: Here's a dame strangled her hubby with wire. Claimed she didn't like him. Why don't you brain Sam with an axe some night?

HENNIE: Why don't you lay an egg, Axelrod?

MOE: I laid a few in my day, Feinschreiber. Hard-boiled ones too.

HENNIE: Yeah?

MOE: Yeah. You wanna know what I see when I look in your eyes?

HENNIE: No.

MOE: Ted Lewis playing the clarinet – some of those high crazy notes! Christ, you coulda had a guy with some guts instead of a cluck stands around boilin' baby nipples.

HENNIE: Meaning you?

MOE: Meaning me, sweetheart.

HENNIE: Think you're pretty good.

MOE: You'd know if I slept with you again.

HENNIE: I'll smack your face in a minute.

MOE: You do and I'll break your arm. [*Holds up paper.*] Take a look. [*Reads*] 'Ten-day luxury cruise to Havana.' That's the stuff you coulda had. Put up at ritzy hotels, frenchie soap, champagne. Now you're tied down to 'Snake-Eye' here. What for? What's it get you? . . . a 2 by 4 flat on 108th Street . . . a pain in the bustle it gets you.

HENNIE: What's it to you?

MOE: I know you from the old days. How you like to spend it!

What I mean! Lizard-skin shoes, perfume behind the ears. ...
You're in a mess, Paradise! Paradise – that's a hot one – yah, crazy
to eat a knish at your own wedding.

HENNIE: I get it – you're jealous. You can't get me.

MOE: Don't make me laugh.

HENNIE: Kid Jailbird's been trying to make me for years. You'd give
your other leg. I'm hooked? Maybe, but you're in the same boat.
Only it's worse for you. I don't give a damn no more, but you
gotta yen makes you –

MOE: Don't make me laugh.

HENNIE: Compared to you I'm sittin' on top of the world.

MOE: You're losing your looks. A dame don't stay young forever.

HENNIE: You're a liar. I'm only twenty-four.

MOE: When you comin' home to stay?

HENNIE: Wouldn't you like to know?

MOE: I'll get you again.

HENNIE: Think so?

MOE: Sure, whatever goes up comes down. You're easy – you remember – two for a nickel – a pushover! [*Suddenly she slaps him.
They both seem stunned.*] What's the idea?

HENNIE: Go on ... break my arm.

MOE [*as if saying 'I love you'*]: Listen, lousy.

HENNIE: Go on, do something!

MOE: Listen –

HENNIE: You're so damn tough!

MOE: You like me. [*He takes her.*]

HENNIE: Take your hand off! [*Pushes him away.*] Come around when
it's a flood again and they put you in the ark with the animals.
Not even then – if you was the last man!

MOE: Baby, if you had a dog I'd love the dog.

HENNIE: Gorilla! [*Exits.* RALPH *enters.*]

RALPH: Were you here before?

MOE [*sits*]: What?

RALPH: When the call came for me?

MOE: What?

RALPH: The call came.

[JACOB *enters.*]

MOE [*rubbing his leg*]: No.

JACOB: Don't worry, Ralphie, she'll call back.

RALPH: Maybe not. I think somethin's the matter.

JACOB: What?

RALPH: I don't know. I took her home from the movie last night.
   She asked me what I'd think if she went away.

JACOB: Don't worry, she'll call again.

RALPH: Maybe not, if Mom insulted her. She gets it on both ends,
   the poor kid. Lived in an orphan asylum most of her life. They
   shove her around like an empty freight train.

JACOB: After dinner go see her.

RALPH: Twice they kicked me down the stairs.

JACOB: Life should have some dignity.

RALPH: Every time I go near the place I get heart failure. The uncle
   drives a bus. You oughta see him – like Babe Ruth.

MOE: Use your brains. Stop acting like a kid who still wets the bed.
   Hire a room somewhere – a club room for two members.

RALPH: Not that kind of proposition, Moe.

MOE: Don't be a bush leaguer all your life.

RALPH: Cut it out!

MOE [*on a sudden upsurge of emotion*]: Ever sleep with one? Look at 'im
   blush.

RALPH: You don't know her.

MOE: I seen her – the kind no one sees undressed till the undertaker
   works on her.

RALPH: Why give me the needles all the time? What'd I ever do to
   you?

MOE: Not a thing. You're a nice kid. But grow up! In life there's two
   kinds – the men that's sure of themselves and the ones who ain't!
   It's time you quit being a selling-plater and got in the first
   class.

JACOB: And you, Axelrod?

MOE [*to Jacob*]: Scratch your whiskers! [*To Ralph*] Get independent. Get what-it-takes and be yourself. Do what you like.

RALPH: Got a suggestion?

　　[MORTY *enters, eating.*]

MOE: Sure, pick out a racket. Shake down the coconuts. See what that does.

MORTY: We know what it does – puts a pudding on your nose! Sing Sing! Easy money's against the law. Against the law don't win. A racket is illegitimate, no?

MOE: It's all a racket – from horse racing down. Marriage, politics, big business – everybody plays cops and robbers. You, you're a racketeer yourself.

MORTY: Who? Me? Personally I manufacture dresses.

MOE: Horse feathers!

MORTY [*seriously*]: Don't make such remarks to me without proof. I'm a great one for proof. That's why I made a success of business. Proof – put up or shut up, like a game of cards. I heard this remark before – a rich man's a crook who steals from the poor. Personally, I don't like it. It's a big lie!

MOE: If you don't like it, buy yourself a fife and drum – and go fight your own war.

MORTY: Sweatshop talk. Every Jew and Wop in the shop eats my bread and behind my back says, 'a sonofabitch'. I started from a poor boy who worked on an ice wagon for two dollars a week. Pop's right here – he'll tell you. I made it honest. In the whole industry nobody's got a better name.

JACOB: It's an exception, such success.

MORTY: Ralph can't do the same thing?

JACOB: No, Morty, I don't think. In a house like this he don't realize even the possibilities of life. Economics comes down like a ton of coal on the head.

MOE: Red rover, red rover, let Jacob come over!

JACOB: In my day the propaganda was for God. Now it's for success.

A boy don't turn around without having shoved in him he should make success.

MORTY: Pop, you're a comedian, a regular Charlie Chaplin.

JACOB: He dreams all night of fortunes. Why not? Don't it say in the movies he should have a personal steamship, pyjamas for fifty dollars a pair and a toilet like a monument? But in the morning he wakes up and for ten dollars he can't fix the teeth. And millions more worse off in the mills of the South – starvation wages. The blood from the worker's heart.

[MORTY *laughs loud and long.*]

Laugh, laugh ... tomorrow not.

MORTY: A real, a real Boob McNutt you're getting to be.

JACOB: Laugh, my son. ...

MORTY: Here is the North, Pop.

JACOB: North, South, it's one country.

MORTY: The country's all right. A duck quacks in every pot!

JACOB: You never heard how they shoot down men and women which ask a better wage? Kentucky 1932?

MORTY: That's a pile of chopped liver, Pop.

[BESSIE *and others enter.*]

JACOB: Pittsburgh, Passaic, Illinois – slavery – it begins where success begins in a competitive system.

[MORTY *howls with delight.*]

MORTY: Oh Pop, what are you bothering? Why? Tell me why? Ha ha ha. I bought you a phonograph ... stick to Caruso.

BESSIE: He's starting up again.

MORTY: Don't bother with Kentucky. It's full of moonshiners.

JACOB: Sure, sure –

MORTY: You don't know practical affairs. Stay home and cut hair to fit the face.

JACOB: It says in the Bible how the Red Sea opened and the Egyptians went in and the sea rolled over them. [*Quotes two lines of Hebrew.*] In this boy's life a Red Sea will happen again. I see it!

MORTY: I'm getting sore, Pop, with all this sweatshop talk.

BESSIE: He don't stop a minute. The whole day, like a phonograph.

MORTY: I'm surprised. Without a rich man you don't have a roof over your head. You don't know it?

MYRON: Now you can't bite the hand that feeds you.

RALPH: Let him alone – he's right!

BESSIE: Another county heard from.

RALPH: It's the truth. It's –

MORTY: Keep quiet, snotnose!

JACOB: For sure, charity, a bone for an old dog. But in Russia an old man don't take charity so his eyes turn black in his head. In Russia they got Marx.

MORTY [*scoffingly*]: Who's Marx?

MOE: An outfielder for the Yanks.

[MORTY *howls with delight.*]

MORTY: Ha ha ha, it's better than the jokes. I'm telling you. This is Uncle Sam's country. Put it in your pipe and smoke it.

BESSIE: Russia, he says! Read the papers.

SAM: Here is opportunity.

MYRON: People can't believe in God in Russia. The papers tell the truth, they do.

JACOB: So you believe in God . . . you got something for it? You! You worked for all the capitalists. You harvested the fruit from your labour? You got God! But the past comforts you? The present smiles on you, yes? It promises you the future something? Did you find a piece of earth where you could live like a human being and die with the sun on your face? Tell me, yes, tell me. I would like to know myself. But on these questions, on this theme – the struggle for existence – you can't make an answer. The answer I see in your face . . . the answer is your mouth can't talk. In this dark corner you sit and you die. But abolish private property!

BESSIE [*settling the issue*]: Noo, go fight City Hall!

MORTY: He's drunk!

JACOB: I'm studying from books a whole lifetime.

MORTY: That's what it is – he's drunk. What the hell does all that mean?

JACOB: If you don't know, why should I tell you.

MORTY [*triumphant at last*]: You see? Hear him? Like all those nuts, don't know what they're saying.

JACOB: I know, I know.

MORTY: Like Boob McNutt you know! Don't go in the park, Pop – the squirrels'll get you. Ha, ha, ha . . .

BESSIE: Save your appetite, Morty. [*To Myron*] Don't drop the duck.

MYRON: We're ready to eat, Momma.

MORTY [*to Jacob*]: Shame on you. It's your second childhood.
[*Now they file out.* MYRON *first with the duck, the others behind him.*]

BESSIE: Come eat. We had enough for one day. [*Exits.*]

MORTY: Ha, ha, ha. Quack, quack. [*Exits.*]
[JACOB *sits there trembling and deeply humiliated.* MOE *approaches him and thumbs the old man's nose in the direction of the dining-room.*]

MOE: Give 'em five. [*Takes his hand away.*] They got you pasted on the wall like a picture, Jake. [*He limps out to seat himself at the table in the next room.*]

JACOB: Go eat, boychick. [RALPH *comes to him.*] He gives me eat, so I'll climb in a needle. One time I saw an old horse in summer . . . he wore a straw hat . . . the ears stuck out on top. An old horse for hire. Give me back my young days . . . give me fresh blood . . . arms . . . give me –
[*The telephone rings. Quickly* RALPH *goes to it.* JACOB *pulls the curtains and stands there, a sentry on guard.*]

RALPH: Hello? . . . Yeah, I went to the store and came right back, right after you called. [*Looks at Jacob.*]

JACOB: Speak, speak. Don't be afraid they'll hear.

RALPH: I'm sorry if Mom said something. You know how excitable Mom is . . . Sure! What? . . Sure, I'm listening. . . . Put on the radio, Jake.

[JACOB *does so. Music comes in and up, a tango, grating with an in-sistent nostalgic pulse. Under the cover of the music* RALPH *speaks more freely.*]

Yes ... yes ... What's the matter? Why're you crying? What happened? [*To Jacob*] She's putting her uncle on. Yes? ... Listen, Mr Hirsch, what're you trying to do? What's the big idea? Honest to God. I'm in no mood for joking! Lemme talk to her! Gimme Blanche! [*Waits.*] Blanche? What's this? Is this a joke? Is that true? I'm coming right down! I know, but – You wanna do that? ... I know, but – I'm coming down ... tonight! Nine o'clock ... sure ... sure ... sure. ... [*Hangs up.*]

JACOB: What happened?

MORTY [*enters*]: Listen, Pop. I'm surprised you didn't – [*He howls, shakes his head in mock despair, exits.*]

JACOB: Boychick, what?

RALPH: I don't get it straight. [*To Jacob*] She's leaving. ...

JACOB: Where?

RALPH: Out West – To Cleveland.

JACOB: Cleveland?

RALPH: ... In a week or two. Can you picture it? It's a put-up job. But they can't get away with that.

JACOB: We'll find something.

RALPH: Sure, the angels of heaven'll come down on her uncle's cab and whisper in his ear.

JACOB: Come eat. ... We'll find something.

RALPH: I'm meeting her tonight, but I know – [BESSIE *throws open the curtain between the two rooms and enters.*]

BESSIE: Maybe we'll serve for you a special blue-plate supper in the garden?

JACOB: All right, all right. [BESSIE *goes over to the window, levels the shade and on her way out, clicks off the radio.*]

MORTY [*within*]: Leave the music, Bessie. [*She clicks it on again, looks at them, exits.*]

RALPH: I know ...

JACOB: Don't cry, boychick. [*Goes over to Ralph.*] Why should you make like this? Tell me why you should cry, just tell me. . . .

[JACOB *takes Ralph in his arms and both, trying to keep back the tears, trying fearfully not to be heard by the others in the dining-room, begin crying.*]

You mustn't cry. . . .

[*The tango twists on. Inside the clatter of dishes and the clash of cutlery sound.* MORTY *begins to howl with laughter.*]

Curtain

SCENE 2

That night. The dark dining-room.

[*As the curtain rises* JACOB *is heard in his lighted room, reading from a sheet, declaiming aloud as if to an audience.*]

JACOB: They are there to remind us of the horrors – under those crosses lie hundreds of thousands of workers and farmers who murdered each other in uniform for the greater glory of capitalism. [*Comes out of his room.*] The new imperialist war will send millions to their death, will bring prosperity to the pockets of the capitalist – aie, Morty – and will bring only greater hunger and misery to the masses of workers and farmers. The memories of the last world slaughter are still vivid in our minds. [*Hearing a noise he quickly retreats to his room.* RALPH *comes in from the street. He sits with hat and coat on.* JACOB *tentatively opens door and asks*] Ralphie?

RALPH: It's getting pretty cold out.

JACOB [*enters room fully, cleaning hair clippers*]: We should have steam till twelve instead of ten. Go complain to the Board of Health.

RALPH: It might snow.

JACOB: It don't hurt . . . extra work for men.

RALPH: When I was a kid I laid awake at nights and heard the sounds of trains ... far-away lonesome sounds ... boats going up and down the river. I used to think of all kinds of things I wanted to do. What was it, Jake? Just a bunch of noise in my head?

JACOB [*waiting for news of the girl*]: You wanted to make for yourself a certain kind of world.

RALPH: I guess I didn't. I'm feeling pretty, pretty low.

JACOB: You're a young boy and for you life is all in front like a big mountain. You got feet to climb.

RALPH: I don't know how.

JACOB: So you'll find out. Never a young man had such opportunity like today. He could make history.

RALPH: Ten p.m. and all is well. Where's everybody?

JACOB: They went.

RALPH: Uncle Morty too?

JACOB: Hennie and Sam he drove down.

RALPH: I saw her.

JACOB [*alert and eager*]: Yes, yes, tell me.

RALPH: I waited in Mount Morris Park till she came out. So cold I did a buck'n wing to keep warm. She's scared to death.

JACOB: They made her?

RALPH: Sure. She wants to go. They keep yelling at her – they want her to marry a millionaire, too.

JACOB: You told her you love her?

RALPH: Sure. 'Marry me,' I said. 'Marry me tomorrow.' On sixteen bucks a week. On top of that I had to admit Mom'd have Uncle Morty get me fired in a second.... Two can starve as cheap as one!

JACOB: So what happened?

RALPH: I made her promise to meet me tomorrow.

JACOB: Now she'll go in the West?

RALPH: I'd fight the whole goddam world with her, but not her. No guts. The hell with her. If she wantsa go – all right – I'll get along.

JACOB: For sure, there's more important things than girls. ...

RALPH: You said a mouthful ... and maybe I don't see it. She'll see what I can do. No one stops me when I get going. ...

[*Near to tears, he has to stop.* JACOB *examines his clippers very closely.*]

JACOB: Electric clippers never do a job like by hand.

RALPH: Why won't Mom let us live here?

JACOB: Why? Why? Because in a society like this today people don't love. Hate!

RALPH: Gee, I'm no bum who hangs around pool parlours. I got the stuff to go ahead. I don't know what to do.

JACOB: Look on me and learn what to do, boychick. Here sits an old man polishing tools. You think maybe I'll use them again! Look on this failure and see for seventy years he talked, with good ideas, but only in the head. It's enough for me now I should see your happiness. This is why I tell you – DO! Do what is in your heart and you carry in yourself a revolution. But you should act. Not like me. A man who had golden opportunities but drank instead a glass tea. No. . . . [*A pause of silence.*]

RALPH [*listening*]: Hear it? The Boston air mail plane. Ten minutes late. I get a kick the way it cuts across the Bronx every night. [*The bell rings:* SAM, *excited, dishevelled, enters.*]

JACOB: You came back so soon?

SAM: Where's Mom?

JACOB: Mom? Look on the chandelier.

SAM: Nobody's home.

JACOB: Sit down. Right away they're coming. You went in the street without a tie?

SAM: Maybe it's a crime.

JACOB: Excuse me.

RALPH: You had a fight with Hennie again?

SAM: She'll fight once . . . some day. . . . [*Lapses into silence.*]

JACOB: In my day the daughter came home. Now comes the son-in-law.

SAM: Once too often she'll fight with me, Hennie. I mean it. I mean it like anything. I'm a person with a bad heart. I sit quiet, but inside I got a –

RALPH: What happened?

SAM: I'll talk to Mom. I'll see Mom.

JACOB: Take an apple.

SAM: Please . . . he tells me apples.

RALPH: Why hop around like a billiard ball?

SAM: Even in a joke she should dare say it.

JACOB: My grandchild said something?

SAM: To my father in the old country they did a joke . . . I'll tell you: One day in Odessa he talked to another Jew on the street. They didn't like it, they jumped on him like a wild wolf.

RALPH: Who?

SAM: Cossacks. They cut off his beard. A Jew without a beard! He came home – I remember like yesterday how he came home and went in bed for two days. He put like this the cover on his face. No one should see. The third morning he died.

RALPH: From what?

SAM: From a broken heart. . . . Some people are like this. Me too. I could die like this from shame.

JACOB: Hennie told you something?

SAM: Straight out she said it – like a lightning from the sky. The baby ain't mine. She said it.

RALPH: Don't be a dope.

JACOB: For sure, a joke.

RALPH: She's kidding you.

SAM: She should kid a policeman, not Sam Feinschreiber. Please . . . you don't know her like me. I wake up in the night-time and she sits watching me like I don't know what. I make a nice living from the store. But it's no use – she looks for a star in the sky. I'm afraid like anything. You could go crazy from less even. What I shall do I'll ask Mom.

JACOB: 'Go home and sleep,' she'll say. 'It's a bad dream.'

SAM: It don't satisfy me more, such remarks, when Hennie could kill in the bed.

[JACOB *laughs*.]

Don't laugh. I'm so nervous – look, two times I weighed myself on the subway station. [*Throws small cards to table.*]

JACOB [*examining one*]: One hundred and thirty-eight – also a fortune. [*Turns it and reads*] 'You are inclined to deep thinking, and have a high admiration for intellectual excellence and inclined to be very exclusive in the selection of friends.' Correct! I think maybe you got mixed up in the wrong family, Sam.

[MYRON *and* BESSIE *now enter.*]

BESSIE: Look, a guest! What's the matter? Something wrong with the baby? [*Waits.*]

SAM: No.

BESSIE: Noo?

SAM [*in a burst*]: I wash my hands from everything.

BESSIE: Take off your coat and hat. Have a seat. Excitement don't help. Myron, make tea. You'll have a glass tea. We'll talk like civilized people. [MYRON *goes.*] What is it, Ralph, you're all dressed up for a party? [*He looks at her silently and exits. To Sam*] We saw a very good movie, with Wallace Beery. He acts like life, very good.

MYRON [*within*]: Polly Moran too.

BESSIE: Polly Moran too – a woman with a nose from here to Hunts Point, but a fine player. Poppa, take away the tools and the books.

JACOB: All right. [*Exits to his room.*]

BESSIE: Noo, Sam, why do you look like a funeral?

SAM: I can't stand it. . . .

BESSIE: Wait. [*Yells*] You took up Tootsie on the roof.

JACOB [*within*]: In a minute.

BESSIE: What can't you stand?

SAM: She said I'm a second fiddle in my own house.

BESSIE: Who?

SAM: Hennie. In the second place, it ain't my baby, she said.

BESSIE: What? What are you talking?

[MYRON *enters with dishes.*]

SAM: From her own mouth. It went like a knife in my heart.

BESSIE: Sam, what're you saying?

SAM: Please, I'm making a story? I fell in the chair like a dead.

BESSIE: Such a story you believe?

SAM: I don't know.

BESSIE: How you don't know?

SAM: She told me even the man.

BESSIE: Impossible!

SAM: I can't believe myself. But she said it. I'm a second fiddle, she said. She made such a yell everybody heard for ten miles.

BESSIE: Such a thing Hennie should say – impossible!

SAM: What should I do? With my bad heart such a remark kills.

MYRON: Hennie don't feel well, Sam. You see, she –

BESSIE: What then? – a sick girl. Believe me, a mother knows. Nerves. Our Hennie's got a bad temper. You'll let her she says anything. She takes after me – nervous. [*To Myron*] You ever heard such a remark in all your life? She should make such a statement! Bughouse.

MYRON: The little one's been sick all these months. Hennie needs a rest. No doubt.

BESSIE: Sam don't think she means it –

MYRON: Oh, I know he don't, of course –

BESSIE: I'll say the truth, Sam. We didn't half the time understand her ourselves. A girl with her own mind. When she makes it up, wild horses wouldn't change her.

SAM: She don't love me.

BESSIE: This is sensible, Sam?

SAM: Not for a nickel.

BESSIE: What do you think? She married you for your money? For your looks? You ain't no John Barrymore, Sam. No, she liked you.

SAM: Please, not for a nickel.

[JACOB *stands in the doorway.*]

BESSIE: We stood right here the first time she said it. 'Sam Feinschreiber's a nice boy,' she said it, 'a boy he's got good common sense, with a business head.' Right here she said it, in this room. You sent her two boxes of candy together, you remember?

MYRON: Loft's candy.

BESSIE: This is when she said it. What do you think?

MYRON: You were just the only boy she cared for.

BESSIE: So she married you. Such a world ... plenty of boy friends she had, believe me!

JACOB: A popular girl. ...

MYRON: Y-e-s.

BESSIE: I'll say it plain out – Moe Axelrod offered her plenty – a servant, a house ... she don't have to pick up a hand.

MYRON: Oh, Moe? Just wild about her. ...

SAM: Moe Axelrod? He wanted to –

BESSIE: But she didn't care. A girl like Hennie you don't buy. I should never live to see another day if I'm telling a lie.

SAM: She was kidding me.

BESSIE: What then? You shouldn't be foolish.

SAM: The baby looks like my family. He's got Feinschreiber eyes.

BESSIE: A blind man could see it.

JACOB: Sure ... sure ...

SAM: The baby looks like me. Yes ...

BESSIE: You could believe me.

JACOB: Any day. ...

SAM: But she tells me the man. She made up his name too?

BESSIE: Sam, Sam, look in the phone book – a million names.

MYRON: Tom, Dick, and Harry.

[JACOB *laughs quietly, soberly.*]

BESSIE: Don't stand around, Poppa. Take Tootsie on the roof. And you don't let her go under the water tank.

JACOB: Schmah Yisroeal. Behold! [*Quietly laughing he goes back into his room, closing the door behind him.*]

SAM: I won't stand he should make insults. A man eats out his –

BESSIE: No, no, he's an old man – a second childhood. Myron, bring in the tea. Open a jar of raspberry jelly.

[MYRON *exits.*]

SAM: Mom, you think –?

BESSIE: I'll talk to Hennie. It's all right.

SAM: Tomorrow, I'll take her by the doctor.

[RALPH *enters.*]

BESSIE: Stay for a little tea.

SAM: No, I'll go home. I'm tired. Already I caught a cold in such weather. [*Blows his nose.*]

MYRON [*entering with stuffs*]: Going home?

SAM: I'll go in bed. I caught a cold.

MYRON: Teddy Roosevelt used to say, 'When you have a problem, sleep on it.'

BESSIE: My Sam is no problem.

MYRON: I don't mean . . . I mean he said –

BESSIE: Call me tomorrow, Sam.

SAM: I'll phone supper time. Sometime I think there's something funny about me.

[MYRON *sees him out. In the following pause Caruso is heard singing within.*]

BESSIE: A bargain! Second fiddle. By me he don't even play in the orchestra – a man like a mouse. Maybe she'll lay down and die 'cause he makes a living?

RALPH: Can I talk to you about something?

BESSIE: What's the matter – I'm biting you?

RALPH: It's something about Blanche.

BESSIE: Don't tell me.

RALPH: Listen now –

BESSIE: I don't wanna know.

RALPH: She's got no place to go.

BESSIE: I don't want to know.

RALPH: Mom, I love this girl. . . .

BESSIE: So go knock your head against the wall.

RALPH: I want her to come here. Listen, Mom, I want you to let her live here for a while.

BESSIE: You got funny ideas, my son.

RALPH: I'm as good as anyone else. Don't I have some rights in the

world? Listen, Mom, if I don't do something, she's going away.
Why don't you do it? Why don't you let her stay here for a few
weeks? Things'll pick up. Then we can –

BESSIE: Sure, sure. I'll keep her fresh on ice for a wedding day.
That's what you want?

RALPH: No, I mean you should –

BESSIE: Or maybe you'll sleep here in the same bed without marriage.
[JACOB *stands in his doorway, dressed.*]

RALPH: Don't say that, Mom. I only mean . . .

BESSIE: What you mean, I know . . . and what I mean I also know.
Make up your mind. For your own good, Ralphie. If she dropped
in the ocean, I don't lift a finger.

RALPH: That's all, I suppose.

BESSIE: With me it's one thing – a boy should have respect for his
own future. Go to sleep, you look tired. In the morning you'll
forget.

JACOB: 'Awake and sing, ye that dwell in dust; and the earth shall
cast out the dead.' It's cold out?

MYRON: Oh, yes.

JACOB: I'll take up Tootsie now.

MYRON [*eating bread and jam*]: He come on us like the wild man of
Borneo, Sam. I don't think Hennie was fool enough to tell him
the truth like that.

BESSIE: Myron! [*A deep pause.*]

RALPH: What did he say?

BESSIE: Never mind.

RALPH: I heard him. I heard him. You don't needa tell me.

BESSIE: Never mind.

RALPH: You trapped that guy.

BESSIE: Don't say another word.

RALPH: Just have respect? That's the idea?

BESSIE: Don't say another word. I'm boiling over ten times inside.

RALPH: You won't let Blanche here, huh. I'm not sure I want her.
You put one over on that little shrimp. The cat's whiskers, Mom?

BESSIE: I'm telling you something!

RALPH: I got the whole idea. I get it so quick my head's swimming. Boy, what a laugh! I suppose you know about this, Jake?

JACOB: Yes.

RALPH: Why didn't you do something?

JACOB: I'm an old man.

RALPH: What's that got to do with the price of bonds? Sits around and lets a thing like that happen! You make me sick too.

MYRON [*after a pause*]: Let me say something, son.

RALPH: Take your hand away! Sit in a corner and wag your tail. Keep on boasting you went to law school for two years.

MYRON: I want to tell you –

RALPH: You never in your life had a thing to tell me.

BESSIE [*bitterly*]: Don't say a word. Let him, let him run and tell Sam. Publish in the papers, give a broadcast on the radio. To him it don't matter his family sits with tears pouring from the eyes. [*To Jacob*] What are you waiting for? I didn't tell you twice already about the dog? You'll stand around with Caruso and make a bughouse. It ain't enough all day long. Fifty times I told you I'll break every record in the house. [*She brushes past him, breaks the records, comes out.*] The next time I say something you'll maybe believe it. Now maybe you learned a lesson. [*Pause.*]

JACOB [*quietly*]: Bessie, new lessons . . . not for an old dog.
  [*MOE enters.*]

MYRON: You didn't have to do it, Momma.

BESSIE: Talk better to your son, Mr Berger! Me, I don't lay down and die for him and Poppa no more. I'll work like a nigger? For what? Wait, the day comes when you'll be punished. When it's too late you'll remember how you sucked away a mother's life. Talk to him, tell him how I don't sleep at night. [*Bursts into tears and exits.*]

MOE [*sings*]:
  'Good-bye to all your sorrows.
  You never hear them talk about the war,
  In the land of Yama Yama. . . .'

MYRON: Yes, Momma's a sick woman, Ralphie.

RALPH: Yeah?

MOE: We'll be out of the trenches by Christmas. Putt, putt, putt ... here, stinker. ... [*Picks up Tootsie, a small, white poodle that just then enters from the hall.*] If there's reincarnation in the next life I wanna be a dog and lay in a fat lady's lap. Barrage over? How 'bout a little pinochle, Pop?

JACOB: Nnno.

RALPH [*taking dog*]: I'll take her up. [*Conciliatory*]

JACOB: No, I'll do it. [*Takes dog.*]

RALPH [*ashamed*]: It's cold out.

JACOB: I was cold before in my life. A man sixty-seven. ... [*Strokes the dog.*] Tootsie is my favourite lady in the house. [*He slowly passes across the room and exits. A settling pause.*]

MYRON: She cried all last night – Tootsie – I heard her in the kitchen like a young girl.

MOE: Tonight I could do something. I got a yen ... I don't know.

MYRON [*rubbing his head*]: My scalp is impoverished.

RALPH: Mom bust all his records.

MYRON: She didn't have to do it.

MOE: Tough tit! Now I can sleep in the morning. Who the hell wantsa hear a wop air his tonsils all day long!

RALPH [*handling the fragments of a record*]: 'O Paradiso!'

MOE [*gets cards*]: It's snowing out, girls.

MYRON: There's no more big snows like in the old days. I think the whole world's changing. I see it, right under our very eyes. No one hardly remembers any more when we used to have gaslight and all the dishes had little fishes on them.

MOE: It's the system, girls.

MYRON: I was a little boy when it happened – the Great Blizzard. It snowed three days without a stop that time. Yes, and the horse cars stopped. A silence of death was on the city and little babies got no milk ... they say a lot of people died that year.

MOE [*singing as he deals himself cards*]:

167

'Lights are blinking while you're drinking,
That's the place where the good fellows go.
Good-bye to all your sorrows,
You never hear them talk about the war,
In the land of Yama Yama
Funicalee, funicala, funicalo. . . .'

MYRON: What can I say to you, Big Boy?

RALPH: Not a damn word.

[MOE *goes 'ta ra ta ra' throughout.*]

MYRON: I know how you feel about all those things, I know.

RALPH: Forget it.

MYRON: And your girl. . . .

RALPH: Don't soft soap me all of a sudden.

MYRON: I'm not foreign born. I'm an American, and yet I never got close to you. It's an American father's duty to be his son's friend.

RALPH: Who said that – Teddy R.?

MOE [*dealing cards*]: You're breaking his heart, 'Litvak'.

MYRON: It just happened the other day. The moment I began losing my hair I just knew I was destined to be a failure in life . . . and when I grew bald I was. Now isn't that funny, Big Boy?

MOE: It's a pisscutter!

MYRON: I believe in Destiny.

MOE: You get what-it-takes. Then they don't catch you with your pants down. [*Sings out*] Eight of clubs . . .

MYRON: I really don't know. I sold jewellery on the road before I married. It's one thing to – Now here's a thing the druggist gave me. [*Reads*] 'The Marvel Cosmetic Girl of Hollywood is going on the air. Give this charming little radio singer a name and win five thousand dollars. If you will send –'

MOE: Your old man still believes in Santy Claus.

MYRON: Someone's got to win. The government isn't gonna allow everything to be a fake.

MOE: It's a fake. There ain't no prizes. It's a fake.

MYRON: It says –

RALPH [*snatching it*]: For Christ's sake, Pop, forget it. Grow up. Jake's
right – everybody's crazy. It's like a zoo in this house. I'm going to
bed.

MOE: 'In the land of Yama Yama. . . .' [*Goes on with 'ta ra'.*]

MYRON: Don't think life's easy with Momma. No, but she means for
your good all the time. I tell you she does, she –

RALPH: Maybe, but I'm going to bed.

   [*Downstairs doorbell rings violently.*]

MOE [*ring*]: Enemy barrage begins on sector eight seventy-five.

RALPH: That's downstairs.

MYRON: We ain't expecting anyone this hour of the night.

MOE:
   'Lights are blinking while you're drinking,
   That's the place where the good fellows go.
   Good-bye to ta ra tara ra,' etc.

RALPH: I better see who it is.

MYRON: I'll tick the button. [*As he starts, the apartment doorbell begins
ringing, followed by large knocking. MYRON goes out.*]

RALPH: Who's ever ringing means it.

   [*A loud excited voice outside.*]

MOE:
   'In the land of Yama Yama,
   Funicalee, funicalo, funic –'
      [*MYRON enters followed by SCHLOSSER the janitor. BESSIE cuts in
      from the other side.*]

BESSIE: Who's ringing like a lunatic?

RALPH: What's the matter?

MYRON: Momma . . .

BESSIE: Noo, what's the matter?

   [*Downstairs bell continues.*]

RALPH: What's the matter?

BESSIE: Well, well . . . ?

MYRON: Poppa. . . .

BESSIE: What happened?

SCHLOSSER: He shlipped maybe in de snow.

RALPH: Who?

SCHLOSSER [to Bessie]: Your fadder fall off de roof. . . . *Ja*
   [*A dead pause.* RALPH *then runs out.*]

BESSIE [dazed]: Myron. . . . Call Morty on the phone . . . call him.
   [MYRON *starts for phone.*] No I'll do it myself. I'll . . . do it. [MYRON
   exits.]

SCHLOSSER [standing stupidly]: Since I was in dis country . . . I was
   pudding out de ash can . . . The snow is vet. . . .

MOE [to Schlosser]: Scram.
   [SCHLOSSER *exits.* BESSIE *goes blindly to the phone, fumbles and
   gets it.* MOE *sits quietly, slowly turning cards over, but watching her.*]

BESSIE: He slipped. . . .

MOE [deeply moved]: Slipped?

BESSIE: I can't see the numbers. Make it, Moe, make it. . . .

MOE: Make it yourself. [*He looks at her and slowly goes back to his game
   of cards with shaking hands.*]

BESSIE: Riverside 7 – . . . [*Unable to talk she dials slowly. The dial
   whizzes on.*]

MOE: Don't . . . make me laugh. . . . [*He turns over cards.*]

Curtain

ACT THREE

A week later in the dining-room.

> [MORTY, BESSIE, *and* MYRON *eating. Sitting in the front room is* MOE *marking a 'dope sheet', but really listening to the others.*]

BESSIE: You're sure he'll come tonight – the insurance man?

MORTY: Why not? I shtupped him a ten-dollar bill. Everything's hot delicatessen.

BESSIE: Why must he come so soon?

MORTY: Because you had a big expense. You'll settle once and for all. I'm a great boy for making hay while the sun shines.

BESSIE: Stay till he'll come, Morty. . . .

MORTY: No, I got a strike downtown. Business don't stop for personal life. Two times already in the past week those bastards threw stink bombs in the showroom. Wait! We'll give them strikes – in the kishkas we'll give them . . .

BESSIE: I'm a woman. I don't know about policies. Stay till he comes.

MORTY: Bessie – sweetheart, leave me live.

BESSIE: I'm afraid, Morty.

MORTY: Be practical. They made an investigation. Everybody knows Pop had an accident. Now we'll collect.

MYRON: Ralphie don't know Papa left his insurance in his name.

MORTY: It's not his business. And I'll tell him.

BESSIE: The way he feels. [*Enter* RALPH *into front room.*] He'll do something crazy. He thinks Poppa jumped off the roof.

MORTY: Be practical, Bessie. Ralphie will sign when I tell him. Everything is peaches and cream.

BESSIE: Wait for a few minutes. . . .

MORTY: Look, I'll show you in black on white what the policy says. *For God's sake, leave me live!* [*Angrily exits to kitchen. In parlour,* MOE *speaks to Ralph who is reading a letter.*]

MOE: What's the letter say?

RALPH: Blanche won't see me no more, she says. I couldn't care very much, she says. If I didn't come like I said. . . . She'll phone before she leaves.

MOE: She don't know about Pop?

RALPH: She won't ever forget me she says. Look what she sends me . . . a little locket on a chain . . . if she calls I'm out.

MOE: You mean it?

RALPH: For a week I'm trying to go in his room. I guess he'd like me to have it, but I can't. . . .

MOE: Wait a minute! [*Crosses over.*] They're trying to rook you – a freeze-out.

RALPH: Who?

MOE: That bunch stuffin' their gut with hot pastrami. Morty in particular. Jake left the insurance – three thousand dollars – for you.

RALPH: For me?

MOE: Now you got wings, kid. Pop figured you could use it. That's why . . .

RALPH: That's why what?

MOE: It ain't the only reason he done it.

RALPH: He done it?

MOE: You think a breeze blew him off?
    [HENNIE *enters and sits.*]

RALPH: I'm not sure what I think.

MOE: The insurance guy's coming tonight. Morty 'shtupped' him.

RALPH: Yeah?

MOE: I'll back you up. You're dead on your feet. Grab a sleep for yourself.

RALPH: No!

MOE: Go on! [*Pushes boy into room.*]

SAM [*whom Morty has sent in for the paper*]: Morty wants the paper.

HENNIE: So?

SAM: You're sitting on it. [*Gets paper.*] We could go home now, Hennie! Leon is alone by Mrs Strasberg a whole day.

HENNIE: Go on home if you're so anxious. A full tub of diapers is waiting.

SAM: Why should you act this way?

HENNIE: 'Cause there's no bones in ice-cream. Don't touch me.

SAM: Please, what's the matter . . . ?

MOE: She don't like you. Plain as the face on your nose. . . .

SAM: To me, my friend, you talk a foreign language.

MOE: A quarter you're lousy. [SAM *exits.*] Gimme a buck, I'll run it up to ten.

HENNIE: Don't do me no favours.

MOE: Take a chance. [*Stopping her as she crosses to doorway.*]

HENNIE: I'm a pushover.

MOE: I say lotsa things. You don't know me.

HENNIE: I know you – when you knock 'em down you're through.

MOE [*sadly*]: You still don't know me.

HENNIE: I know what goes in your wise-guy head.

MOE: Don't run away. . . . I ain't got hydrophobia. Wait. I want to tell you. . . . I'm leaving.

HENNIE: Leaving?

MOE: Tonight. Already packed.

HENNIE: Where?

MORTY [*as he enters followed by the others*]: My car goes through snow like a dose of salts.

BESSIE: Hennie, go eat. . . .

MORTY: Where's Ralphie?

MOE: In his new room. [*Moves into dining-room.*]

MORTY: I didn't have a piece of hot pastrami in my mouth for years.

BESSIE: Take a sandwich, Hennie. You didn't eat all day. . . . [*At window*] A whole week it rained cats and dogs.

MYRON: Rain, rain, go away. Come again some other day. [*Puts shawl on her.*]

MORTY: Where's my gloves?

SAM [*sits on stool*]: I'm sorry the old man lays in the rain.

MORTY: Personally, Pop was a fine man. But I'm a great boy for an honest opinion. He had enough crazy ideas for a regiment.

MYRON: Poppa never had a doctor in his whole life. . . .

[*Enter* RALPH.]

MORTY: He had Caruso. Who's got more from life?

BESSIE: Who's got more? . . .

MYRON: And Marx he had.

[MYRON *and* BESSIE *sit on sofa.*]

MORTY: Marx! Some say Marx is the new God today. Maybe I'm wrong. Ha ha ha. . . . Personally I counted my ten million last night. . . . I'm sixteen cents short. So tomorrow I'll go to Union Square and yell no equality in the country! Ah, it's new generation.

RALPH: You said it!

MORTY: What's the matter, Ralphie? What are you looking funny?

RALPH: I hear I'm left insurance and the man's coming tonight.

MORTY: Poppa didn't leave no insurance for you.

RALPH: What?

MORTY: In your name he left it – but not for you.

RALPH: It's my name on the paper.

MORTY: Who said so?

RALPH [*to his mother*]: The insurance man's coming tonight?

MORTY: What's the matter?

RALPH: I'm not talking to you. [*To his mother*] Why?

BESSIE: I don't know why.

RALPH: He don't come in this house tonight.

MORTY: That's what *you* say.

RALPH: I'm not talking to you, Uncle Morty, but I'll tell you, too, he don't come here tonight when there's still mud on a grave. [*To his mother*] Couldn't you give the house a chance to cool off?

MORTY: Is this a way to talk to your mother?

RALPH: Was that a way to talk to your father?

MORTY: Don't be so smart with me, Mr Ralph Berger!

RALPH: Don't be so smart with *me*.

MORTY: What'll you do? I say he's coming tonight. Who says no?

MOE [*suddenly, from the background*]: Me.

MORTY: Take a back seat, Axelrod. When you're in the family —

MOE: I got a little document here. [*Produces paper.*] I found it under his pillow that night. A guy who slips off a roof don't leave a note before he does it.

MORTY [*starting for Moe after a horrified silence*]: Let me see this note.

BESSIE: Morty, don't touch it!

MOE: Not if you crawled.

MORTY: It's a fake. Poppa wouldn't —

MOE: Get the insurance guy here and we'll see how — [*The bell rings.*] Speak of the devil. . . . Answer it, see what happens. [MORTY *starts for the ticker.*]

BESSIE: Morty, don't!

MORTY [*stopping*]: Be practical, Bessie.

MOE: Sometimes you don't collect on suicides if they know about it.

MORTY: You should let . . . You should let him. . . [*A pause in which all seem dazed. Bell rings insistently.*]

MOE: Well, we're waiting.

MORTY: Give me the note.

MOE: I'll give you the head off your shoulders.

MORTY: Bessie, you'll stand for this? [*Points to Ralph.*] Pull down his pants and give him with a strap.

RALPH [*as bell rings again*]: How about it?

BESSIE: Don't be crazy. It's not my fault. Morty said he should come tonight. It's not nice so soon. I didn't —

MORTY: I said it? Me?

BESSIE: Who then?

MORTY: You didn't sing a song in my ear a whole week to settle quick?

BESSIE: I'm surprised. Morty, you're a big liar.

MYRON: Momma's telling the truth, she is!

MORTY: Lissen. In two shakes of a lamb's tail, we'll start a real fight and then nobody won't like nobody. Where's my fur gloves? I'm going downtown. [*To Sam*] You coming? I'll drive you down.

HENNIE [*to Sam, who looks questioningly at her*]: Don't look at me. Go home if you want.

SAM: If you're coming soon, I'll wait.

HENNIE: Don't do me any favours. Night and day he pesters me.

MORTY: You made a cushion – sleep!

SAM: I'll go home. I know ... to my worst enemy I don't wish such a life –

HENNIE: Sam, keep quiet.

SAM [*quietly; sadly*]: No more free speech in America? [*Gets his hat and coat.*] I'm a lonely person. Nobody likes me.

MYRON: I like you, Sam.

HENNIE [*going to him gently; sensing the end*]: Please go home, Sam. I'll sleep here.... I'm tired and nervous. Tomorrow I'll come home. I love you ... I mean it. [*She kisses him with real feeling.*]

SAM: I would die for you. ... [*He looks at her. Tries to say something, but his voice chokes up with a mingled feeling. He turns and leaves the room.*]

MORTY: A bird in the hand is worth two in the bush. Remember I said it. Good night. [*Exits after Sam.*]

[HENNIE *sits depressed.* BESSIE *goes up and looks at the picture calendar again.* MYRON *finally breaks the silence.*]

MYRON: Yesterday a man wanted to sell me a saxophone with pearl buttons. But I –

BESSIE: It's a beautiful picture. In this land, nobody works. ... Nobody worries. ... Come to bed, Myron. [*Stops at the door, and says to Ralph*] Please don't have foolish ideas about the money.

RALPH: Let's call it a day.

BESSIE: It belongs for the whole family. You'll get your teeth fixed –

RALPH: And a pair of black and white shoes?

BESSIE: Hennie needs a vacation. She'll take two weeks in the mountains and I'll mind the baby.

RALPH: I'll take care of my own affairs.

BESSIE: A family needs for a rainy day. Times is getting worse.

Prospect Avenue, Dawson, Beck Street – every day furniture's on the sidewalk.

RALPH: Forget it, Mom.

BESSIE: Ralphie, I worked too hard all my years to be treated like dirt. It's no law we should be stuck together like Siamese twins. Summer shoes you didn't have, skates you never had, but I bought a new dress every week. A lover I kept – Mr Gigolo! Did I ever play a game of cards like Mrs Marcus? Or was Bessie Berger's children always the cleanest on the block! Here I'm not only the mother, but also the father. The first two years I worked in a stocking factory for six dollars while Myron Berger went to law school. If I didn't worry about the family who would? On the calendar it's a different place, but here without a dollar you don't look the world in the eye. Talk from now to next year – this is life in America.

RALPH: Then it's wrong. It don't make sense. If life made you this way, then it's wrong!

BESSIE: Maybe you wanted me to give up twenty years ago. Where would you be now? You'll excuse my expression – a bum in the park!

RALPH: I'm not blaming you, Mom. Sink or swim – I see it. But it can't stay like this.

BESSIE: My foolish boy. . . .

RALPH: No, I see every house lousy with lies and hate. He said it, Grandpa – Brooklyn hates the Bronx. Smacked on the nose twice a day. But boys and girls can get ahead like that, Mom. We don't want life printed on dollar bills, Mom!

BESSIE: So go out and change the world if you don't like it.

RALPH: I will! And why? 'Cause life's different in my head. Gimme the earth in two hands. I'm strong. There . . . hear him? The air mail off to Boston. Day or night, he flies away, a job to do. That's us and it's no time to die.

[*The aeroplane sound fades off as* MYRON *gives alarm clock to Bessie which she begins to wind.*]

BESSIE: 'Mom, what does she know? She's old-fashioned!' But I'll tell you a big secret: My whole life I wanted to go away too, but with children a woman stays home. A fire burned in *my* heart too, but now it's too late. I'm no spring chicken. The clock goes and Bessie goes. Only my machinery can't be fixed. [*She lifts a button: the alarm rings on the clock; she stops it, says* 'Good night' *and exits.*]

MYRON: I guess I'm no prize bag. . . .

BESSIE [*from within*]: Come to bed, Myron.

MYRON [*tears pages off calendar*]: Hmmm. . . . [*Exits to her.*]

RALPH: Look at him, draggin' after her like an old shoe.

MOE: Punch drunk. [*Phone rings.*] That's for me. [*At phone*] Yeah? . . . Just a minute. [*To Ralph*] Your girl . . .

RALPH: Jeez, I don't know what to say to her.

MOE: Hang up?

    [RALPH *slowly takes phone.*]

RALPH: Hello. . . Blanche, I wish. . . I don't know what to say. . . . Yes . . . Hello? . . . [*Puts phone down.*] She hung up on me . . . .

MOE: Sorry?

RALPH: No girl means anything to me until . . .

MOE: Till when?

RALPH: Till I can take care of her. Till we don't look out on an air-shaft. Till we can take the world in two hands and polish off the dirt.

MOE: That's a big order.

RALPH: Once upon a time I thought I'd drown to death in bolts of silk and velour. But I grew up these last few weeks. Jake said a lot.

MOE: Your memory's okay?

RALPH: But take a look at this. [*Brings armful of books from Jacob's room – dumps them on table.*] His books, I got them too – the pages ain't cut in half of them.

MOE: Perfect.

RALPH: Does it prove something? Damn tootin'! A ten-cent nail-file cuts them. Uptown, downtown, I'll read them on the way. Get a big lamp over the bed. [*Picks up one.*] My eyes are good. [*Puts book in pocket.*] Sure, inventory tomorrow. Coletti to Driscoll to Berger – that's how we work. It's a team down the warehouse. Driscoll's a show-off, a wiseguy, and Joe talks pigeons day and night. But they're like me, looking for a chance to get to first base too. Joe razzed me about my girl. But he don't know why. I'll tell him. Hell, he might tell me something I don't know. Get teams together all over. Spit on your hands and get to work. And with enough teams together maybe we'll get steam in the warehouse so our fingers don't freeze off. Maybe we'll fix it so life won't be printed on dollar bills.

MOE: Graduation Day.

RALPH [*starts for door of his room, stops*]: Can I have ... Grandpa's note?

MOE: Sure you want it?

RALPH: Please – [MOE *gives it.*] It's blank!

MOE [*taking note back and tearing it up*]: That's right.

RALPH: Thanks! [*Exits.*]

MOE: The kid's a fighter! [*To Hennie*] Why are you crying?

HENNIE: I never cried in my life. [*She is now.*]

MOE [*starts for door. Stops*]: You told Sam you love him. ...

HENNIE: If I'm sore on life, why take it out on him?

MOE: You won't forget me to your dyin' day – I was the first guy. Part of your insides. You won't forget. I wrote my name on you – indelible ink!

HENNIE: One thing I won't forget – how you left me crying on the bed like I was two for a cent!

MOE: Listen, do you think –

HENNIE: Sure. Waits till the family goes to the open-air movie. He brings me perfume. ... He grabs my arms –

MOE: You won't forget me!

HENNIE: How you left the next week?

MOE: So I made a mistake. For Chris' sake, don't act like the Queen of Roumania!

HENNIE: Don't make me laugh!

MOE: What the hell do you want, my head on a plate?! Was my life so happy? Chris', my old man was a bum. I supported the whole damn family – five kids and Mom. When they grew up they beat it the hell away like rabbits. Mom died. I went to the war; got clapped down like a bedbug; woke up in a room without a leg. What the hell do you think, anyone's got it better than you? I never had a home either. I'm lookin' too!

HENNIE: So what?!

MOE: So you're it – you're home for me, a place to live! That's the whole parade, sickness, eating out your heart! Sometimes you meet a girl – she stops it – that's love. . . . So take a chance! Be with me, Paradise. What's to lose?

HENNIE: My pride!

MOE [*grabbing her*]: What do you want? Say the word – I'll tango on a dime. Don't gimme ice when your heart's on fire!

HENNIE: Let me go!

[*He stops her.*]

MOE: WHERE!

HENNIE: What do you want, Moe, what do you want?

MOE: You!

HENNIE: You'll be sorry you ever started –

MOE: You!

HENNIE: Moe, lemme go – [*Trying to leave*] I'm getting up early – lemme go.

MOE: No! . . . I got enough fever to blow the whole damn town to hell. [*He suddenly releases her and half-stumbles backwards. Forces himself to quiet down.*] You wanna go back to him? Say the word. I'll know what to do. . . .

HENNIE [*helplessly*]: Moe, I don't know what to say.

MOE: Listen to me.

HENNIE: What?

MOE: Come away. A certain place where it's moonlight and roses. We'll lay down, count stars. Hear the big ocean making noise. You lay under the trees. Champagne flows like –

[*Phone rings, MOE finally answers the telephone.*]

Hello? . . . Just a minute. [*Looks at Hennie.*]

HENNIE: Who is it?

MOE: Sam.

HENNIE [*starts for phone, but changes her mind*]: I'm sleeping. . . .

MOE [*in phone*]: She's sleeping. . . . [*Hangs up. Watches* HENNIE *who slowly sits.*] He wants you to know he got home okay. . . . What's on your mind?

HENNIE: Nothing.

MOE: Sam?

HENNIE: They say it's a palace on those Havana boats.

MOE: What's on your mind?

HENNIE [*trying to escape*]: Moe, I don't care for Sam – I never loved him –

MOE: But your kid – ?

HENNIE: All my life I waited for this minute.

MOE [*holding her*]: Me too. Made believe I was talkin' just bedroom golf, but you and me forever was what I meant! Christ, baby, there's one life to live! Live it!

HENNIE: Leave the baby?

MOE: Yeah!

HENNIE: I can't. . . .

MOE: You can!

HENNIE: No . . .

MOE: But you're not sure!

HENNIE: I don't know.

MOE: Make a break or spend the rest of your life in a coffin.

HENNIE: Oh God, I don't know where I stand.

MOE: Don't look up there. Paradise, you're on a big boat headed south. No more pins and needles in your heart, no snake juice squirted in your arm. The whole world's green grass and when you cry it's because you're happy.

HENNIE: Moe, I don't know. . . .

MOE: Nobody knows, but you do it and find out. When you're scared the answer's zero.

HENNIE: You're hurting my arm.

MOE: The doctor said it – cut off your leg to save your life! And they done it – one thing to get another.

[*Enter* RALPH.]

RALPH: I didn't hear a word, but do it, Hennie, do it!

MOE: Mom can mind the kid. She'll go on forever, Mom. We'll send money back, and Easter eggs.

RALPH: I'll be here.

MOE: Get your coat ... get it.

HENNIE: Moe!

MOE: I know ... but get your coat and hat and kiss the house good-bye.

HENNIE: The man I love. .... [MYRON *entering*.] I left my coat in Mom's room. [*Exits*.]

MYRON: Don't wake her up, Beauty. Momma fell asleep as soon as her head hit the pillow. I can't sleep. It was a long day. Hmmm. [*Examines his tongue in buffet mirror*.] I was reading the other day a person with a thick tongue is feeble-minded. I can do anything with my tongue. Make it thick, flat. No fruit in the house lately. Just a lone apple. [*He gets apple and paring knife and starts paring*.] Must be something wrong with me – I say I won't eat but I eat. [HENNIE *enters dressed to go out*.] Where you going, little Red Riding Hood?

HENNIE: Nobody knows, Peter Rabbit.

MYRON: You're looking very pretty tonight. You were a beautiful baby too. 1910, that was the year you was born. The same year Teddy Roosevelt come back from Africa.

HENNIE: Gee, Pop; you're such a funny guy.

MYRON: He was a boisterous man, Teddy. Good night. [*He exits, paring apple*.]

RALPH: When I look at him, I'm sad. Let me die like a dog, if I can't get more from life.

HENNIE: Where?

RALPH: Right here in the house! My days won't be for nothing. Let

Mom have the dough. I'm twenty-two and kickin'! I'll get along. Did Jake die for us to fight about nickels? No! 'Awake and sing,' he said. Right here he stood and said it. The night he died, I saw it like a thunderbolt! I saw he was dead and I was born! I swear to God, I'm one week old! I want the whole city to hear it – fresh blood, arms. We got 'em. We're glad we're living.

MOE: I wouldn't trade you for two pitchers and an outfielder. Hold the fort!

RALPH: So long.

MOE: So long.

[*They go and* RALPH *stands full and strong in the doorway seeing them off as the curtain slowly falls.*]

Curtain

THE BIG KNIFE

For
M. V. LEOF, M.D.,
in his seventy-eighth year,
with love

SCENES

Act One
A summer afternoon.

Act Two
Late one night, the following week.

Act Three
1. Late afternoon, a few days later.
2. An hour later.

———

The action takes place in the playroom of Charlie
Castle's Beverly Hills house, in the present day.

p 212 Hollywood ethic
           ↑
        integrity

p 249 Vitamin D
p. 251

ACT ONE

Time: The present.

Place: The 'Playroom' of Charles Castle's house in Beverly Hills, California.

The comfortable easy furniture, a small but laden bar, a large phonograph, a miniature piano, various games and a card table, rich drapes and rugs – all express ease, casual luxury and good taste.

A number of good paintings hang on the walls and add to the quality of the room; these include a good, typical Utrillo, a large impressive head of a clown by Rouault, and a typical Modigliani.

Two large windows open up one side of the room; between them a screen door opens out on an expansive lawn. Opposite, and far downstage, a softly contoured archway, underlined by two ascending steps, leads to the rest of the roomy, airy house. Beyond the archway a practical iron staircase spirals upward to a landing, a frequently used back stairs.

[*The room is empty when the curtain rises. Drapes are half-drawn to shield out the intense mid-day sun. The automatic phonograph entertains the airy emptiness with a snatch of French operetta, a love duet by two eminent Parisian players. A moment later* RUSSELL, *the negro butler, enters and collects soiled glasses from the bar. He is a simple, sincere man who finds pleasure in everything; he is proud and happy to be working in this home.*

As he starts out of the room BUDDY BLISS *enters. In publicity work, a friend of Charlie Castle,* BLISS *is of humourless sturdiness, an intent and hopeful (or shall we say hopeless?) believer in facts and self-improvement. In adjustment to Charlie, he is mostly an eager, grateful, and nervous failure; he is dense and stubborn too. Some would call him 'a nice, American boy'.*

RUSSELL *asks:* 'Anything I can get you, Mr Bliss?' *Unheeding,* BUDDY *paces nervously, jerkily lighting a cigarette.* RUSSELL *goes. and a moment later, stuffing a telegram in one pocket,* CHARLIE

CASTLE *enters. He looks around his room, his evident anger and annoyance changing for a moment to surprise.*

CHARLIE CASTLE, *the famous movie star, is virile and instant, sensitive and aware, although frequently, as now, he is apt to mask his best qualities behind a cynical, guying manner and certain jazzy small-talk. He knows how to use an abruptly disarming charm and he understands the value of candour. He is a very successful man and this sits on him with a certain relaxed gravity. He is a 'going concern' and he knows and acts it.*]

CHARLIE: Where's Patty?

BUDDY: Powdering her nose.

CHARLIE: Why are you so pale, Bud? You take this so big?

BUDDY: I work for the studio, Charles. You're a big star – I'm supposed to keep you out of trouble. [*Speaking quickly, he has dropped his voice; Patty will return in a moment.*]

CHARLIE: That doesn't give her the right to insult me at my own lunch table, Bud. She keeps coming at me with those great big lobster claws, and Mr Castle, he don't like it!

BUDDY: All I'm trying to do is ease the situation. As an old friend, if you don't mind me saying so – you can't talk that way to Patty Benedict. Hell, Charles, eighteen million people read her column every day. For the love of Pete, take it easy till I get her out of here!

CHARLIE: Did you hear that stuff she started about my wife? She was edging up all through the lunch – what about the separation rumours? I could hear it clicking in her head, like knitting needles.

BUDDY: I'll have her out of here in five minutes flat.

CHARLIE: What a life you publicity men lead! It makes me wonder if I was being friendly when I got you the job.

BUDDY [*fondly*]: What a guy! After all you've done for me – ?

CHARLIE [*soberly*]: I think, Bud, the shoe is on the other foot. [*Quickly, looking off*] Uh Uh! Put the leash around my neck – here comes Malignant Maggie! [*Then, gaily*] Patty, darling, quench your thirst?

[*He is all gayness and glitter as* PATTY *enters, a mask assumed and played lightly and guyingly, except when her back is turned.* PATTY BENEDICT *is a famous movie columnist. She is authoritative, cynical, and assured, insolently appraising; the world of Hollywood is surely her intimidated oyster.*]

PATTY: Light my cigarette, Chuck. ... Thanks. [CHARLIE *has beaten* BUDDY *to the cigarette.*] What is that, the radio?

CHARLIE: No, it's a record – love scene from a fancy French operetta.

PATTY: Shut the damn thing off.

[CHARLIE, *exchanging glances with* BUDDY, *does so;* PATTY *sits.*]

It's a hot and lazy afternoon ... cool in here. ...

CHARLIE [*going to the bar*]: Who wants what from the lemonade stand?

PATTY [*unheeding*]: I like the airiness of this room. ...

[BUDDY *indicates that he won't have a drink;* CHARLIE *makes a highball.*]

French paintings, dear one?

CHARLIE: Yeah.

PATTY: Don't you buy American any more?

CHARLIE: Let nothing you dismay, little chum. I don't know one painter from another.

BUDDY [*helpfully*]: He doesn't know one painter from another.

CHARLIE: I wouldn't want my fans saying I've gone arty, would I? They're my wife's hobby.

BUDDY: Marion's hobby.

[PATTY *flicks an annoyed look at Buddy as* CHARLIE *comes down with his drink.*]

PATTY: How long do I know you, Chuck?

CHARLIE [*pert and playful*]: A fat nine or ten years.

PATTY: The first time we met, all you'd talk about was F.D.R.

CHARLIE: I believed in F.D.R.

PATTY: I *still* need an angle for my Sunday piece . . . what do you believe in now?

CHARLIE: What we had for lunch – roast beef, rare!

PATTY [*ominously*]: You're lots smarter, child, than you used to be.

CHARLIE [*over-gracious*]: I had to learn, Patricia.

BUDDY: Charlie's slogan – if you got a message send for Western Union.

[PATTY *flicks another look at Buddy and stands.*]

PATTY: Well, here's the afternoon burnt to a crisp, and still no Sunday piece. How is your new picture, any good?

CHARLIE: I wouldn't kid *you*, Patty; another armful of roses and a basket of kittens.

PATTY: Anything on your new contract yet?

CHARLIE [*looking quickly to Buddy*]: No.

PATTY: Marcus Hoff told me last week that you were about to re-sign.

CHARLIE: He's the head of the studio, isn't he? It doesn't cost him anything to dream.

PATTY: Are you and Marcus feuding . . . ?

CHARLIE [*lightly*]: Now, darling, why would I feud with Uncle Hoff?

BUDDY [*quickly*]: Mr Hoff has always been more like a father to Charles.

PATTY [*ignoring Buddy*]: I'm trying to remember your real name. Kress?

BUDDY: Cass – Charles Cass.

CHARLIE: I hooked my stage name from an uncle. His name was Schloss – Castle in German.

PATTY [*dryly*]: What made you honour your uncle to that high degree?

CHARLIE: He merely raised me after my parents died.

BUDDY [*helping*]: In Philly, wasn't it?

CHARLIE: Philadelphia, yep. They were awfully poor, my aunt and uncle. [*Pausing*] I made money too late to be able to help them. I regret that. .... [*Softly, pausing*] We're homesick all our lives, but adults don't talk about it, do they? [*Turning*] Buddy, did you read much as a kid?

BUDDY: As a kid? Not unless they hit me with a whip!

CHARLIE: My uncle's books – for that neighbourhood – I'll bet he had a thousand! He had a nose for the rebels – London, Upton Sinclair – all the way back to Ibsen and Hugo. Hugo's the one who helped me nibble my way through billions of polly seeds. Sounds grandiose, but Hugo said to me: 'Be a good boy, Charles. Love people, do good, help the lost and fallen, make the world happy, if you can!' [*Quickly, looking at Patty*] I know before you say it, dear – too fruity. I buy it all back.

[PATTY *smiles thinly, turns, and starts out; but abruptly she turns.*]

PATTY: Now let me have the truth, Chuck, before I go, about the separation rumours.

CHARLIE [*laughing*]: That Patty cake – she's always trying to tag me! [*Turning*] Get out of that jury box, darling – there's no basis in fact for the rumours. Marion has the kid at the beach because of the polio scare.

PATTY [*forcefully*]: Chuck, I don't think I'd ever forgive you if someone else published your divorce story before I did. I hope you understand that.

BUDDY [*in background*]: He understands that. ....

PATTY: What about her politics, your wife's?

CHARLIE [*temper slipping*]: Politics? That's another nasty rumour. Maybe Marion gave them some campaign money, but she didn't, so far as I know.

BUDDY [*nervously*]: What Charles is trying to say – Marion comes from fine, old American stock.

CHARLIE: They got here with the cricket and the mouse.

BUDDY: Her father's history books are read in every college in the land –

CHARLIE [*flatly*]: And, anyway, that's her right!

PATTY [*sharply*]: What's her right?

BUDDY: Patty, what Charles means by that –

[PATTY *turns with icy annoyance on Buddy*.]

PATTY: Shut up for five minutes! I want my gossip from the horse's mouth, not its tail!

[*Flushing,* BUDDY *steps back nervously*.]

CHARLIE [*soothingly*]: Come on, Patty, you know it's his living – let's be democratic. [*To Buddy*] Mix yourself a drink.

[PATTY *turns angrily on Charlie while* BUDDY *goes back to the bar and nervously putters there*.]

PATTY: You're just too itsy-bitsy coy for me today! And while we're on the subject, why did the studio give him back his job?

CHARLIE: Buddy's a first-rate publicity man. He's an old personal friend, too.

PATTY [*sarcastically*]: Oh, yes, you were his character witness last year – you paid his legal fees. But why did the studio give him back his job after that scandalous mess?

CHARLIE [*sober and wary now*]: I don't get your point, Patty. Buddy went to jail for ten months. It's all past and forgotten.

PATTY: It's not forgotten if I choose to revive it!

CHARLIE [*appealingly*]: Darling, why would you do that?

PATTY: Some of you seem to forget that this place has to keep its skirts clean. This boy steals your car from a studio Christmas party. He drives along, half-drunk –

CHARLIE: He wasn't drunk – that was cleared in court. And, as my friend, he had a right to *borrow* my car.

PATTY: The fact remains – he hit and ran! He killed that child in your car! How friendly did you feel when Big Brains here ditched the car on your back lawn and the police walked in that Christmas Eve? All he did, your dear friend, was to almost ruin a career out of the story books!

CHARLIE: I think we can be human enough to forgive that. Jitters and all, didn't he step up and take the blame in time?

PATTY: But I still call it damn poor public relations to give him back his job!

CHARLIE [*oily now*]: Patty, with all the yawping in the world, why would you want to wake this sleeping dog?

PATTY [*pausing*]: I'll make you a swap. What about your marriage? [*She watches him keenly. He hesitates;* BUDDY *turns.*]

CHARLIE [*quietly, smiling*]: No, Hubbard, that cupboard is bare. . . .

PATTY [*smirking*]: That's your answer, Chuck. . . .

CHARLIE [*putting his arm around her*]: Now, Patty, thanks for the visit. Be well and strong. God bless, but please don't rake up the past. [*She smiles thinly and starts out. At this moment* MARION CASTLE *comes down the spiral stairs.* CHARLIE *is surprised but calls cheerfully:*] Here's Marion now! I didn't know she was in the house. Come down, dear . . . say hello to Patty Benedict.

MARION: Hello, Miss Benedict. I came in town to shop.

PATTY [*appraisingly*]: Hello, Mrs Castle. . . .

BUDDY: Hello, Marion.

MARION: Hello, Buddy, I came in town to shop. [*She and* CHARLIE *are both flustered.*] Oh, there's an eighth horror in the world. It needs publicity – what laundries do to sheets and pillow cases! Every month I buy a dozen!

PATTY [*unsmiling*]: Why don't you try the Martell Stores? They sell a fine percale sheet at a really modest price. Do you and Charlie use a double bed, or is that a foolish question, since you're separated now? You *are* separated, aren't you?

CHARLIE [*laughing*]: Patty, you take the cake for persistence!

PATTY: We're all sensible, sophisticated folk. There's no use wearing crêpe. Divorce is as common as the ordinary head-cold.

MARION [*sharply*]: I'm not sophisticated, Miss Benedict, and it's none of your business!

PATTY: And you're the child who'll tell me?

CHARLIE: Just a minute –

MARION: Yes! I'm the one in town who's not afraid to tell you to mind your own business!

CHARLIE [*helplessly*]: Marion, listen . . .

PATTY: Well, I'm so glad we've come to an understanding at last.

CHARLIE: Marion!

PATTY: No more fuss. I know when I've worn out my welcome.
[PATTY *exits smartly,* CHARLIE *following her after a baleful glance at Marion's back.*]

BUDDY: Marion, gosh! For the love of Pete –! [*He hurries after the others.*]

[*Showing defiance, anger, and spunk at the moment,* MARION CASTLE *pours herself a glass of sherry. She is a smart and good-looking thirty-two years' accumulation of woman and sensibility. Frequently now her face wears an expression of bemused sadness. Normally she is an alert, intelligent, feminine woman; at present we may expect to surprise in her face and manner something rueful, anxious, and nervous.* CHARLIE *returns and looks at her for a silent moment.*]

CHARLIE: Tell me, Angel, what the hell did you think you were doing?

MARION: I'll tell her lots more if she plays Lady Pry again!

CHARLIE: I'm in the movie business, darling. I can't afford these acute attacks of integrity.

MARION [*eyeing him*]: Why don't you talk to me the way you talk to her?

CHARLIE: How do I talk to her?

MARION: Your mouth is liquid honey.

CHARLIE: I'm insincere with her.

MARION [*archly*]: Husband dear, be insincere with me. ...

CHARLIE: Would you use your brain, darling? Free speech is the highest-paid luxury in this country today. Patty's got eighteen million readers. Why antagonize her? Where's the sense?

MARION: From time to time I believe in being completely senseless. I'm a human being, a woman, not a diplomat. Doesn't it make you blench to say 'God bless' to Patty Benedict? But, of course, you're not sincere.

CHARLIE: Don't you think you're exaggerating a teenie-weenie bit?

MARION: I'll stop ... [*She opens her purse and takes a pill from a little box.*]

CHARLIE: What's that pill? Don't you feel well?

MARION: Half-grain codeine. That's what I went upstairs for.

[CHARLIE *puts his glass on the bar and looks in her purse.*]

CHARLIE: What's in the other box?

MARION: A pill that runs a little faster. . . .

CHARLIE: What do you do, Angel, eat these pills like candy? They're dangerous drugs!

MARION: Don't you take drugs, Handsome, to put yourself to sleep and pep you up?

CHARLIE [*nettled*]: Sure, if I'm low or tired, but not in ten assorted flavours!

MARION: Migraines and sinus never bother solid Charlie. Don't you know the fancy world you live in yet? What can a doctor do if the women come to his office looking for life? Can he give them life? So they settle for easy solutions, fifty in a bottle – pills and twenty-dollar injections.

CHARLIE: For what?

MARION: For a substitute for a normal, happy life. I know all about it – I saw it in a movie. . . .

[*Lapsing again,* MARION *walks to the Rouault painting.* CHARLIE, *a little sheepish, says of the picture:*]

CHARLIE: I'm beginning to like that picture. You're right – it broods. This Rouault guy may make the Olympics Team. [*Then, apologetically*] I had no idea, all those pills ...

[RUSSELL *enters with clean glasses for the bar.*]

RUSSELL: Why, Mrs Castle, didn't see you come in – it's a real pleasure!

MARION: Thanks, Russell. How's Lucille?

RUSSELL: She's gonna be mighty glad to see you.

MARION: I'll come back to the kitchen before I leave.

[*Smiling and pleased,* RUSSELL *leaves.*]

You're supposed to have Billy this week.

CHARLIE [*quickly*]: I was about to ask – how is my son, Mommy?

MARION: Billy's fine, but I can't send him in without the nurse, and she won't work with Negroes.

CHARLIE: Fire her! The hell with *that*!

MARION: Except I'm too tired just now to break in another nurse. I'm in the mood to sleep the clock around – as if I were pregnant.

[CHARLIE *goes to the bar and makes a drink.*]

CHARLIE: I haven't seen you for two weeks, Angel. ...

MARION: Three, Handsome.

CHARLIE [*uneasily*]: Three? Really?

MARION: Really, three.

CHARLIE [*pausing*]: Are you lonely out at the beach?

MARION: Yes ...

CHARLIE: Very lonely?

MARION [*with a moue*]: Medium rare.

[*He comes down with his drink.*]

CHARLIE [*earnestly*]: Marion, in the whole world I care about only three and a half people: You, little Billy, Hank Teagle ... and the half a man that's me. Marion, be as brutally frank as you like. Why don't you come back? Does that hurt?

[*Seated,* MARION *is rubbing her forehead. Without waiting,* CHARLIE *steps behind her and begins massaging her forehead with his finger tips; she yields.*]

MARION: I'm going for a treatment in twenty minutes.

CHARLIE: Marion, I can change, I know I can make you happy.

MARION: How, darling, how can you change in the twelfth year of this fantastic career? Why did I leave you once before? Why don't I come back *this* time? Because a man, darling, can live only two ways – either married or like a bachelor. But all you want, Charlie, is the best features of both.

CHARLIE: Marion, you don't think that those occasional girls –

MARION: Oh, yes, I *do* think those occasional girls! Surprised?

[MARION *smiles at this herself.* CHARLIE *massages in slow silence.*]

Charlie Cass was a wonder and I was Mrs Cass. Now you're Hoff's Mr Castle.

CHARLIE [*stiffly*]: Sorry, sweet, I don't buy that – I don't belong to Marcus Hoff.

MARION: What about the new contract?

CHARLIE: I'm far from perfect, but you're making a big mistake if you think you can face the wide world alone. Don't tell me you have little Billy – he still eats a grape in four bites! You don't have a family – you don't even have a confidant, unless it's Hank Teagle, and he's *my* friend as much as yours.

MARION: Hank asked me to marry him last night.

[CHARLIE *slowly stops massaging.*]

CHARLIE: And . . . what did you say?

MARION: Nothing.

CHARLIE: He's got his goddam nerve!

MARION: All he said was *if*.

CHARLIE [*bitterly*]: Repeat that – there was so much traffic going by!

MARION: I tried to avoid this conversation.

CHARLIE: Okay you win! Famous husband remarks – you win!

[CHARLIE *is gloomily prowling the room by now; he takes a strap watch from his pocket. Tired,* MARION *crosses and takes some soiled glasses to the bar.*]

Don't be such a housewife all the time – leave the glasses where they are! Damn strap's broke on my watch, too. . . .

MARION [*quietly*]: I'll need a cheque for Monday. Bills are coming in.

CHARLIE: I'll have Harold send it from his office.

MARION: Are you renewing with Hoff or not?

CHARLIE: Where the hell does Hank Teagle come off to propose to you?!

MARION: Put Hank aside – he's leaving for New York in two weeks.

CHARLIE: What, to find a forty-cent gin?

MARION: To write a new book. He's been on the wagon for months. Charlie, I want you to believe me; I won't come back if you sign the new contract.

CHARLIE: I never expected to see the day when a three-and-a-half-million-dollar deal would give you chills and fever. . . .

MARION [*earnestly*]: Neither did I. I'm as human as the next one. It's a fabulous deal. But it's for fourteen years and I don't believe in the life that goes with it. Charlie, you're half-asleep right now! I haven't seen you sparkle since the day Billy was born! You used to take sides. Golly, the zest with which you fought. You used to grab your theatre parts and eat 'em like a tiger. Now you act with droopy eyes – they have to call you away from a card game. Charlie, I don't want you to sign that contract – you've given the studio their pound of flesh – you don't owe them anything. We arrived here in a pumpkin coach and we can damn well leave the same way!

CHARLIE: Pulled by a flock of mice? Please! I'm Hoff-Federated's biggest star. I'm worth millions a year to them in ice-cold profits! Hoff's got me by the tail and he won't let go and you know why!

MARION: Tell him you're leaving Hollywood for good. Promise him never to make pictures for anyone else.

CHARLIE [*impatiently*]: Just what do you expect me to do? Pick up, without a backward glance – and what? Go back and act in shows?

MARION: What's wrong with shows? You started in the theatre. We'd go back to New York, yes – the theatre still can give you a reasonable living. And away from this atmosphere of flattery and deceit we might make our marriage work.

CHARLIE: The theatre's a stunted bleeding stump. Even stars have to wait years for one decent play.

MARION: But here, of course, they plan your future, don't they? They buy books out here, idiot's tales! From dividend to dividend, they don't waste your talents for a minute: in your last ten pictures you were electrocuted four times!

CHARLIE [*smirking, sick at heart*]: Listen, monkey, I know I'm a mechanical, capering mouse. But Charlie Cass is still around in dribs and drabs – don't you think he'd like to do a fine play every other year? Don't you think I want our marriage to work? [*Paus-*

ing] But I have to face one horny fact: I'm Hoff's prisoner now, and signing the contract is the ransom fee! [*Nervously, pausing*] I didn't have the nerve that night, in this room ... I made the wrong decision ...

[*They have both dropped their voices by now.* MARION *speaks gently, as if to a child.*]

MARION: Come here, Charlie. Hold my hands. ...

[*He looks across at her, slowly puts down his glass and comes to her, taking her hands in his.*]

[*Gently*] God help me, I often wished you'd lost your nose and ears in the war. [*Smiling*] Then the other women wouldn't want you and I'd have you to myself. I know you, deeply, darling ... I've had you with my morning coffee. [*Pausing*] I know the sleepless nights you've had since Christmas Eve. Look at me, darling. We *both* made a mistake that night in this room.

CHARLIE: You could have pushed me the other way that night.

MARION: You needed sympathy. ... I wasn't strong enough. It was a difficult choice that night. We failed together, but now we have a second chance. It's a gamble – I know what Hoff can do if you refuse to sign.

CHARLIE: You're *sure* you know what he can do?

MARION: Yes, but that's the chance we have to take. We may lose everything we own. This time we have to make the right decision together.

[CHARLIE *turns away, thinking, hesitant, and confused.*]

CHARLIE: Marion, is that what you want me to do ...?

MARION: Yes. I know I'm talking about our lives and your fabulous career. But if you sign, you sink in even deeper than before. Refuse to sign, Charlie.

[*She is watching* CHARLIE *keenly, hopefully. Now, abruptly, he turns back to her, a decision almost made.*]

CHARLIE: All right, I'll try. I haven't agreed to sign. I've been stalling them for months. Nat'll be here any minute. He may come up with some big idea.

[*Both are sad and unsteady, deeply moved.*]

MARION: I like Nat – he's very fatherly – but Hollywood agents aren't worth their weight in feathers.

CHARLIE: Just what you suggested. It may not work with Hoff, but I'll try. I don't want to lose you, Marion.

MARION: Everything is in your hands, Handsome. ...

CHARLIE: We love each other ... you've been faithful to me all these years.

MARION [*archly sad*]: Don't be too sure of that. ...

CHARLIE [*turning away*]: Who could blame you? I don't deserve it.

MARION: From now on I want a man who has the right to blame me. Nowadays, to be faithful ... it gives you that loony, old-fashioned moral grandeur of an equestrian statue in the park. [*Half-smiling*] Poor horse ... [*Then, starting out*] I'll call you later, from the doctor's office. ...

CHARLIE [*morosely*]: Tell the cook again, will ya, to stop sprinkling parsley on everything she cooks.

[*Smiling musingly,* MARION *takes up her purse and drifts out of the room. Dusted down with depression,* CHARLIE, *nervous and grim, finishes his drink. Then he turns impatiently to answer the ringing phone.*]

Yeah! This is Castle. ... [*then*] No, nobody wants any wine! Don't keep calling a man's home for things like that! No, I don't want any wine. [*He slams up the phone as* RUSSELL *enters.*] Boy friend, answer the phone from time to time!

RUSSELL: Mr Castle, you always pick it up before I get there.

CHARLIE: Well, walk a little faster – beat me to it. Geez, I sound unpleasant to myself! [*In the meantime, standing at the bar, he has begun to dial a number.*]

RUSSELL: No, you're just a little edgy. [*Looking out*] Here comes Mr Nat Danziger, the agent.

[NAT DANZIGER *appears at the garden door.*]

NAT: Hello, hello, hello!

CHARLIE: Come in, Nat.

[NAT *drops into a seat, putting aside his hat and an envelope of contracts.*]

NAT: No matter how you slice it up there's never enough time in Hollywood.

CHARLIE [*into the phone*]: Harold? Charlie the Castle. Marion needs a cheque – household. Send it to the beach. Usual amount. No, double it. She's moody – maybe she'd like to buy some clothes. [*Then*] I don't remember what those cheques were for – cards, I think. [*Impatiently*] Well, what am I supposed to do? Ask the government if I can give a hungry writer two hundred bucks? [*Then*] Look, Harold, you're my business manager. That's what I pay you for. I pay *you* to go crazy. [*Listening*] All right! Then get tough and bossy! Someone has to get tough with me before I float away. Sounds girlish, doesn't it?

NAT: Give him my regards.

CHARLIE: Nat sends his best. 'Bye, 'bye. [*Hanging up*] He says I'm broke. I spend too much. He thinks I care. Everybody's annoyed with me, but why complain?

NAT: Since you're at the bar I'll take some Poland water with ice. How's Marion?

CHARLIE: You missed her by a minute.

NAT [*slyly*]: You could tickle me to death by telling me there's a certain little something brewing between you two.

CHARLIE [*soberly*]: Wish I could, Nat.

[NAT *sadly ponders this for a moment.* NAT DANZIGER *is past sixty, with all the qualities of the president of a synagogue. He is tolerant, sympathetic, reliable, and wise in business ways; he is paternal, really concerned for those he loves. He is charitable not on principle alone; much of what he says is tinged with sentiment and religiosity. His confidence and affable authority give him a certain foolish quality. He wants to do the right thing always. He speaks fondly, with a certain grotesque cheerfulness. His motto, 'I serve!'*]

NAT [*sighing*]: Charlie, you and Marion – two sweet human mortals – and you can't settle one little problem.

CHARLIE: Maybe that's why empires are falling, Nat, because just like me millions 'can't settle one little problem'.

NAT [*lightly*]: Who's got time to worry about empires? All I want to to do is live in peace and please my clients.

CHARLIE [*moodily*]: How do we know that America isn't dying of trying to please its clients? Did you ever think of that?

NAT: No, to tell the truth . . .

CHARLIE: What I mean . . . don't you feel it in the air? Don't you see them pushing man off the earth and putting the customer in his place?

NAT: That's a very intelligent remark, Lovey. You brought that out very good. By the way, not to digress, I just left Marcus's office. . . .

CHARLIE: Marion's dead-set against the contract, Nat. From her point of view – it makes me Marcus's prisoner for a lifetime!

[CHARLIE *comes down with two glasses, giving one to Nat.*]

NAT [*worried*]: Yes, but when you sign, Marcus is *your* prisoner, too, for a lifetime. [*Sipping and sighing*] Ah, water when you're thirsty . . .

CHARLIE: I'd be over fifty when this deal runs out.

NAT: That's bad? I'm over sixty! No, believe me, dear sir and friend, without reviewing the contract's various features – why should I bore you? – what are we faced with here? A financial arrangement whereby –

CHARLIE [*morosely*]: The money factor isn't everything.

NAT: Agreed, I agree. But a million dollars is got an awful big mouth.

CHARLIE: Wait a minute, Nat. I know all that. But I can't continue doing these kind of pictures.

NAT: But it's there in black on white – you don't have to! I, me – you don't even see the scripts. I take out these glasses with the oxford frames. [*Doing so*] I settle myself down at night in a cosy Morris chair – although they don't call them Morris chairs any more – *I* approve before *you* even *see* the scripts!

CHARLIE: Don't kid a veteran of the Hollywood wars – we've been doing that the last three years!

204

NAT: But this deal is fool-proof. And rain or shine, for fourteen years, with complete approval of scripts – you can't be touched, you can't be hurt! And it's legal tender for three million, seven hundred and forty-four watermelons!

CHARLIE: But, Nat, if it costs me Marion –

NAT [*promptly*]: Her I'm gonna talk to again. You don't have to tell the old man – she's a little hectic now. But she'll cool down. You'll sign the contract, you're both young –

CHARLIE: You don't hear a word I say, do you?

[NAT *stops and sits back, as patient as an old circus horse, which is what he partly is.*]

NAT: I don't? I'm listening. I wanna hear. Refresh my memory. [*A quick addition*] But one thing – as sure as the Judgement Day! – Charlie Castle is an institution! And, as your humble servant told Marcus Hoff in his own office on Wednesday last – you can't tamper around with an institution!

CHARLIE [*with a smearing smile*]: You'll drive me to suicide, Nat.

NAT: Darling, listen –

CHARLIE: No, I'm goddam annoyed. You never listen to me.

NAT: But I'm listening.

CHARLIE: I DON'T WANT TO SIGN THIS CONTRACT!

[*A pause, silence;* NAT *sips his drink, watching Charlie over his glass.*]

NAT: *You don't.* . . .

CHARLIE: NO!

NAT [*quietly*]: But I thought you agreed to sign it. . . .

CHARLIE: Listening doesn't mean agreement. I *listened* to Marcus, I listened to you – I've been listening till I'm blue in the face, but I didn't agree to sign it!

[NAT *stops, lights his dead cigar, and looks Charlie over shrewdly. Finally:*]

NAT: Don't drink so much, Charlie. . . .

CHARLIE: You can come to my funeral. . . . It'll probably be raining!

NAT [*pausing*]: Charlie, with a tip of my hat to that gentleman – I work for you, not for Marcus. But I'll tell you something. He's sore as a boil – I just came from his office – two hours of Hail Columbia!

CHARLIE: What's he sore about?

NAT: We're stalling! The studio's out on the limb to the extent – a million dollars' worth of literary properties they bought for you over the last few years. Next week he goes to New York and he wants to present your new contract to the board. [*Looking at his watch*] Which all leads up to the fact ... they're dropping in here.

CHARLIE: Who?

NAT: Marcus and Smiley Coy.

CHARLIE [*startled*]: When?

NAT: Any minute, to invite you to the races. I'm here and you're here ... and it's supposed to lead to a show-down. So you see ...

CHARLIE: I don't wanna see Hoff today! I'm playing tennis in twenty minutes.

NAT [*solemnly*]: Lovey, I have to tell you – I'm very troubled. [*Then*] Everybody has a delusion that you're very tough – they mix you up with the parts you play. But I know you better. You're a special, idealistic type. The only thing – business and idealism don't mix – it's oil and water. Darling, you expect too much from yourself. A movie isn't a movie to you – it's a gospel. But you're mistaken, dear sir and friend. In all humility –

CHARLIE: Don't get me wrong, Nat. I live out here like a rajah and I love it! But what about the work? The place is hell on married life! I can't make peace with this place – I don't wanna live under the same blanket with Marcus Hoff and his feudal friends. The colour of their money is getting pale white with blood-shot eyes and I don't want it!

NAT: Charlie, a last few words. We're not in a bargaining position with Marcus now. But I'll do anything you ask me within my power, as the good Lord sits above.

CHARLIE: Get me out of here!

NAT: Never make pictures again? That would be your only chance to get away.

CHARLIE [*pausing*]: Put it in writing – I'll never make pictures again. Would he let me go?

NAT: You're an American institution, Charlie –

CHARLIE [*bitterly*]: Yeah, like a comic strip!

NAT [*gently*]: You're a very big star, Lovey, one of the biggest. No, Marcus won't let you go.

CHARLIE: But suppose I just tore the contract up and moved away?

NAT: What would he do?

CHARLIE: What would he do?

NAT [*slowly*]: God forbid . . . what he would do. Charlie, never underestimate a man because you don't like him. I know Marcus more than thirty years. Before he wore three-hundred-dollar suits and put his old, dead mother's picture on his desk – that mother he got from Central Casting. He's stepped in the tar himself enough, but he always keeps his shoes clean. Until that Christmas Eve you were a free agent. But not as of here and now. . . .

CHARLIE: I didn't want you to call him in that night.

NAT: He was the only one who could help you that night. [*Pausing*] But you still have here on paper a fabulous deal –

CHARLIE [*unhappily*]: We talk and talk and nothing gets settled.

NAT [*quietly*]: Because here there's not two right answers, Lovey, only one. You sign or you go to jail, I'm sorry to say. . . . .

RUSSELL [*entering*]: Mr Hoff and Mr Coy, they are here in person.

[CHARLIE *is pointedly silent.*]

NAT: Send them in.

[RUSSELL *goes,* NAT *stands, clearing his throat.* CHARLIE *puts on dark sun glasses.*]

[*Sotto voce*] Don't let on, namely, I told you a thing. . . .

CHARLIE: Every way is a way to die.

NAT: I'm older – every way is a way to live.

[*Giving Nat a cynical smile,* CHARLIE *goes to the archway and calls out cheerfully.*]

CHARLIE: This is a surprise, gentlemen! Come in, come in. . . .

[*Enter* MARCUS S. HOFF *and* SMILEY COY. HOFF *is a sleek, middle-aged man, full of* amour propre, *suave, ceremonial, and grave, shrewdly pompous, but authoritative and powerful. He knows how to play a part and how to get his way. Easy and assured, he is not stupid; he speaks in a kindly tone.* COY, *of contrasting colours, slim and tall where Hoff is plump and pudgy, is Hoff's perfect tool and factotum. He is elegant, loose-jointed, and deft; he is completely competent, cynical, calm, and courteous; he has many of the witty and amusing characteristics of the professional Irishman, including a certain atmosphere of loneliness.*]

COY: Ah ha, two heads under one hat! What goes on here?

NAT: How are you, Marcus? Smiley . . .?

HOFF: Hello, Charlie. Nat being in my hair so frequently, I don't say hello to him. I didn't expect to find you here, Nat.

NAT [*solemnly*]: I came in out of God's sunshine, that's all.

COY [*to Charlie*]: How did you wake up this morning, Ella?

CHARLIE [*groaning*]: I didn't wake up: I came to!

[CHARLIE, *with his unconscious habit of entertaining studio executives, makes them laugh. Typical Hollywood small talk follows, much of it overlapping.*]

HOFF: Did you hear about Joe Ackermann?

NAT [*quickly attentive*]: No . . .

HOFF [*gravely*]: Cancer.

NAT [*shocked*]: Oh, poor Joe Ackermann. Poor Martha . . . I saw them only the other day. [*Sighing deeply*] I'll have to call them tonight.

HOFF: Charlie, where did you get that beautiful shirt?

CHARLIE: Can't remember, to tell the truth.

HOFF [*feeling it*]: That's a pleasure to put next to your skin. Feel that, Nat. Find me a few like that, Smiley. Charlie, we request the pleasure of your company at the races this afternoon.

CHARLIE [*doubtfully*]: I don't think I can, Marcus. . . .

COY: Sid Benson's running two of his horses.

CHARLIE: How does he do it on four thousand a week?

NAT: Simple. He calls it business –

HOFF: It's worked out, taxwise.

NAT: And Uncle Sam pays the losses.

COY: I'm ready to bar-tend, union regulations permitting. Marcus?

HOFF: A little sparkling water. Don't be a fossil, Charlie. You'll enjoy the afternoon and we'll appreciate your company.

CHARLIE: Thanks, Marcus, but, among other things, I have to sweat out a 'skinful'.

COY: What did Patty Benedict have to say?

CHARLIE [*entertainingly*]: She's a bitch of a dish. Marion happened to drop in a moment and bit her right on the rump.

HOFF [*smiling*]: I, myself, if I had the nose of a dog, how many people I'd bite in the dark. Poor little me. [*Then*] How is Marion?

CHARLIE [*shrugging*]: Umm ...

HOFF: Charlie, I hope for your reconciliation with her as if you were both my own. In ourselves we are nobody, unimportant. But if we can express the Divine Will – and a happy marriage is surely such an expression – we are really living beyond our own selfish aims.

CHARLIE [*simpering*]: Very sweet of you, Marcus. ...

HOFF: Since we're here in friendly conclave ... what about the contract? I'll have to send it to the barbershop – it's growing whiskers.

CHARLIE [*taken aback*]: I'm having trouble with it, Marcus. ...

HOFF [*gravely*]: Trouble? Tell me. I have broad shoulders ... [*Waiting but getting no answer*] People can always speak frankly to me. Charlie, you're in a position which entitles you to make the highest demands. Let me hear your innermost thoughts ...

NAT [*after a pause*]: Charlie has no special demands other than those over which I laboured on and ironed out with your Bill Burton in the many pleasant conferences in his office and mine.

HOFF [*nodding*]: That was *my* distinct impression of the situation, too.

CHARLIE [*coming down*]: Marion doesn't want me to sign the contract.

HOFF [*pausing*]: Well, you are still man and wife – tree and bark – and God has put that together. I can understand. What does Marion want to see in the contract?

CHARLIE: She doesn't want me to sign it.

NAT: Marcus. What –

HOFF [*sharply*]: No, no, let *him* answer, Nat. Why?

[*Posed negligently,* SMILEY COY *listens in the background; part of his job is to seem impartial and friendly to both sides.*]

CHARLIE: It's the whole contract, Marcus – the whole idea of signing for that length of time.

[*There is a silent pause;* HOFF *slowly turns and looks squarely at Nat Danziger, who feels impelled to say:*]

NAT: Marcus, people can always speak frankly to you and that's what Charlie wants to do.

[HOFF *slowly turns and faces Charlie.*]

HOFF: And what do you propose instead . . .?

CHARLIE: I want to leave Hollywood. I'm willing to sign anything, guaranteeing you that I'll never make pictures again. I have nothing against you or Hoff-Federated, but I'm tired – I wanna go away.

HOFF [*quietly*]: You can go on lay-off for six months, even a year.

CHARLIE: No, I wanna leave for good.

HOFF [*pausing*]: I see. . . . [*Then, with the faintest smile, he leans back and closes his eyes.*] Charlie Castle, I easily call to mind our first meeting in my office in the old building. Can you recall what I said at that time . . . ?

CHARLIE [*uneasily*]: Some of the things . . .

HOFF: Pardon me closing my eyes – it helps me see better. [*Pausing*] I see a raw youth, but full of that special vitality of talent. And I said, if memory serves, 'Son, you're gonna be one of the biggest stars in the business,' I says. 'And as sure as God made the green earth, you're gonna run into many problems.' [*He opens his eyes and stares blandly at Charlie, occasionally turning to the others for emphasis.*] 'That's what I'm here for,' I says. 'This business can run itself. They don't need Marcus Hoff until the problems start. But that's the time,' I says, 'when I show them why I earn my salaries. And I'm here for you, Charlie Castle. My advice is always free, given with pleasure. I can't *always* help,' I says, 'but probably *more* than not.' And you came to me, Charlie Castle, more times than one. Is that true?

CHARLIE [*chaffing*]: Yes.

HOFF [*pausing*]: I'm skipping the years of coolness between us. You came to my office no more. The reason why is beyond me. And yet I was always there for you and yours, and the vexing problems, so manifold, of the heat and toil of the day. And on a certain night, in this very room – the law – *it spelled scandal* – I was there for you, too. And I'm here today, Charlie, *now*. I'm gonna indulge in a little story ... and to some of you it isn't news. The woman I called my wife for almost thirty years ... certain facts came home to me. Handling deals – it was the year of the merger, Nat – it was an easy day for me when I could call eight hours' sleep my own. These facts came up, as I say ... my wife, certain scenes, drinking ... a certain hotel in New York ... attempted suicides: I was out of my mind! We brought her back that time – Smiley was good enough to enter my employ the year before – it amounted to the fact, psycho-analysis – thirty or forty thousand dollars down the drain in a single year, but not begrudged. I thought to amuse her with a pleasure boat, the *Alberta*, named after her. But, as God is my witness above – nothing helped! And then one day, in my office – Smiley was there – Frank Lubner, a pioneer in the industry – I drank a light scotch and soda and I began to cry. I don't think I wept like that since I was a boy. Because I saw, by a revelation of pain, that my wife had determined, in her innermost mind, to destroy me and my career out of WILFUL MALICIOUS JEALOUSY! You ask me why? I ask *you* why! But from that day on I realized an essential fact of life: the woman must stay out of her husband's work when he's making her bread and butter! The wife of a man in your position should have the regard and respect to advance his career!

[*At last* NAT *finds a rift to slip through.*]

NAT: Hear me, Marcus . . . Charlie's real worry in the past, and it's a commendable thing in itself, he wanted to make better pictures.

HOFF: I'm not finished, Nat, although I'll discuss that later. [*Turning back to Charlie*] Because sometimes it becomes necessary to separate ourselves . . . from a wife who puts her petty interests before the multiplicity of a great career!

[*A momentary shocked silence is broken by* COY.]

COY: What Marcus means –

HOFF [*sharply*]: I'm aware of what I said! Because I'm already aware that Marion has twice cut herself off from her husband's concern by thoughtless, rumour-provoking retirements to the beach. I leave unmentioned certain reprehensible politics! Or will it be said that Charlie drove her out of his home? Absurd and ridiculous! Or does anyone think –? [*He is suddenly crying, with real tears*] Don't you think –? [*Unable to speak a moment*] Charlie, who can have anything I own . . . the pain of this moment . . . memories . . . to realize what he feels. . . .

[HOFF, *controlling himself, turns away, handkerchiefing his face.* CHARLIE *is disgusted;* NAT *is long-suffering;* SMILEY *is solemn and a moment later brings Hoff fresh water.*]

NAT [*plainly*]: I'm sure everyone understands, Marcus . . . namely . . .

[HOFF *returns; he sits again and clears his throat; in a moment his emotion will change to a brisk, appealing candour.*]

HOFF: As for better pictures, Nat, give me one good reason why a Charlie Castle shouldn't make the best in the world.

NAT: I don't think Charlie is holding out for any particular little thing. I know this boy and –

[HOFF *laughs and turns good-naturedly to Coy.*]

HOFF: You see how it goes, Smiley? They want a bonus tacked on. [*Chuckling*] All right, Nat, my old friend, you get it – an extra twenty-five thousand for every Castle picture we release. [*To Coy*] Make a note for a covering letter. . . .

NAT [*a polite murmur*]: That's very generous, Marcus. . . .

[HOFF *jovially turns to a glum Charlie next.*]

HOFF [*dramatically*]: BUT . . . it doesn't have to leave this room. I don't want the stockholders saying Marcus Hoff is out of his mind . . .

[*As solemn and stolid as an owl,* NAT *looks back at* CHARLIE *who is giving him a tormented stare.*]

So you see, Charlie, I'm like a girl in a summer-time canoe – I can't say no! [*Pausing*] Now what do you find it in your heart to do?

CHARLIE [*pausing*]: I meant what I said. I'm not bargaining with you, Marcus.

[HOFF *looks from Charlie to Nat and back again; his joviality is slowly replaced by something cooler.*]

HOFF: You're not in a bargaining position, Charlie . . . [*Silence. The implied threat is understood by all present.*] But it's true, I can't force you to sign the contract, can I?

[CHARLIE'S *pent-up nervous energy flares out.*]

CHARLIE: But that's just what the hell you're trying to do!

HOFF [*gravely*]: Charlie, I have to take this amiss. I offer you my hand and you spit in my face.

CHARLIE [*bitterly*]: Marcus, I want you to let me go. We don't like each other, I know – but I'll promise you anything to let me go!

HOFF [*pausing*]: I solemnly adjure realism, Charlie. I need your physical presence on the lot – your body, not your good will.

[HOFF *nods to* COY, *who comes down to a table with the contracts.* HOFF *brings out a gold fountain pen.*]

[*Blandly*] I want you to sign these papers with one of the pens that ended the last war. It was used by a great American, General MacArthur.

[CHARLIE *takes the pen and, sitting, looks at it;* NAT *avoids his eyes.*]

CHARLIE: Marcus – I don't give one good goddam for anything you said here today! I love Marion and I don't intend to lose her if I can help it!

HOFF [*quietly*]: Charlie, I can't tell you how many long months of constructive dreaming are in this moment. And I will let nothing or no one stand in the way of that dream!

CHARLIE: I'm asking for the last time – let me go!

HOFF [*shrugging*]: I can't force you to sign . . . .

[*They look at each other,* CHARLIE *and* HOFF, *for one peculiar moment like gross, befuddled animals. Then, the contracts open to the proper pages,* CHARLIE *turns and rips through them with four signatures. Then he stands and walks to the bar.*]

CHARLIE: I'll keep this pen. It's my only proof that the war is over. Or even that it was fought. That's Captain Castle talking! [*He throws down a rapid scotch.*]

HOFF: Charlie, we all love you. You're a peculiar duck, but in a free country that's your right.

COY [*gathering up the contracts*]: Congratulations, Ella. . . .

HOFF: You'll enjoy the races, Charlie – we won't stay too late. No? Well, I'm sorry. Nat, we're driving past your office.

NAT: Thanks, but I'm going out to Culver City.

HOFF: Charlie . . . see? [*Walking past the others,* HOFF *goes to the archway and suddenly stoops and groans, as if staggering with a painful burden on his back.*] See, Charlie? . . . All your troubles and worries . . . on my back. Uh uh! No more worries for you from now on. How I envy you your ease of mind!

[*Bent in half, groaning and grunting with the 'burden',* HOFF *exits.* COY *starts after him, saying easily:*]

COY: What's with you tonight, Ella? That certain party finds herself fascinated.

CHARLIE [*bitterly, turned away*]: Tell her I'll send it by mail!

COY [*smiling*]: Right. 'Bye now.

[COY *goes jauntily on his long legs.* NAT *looks silently at Charlie in the gloomy atmosphere.*]

CHARLIE [*finally*]: The smooth sonofabitch, he twisted my head like I was a ten-cent doll! [*The phone rings;* CHARLIE *answers it reluctantly*.] Hello? Yes, dear . . . Nat's still here.

NAT: For me?

CHARLIE [*whispering*]: Marion ... [*Then, into phone*] Hoff was here. Sweetheart ... I lost ... [*A pause*] Yes, I – hello? Hello?

> [*He slowly cradles the phone, saying: 'She hung up on me'. He sits and puts his face in his hands. It is a moment before Nat knows what to say.*]

NAT: I happen to believe in Marion's good sense, namely. I believe in her and I believe in you. I'll talk to her.

CHARLIE: Don't ...

NAT [*pausing*]: What the heck, Charlie, let's look in the mirror and call a spade a spade. [*Walking around*] Before you know it, the summer is over and Mr September is here and you'll work and forget petty troubles. Work – it's the cream and the essence – work! I'll help you – I'll lay down my life for you ... and that's from the heart!

CHARLIE [*looking up*]: Do me a favour, Nat. I signed the contract? Then omit the heart. The free giving of hearts out here begins to freeze my blood. [*Disgusted*] Boy, if I didn't love people so much ... how I'd hate 'em! [*He comes down with his highball and stumbles slightly.*] Hey, are these the legs that launched a thousand tennis balls!

> [*Smiling, NAT crosses and picks up his hat. He looks up at the Utrillo painting.*]

NAT: A very pretty picture indeed; but, as my devoted wife used to say – she should rest in peace – 'The prettiest picture of all – who'll disagree? – a mirror!' [*Turning*] I'll call you tomorrow, darling....

> [CHARLIE *is sunk in a chair with his drink.* NAT *heads for the archway.*]

NAT [*stopping*]: Oh! I suppose you heard about Miss Dixie Evans?

CHARLIE: Dixie? What's wrong with Dixie?

NAT [*chuckling*]: Ahh, I'll tell you some other time. 'Bye 'bye ...

CHARLIE: 'Bye ...

> [NAT *waves his hands and goes.* CHARLIE, *whose speech has thickened, sips his drink, musing, muttering to himself. He takes off and throws*]

his sun glasses aside. CONNIE BLISS *enters by the screen door right;* CHARLIE *does not see her.*]

CONNIE: Charlie, talking to yourself? Secret vices? It's me, remember?

[CHARLIE, *who has whirled around, drops back.*]

CHARLIE: Look what the wind blew in! Hello, Connie.

CONNIE: Isn't Buddy here?

CHARLIE: He isn't here.

CONNIE[*going to bar*]: His secretary said he was. Why stand on ceremony? I'll mix myself a highball and then I'll leave!

CHARLIE [*muttering*]: Thought I'd play some tennis ....

[*She goes behind the bar to mix a drink.* CHARLIE *closes his eyes.* CONNIE *is handsome and blonde, with lissom, fairly uncovered body; any dress she wears looks like a bathing suit. She would be hard were it not for her disposition to please; but this does not mean that she is undetermined. She minces and coquettes a little, her way of asking for your favour, and she laughs constantly, without effort; finally, her blue-eyed, washed-out candour covers enough slyness; hers is a nimble, jumping mind. In a certain mood, you will find her light and refreshing, a veritable Rhine wine of a person.*]

CONNIE: A thousand-dollar bond couldn't get me out in this sizzling sun, with a racquet in my hand. You should keep your doors locked, Charlie. You could be kidnapped and held for a delicious ransom.

CHARLIE: I'm a prize. . . .

CONNIE: I like these big, silly ice kegs – they're never empty. Charlie, I'm going right home if you fall asleep on me!

[CHARLIE *opens his eyes as she comes down; she sits on the arm of his chair.*]

CHARLIE: I was thinking. . . . [*Eyeing her*] Cigarette?

CONNIE: One of those Turkish ones you get. They're awfully sexy, Turkish ones. Hot weather always makes me frisky. . . . [*Then*] What about you and Marion? Buddy's my husband, but he won't tell me a thing.

CHARLIE: Where'd you come from now, frisky miss?

CONNIE: Lunch at The Players.

CHARLIE: With that second-class neurotic, Wally Weider?

CONNIE [*surprised*]: How did you know?

CHARLIE [*dryly*]: Rumours.

CONNIE: Say, a girl has lunch with a man once and in this town it's a torrid romance. Would I be seen in public if it was?

CHARLIE: No, you'd pull the blinds, if I know you, and I think I do. [CONNIE *laughs heartily.* CHARLIE *gets up and walks, swinging an imaginary tennis racquet.*]

CONNIE: You have to admit one thing about Buddy – he lacks a sense of humour.

CHARLIE: God didn't make us all alike, Connie. [*Stopping his swinging*] You've cornered me at twenty different parties. Why do you sniff me out every time I'm drunk?

CONNIE [*laughing*]: Are you drunk?

CHARLIE: My mood is low, honey, and I'm stewed to the gills.

CONNIE: Is that a warning . . . ?

CHARLIE [*mordantly*]: Yeah, all the red neon lights are on and the sky is full of drunken blackbirds. [*Pausing, harshly*] Now, stop shaking that thing in my face and go home!

CONNIE [*murmuring*]: Why stand on ceremony, Charlie? I find you very attractive.

[*Attracted and repelled,* CHARLIE *looks at her; then he steps forward and takes her by the upper parts of her arms.*]

Darling . . .

CHARLIE: You don't care what you do to your husband, do you?

CONNIE: Do you . . . ? [*Then, twisting away*] No, that hurts, boy friend!

CHARLIE: You're always naked – just to hold you by the soft parts of your arms is a meal. . . .

[*Revolted,* CHARLIE *smirks and drops into his chair.* CONNIE *laughs, and rubs her arm; then she crosses and touches Charlie's ear, stepping back quickly to avoid his upflung arm.*]

CONNIE: You hurt me, darling. I'm a naughty girl – I wish I could say I didn't like it. [*Drinking*] Life's a sweet thing, isn't it? That's what Buddy will never understand. He's not a good-time man, if I may get scientific.

CHARLIE [*unturned*]: Go home, Connie. . . .

[*Instead, she sits and stretchingly luxuriates in a soft chair.*]

CONNIE: Last year I almost left your friend Buddy. But then that terrible thing came up and of course I had to play my part. Particularly since it got so involved.

CHARLIE: What do you mean involved?

CONNIE: Now stop it, Charlie. Don't you think I know Buddy went to prison for you? Don't you think I know *you* killed that child, not Buddy, in the auto accident?

[*He looks at her stupidly, closing one eye.*]

CHARLIE: Buddy told you that?

CONNIE: Let's face it . . . you're the hero of the world to Buddy. He wouldn't tell me a thing like that! He'd just go ahead and go to jail for you. He wouldn't ask his wife! [*Then archly*] That handsome Smiley Coy called Buddy twice that night. He's very important – why would he call Buddy? So tiny Connie put two and two together –

CHARLIE: And got a crooked five . . . ?

CONNIE [*pleasantly shrugging*]: Darling, if that's the way you want it? [*Then*] Not to mince words Buddy's dull to me – very dull and inconvenient.

CHARLIE: What do you want? Support without inconvenience? Haven't you been living on his money all this time?

CONNIE [*easily*]: No, I've been living on your money all this time. . . .

CHARLIE: Once it leaves my hands, it's his, not mine. And stop that gentle rocking like a boat!

CONNIE: Get organized, Charlie, you're drunk. What do you want to be, a saint? There's wonderful hell in you. Let's enjoy it!

CHARLIE: Can't you think beyond the tips of your own toes?

CONNIE [*laughing*]: You're wonderful when you're mad – real jet

218

propulsion! [*Glass extended*] Carbonate me, darling. . . . Oh, I know I'm a naughty girl. Self-service. [*Shrugging, she goes to the bar and fixes her drink.*] Another one for you . . . ?

CHARLIE: No, that liquor's got me in a hurry. . . . [*He stands, baffled and cumbersome, very drunk, shaking his head.*] How did you know Marion wasn't at home?

CONNIE [*lightly*]: Why, she's at the beach, with headaches. She believes in faithful marriage.

CHARLIE: An' whatta you believe . . . what the hell?

[*She returns, rolling her eyes.*]

CONNIE: I like to walk up spiral stairs, just like in a play. . . . [*She steps back, smiling, as he lunges at her.*]

CHARLIE: You . . . I asked you a question . . . whatta you believe in?

CONNIE [*brightly*]: Well, not in gloomy thoughts. In fun, darling, in perfume, in staying young and making love. In goodies of every sort and description. I like snug, draped bedrooms and locked doors, so I can be my naked self. As you desire me, darling. . . .

CHARLIE [*heavily*]: Go home, your mother wants you!

CONNIE [*laughing*]: You know you're a good time, Charlie, just like me!

CHARLIE: I'm not like you, I don't know what I'm like . . . not you. [*Shaking his head*] I'm drunk – umm!

CONNIE: You certainly are. I'll leave when it's dark. Now get upstairs. . . .

CHARLIE [*shoving her violently to the floor*]: Go home, Connie, I don't need you to go to hell with. I can splash up my own mud and neon lights! Go home, Connie.

[CHARLIE *grabs a bottle of scotch from bar and starts up spiral stairs leaving* CONNIE *behind, but in a moment she follows.*]

Slow curtain

ACT TWO

Scene: The same.
Time: Late at night, a week later.

[*With* CONNIE *and* BUDDY BLISS *present,* CHARLIE *and* MARION *have been acting hospitably all evening.* CHARLIE *is rewinding a large reel of 16-mm. film; during the opening moments of the scene he will be moving into a closet the various parts of a home projection apparatus.*
Uneasy, strained and tired, CHARLIE *speaks lightly and over-energetically.* CONNIE *is bored but is covering it by light chatter interrupted by glasses of brandy.* MARION *seems calm and matronly, a gracious hostess who is quietly concentrating on making things move smoothly.*]

CONNIE: No one minds if I take another brandy. . . .

MARION: That's what it's there for. Buddy, there's another bottle of champagne on ice. . . .

BUDDY: Nothing more for me, thanks.

[CONNIE *has gone to the bar.* CHARLIE *looks back over his shoulder.*]

CHARLIE: Buddy, plunge your fist in that humidor and smoke a fresh Havana cigar.

BUDDY: I never was much for cigars, Charles, thanks. Connie doesn't like a man who smokes cigars.

CONNIE [*pertly*]: It depends on who the man is!

CHARLIE [*laughing*]: Ow ow, that was wicked!

BUDDY [*smiling*]: How old is this picture you just ran!

CHARLIE: About eight or nine years. Why?

[CONNIE *comes down and stands behind Buddy's chair.*]

BUDDY: I never seen it before. Ye gods, you had steam.

CONNIE: Charlie's a better actor now than he ever was.

BUDDY: I should say he is. He's a better actor than he ever was!

CHARLIE: You're sweet, Bud, a real friend – solid as an apple. But don't butter my radish when it comes to acting in a piece of four-

220

bit bait like *Tiger on the Town*. I'm an imitation now of what I was ten years ago. How the hell can I grow with these sort of parts? And all the kids who imitate me – they're an imitation of an imitation! That's how it goes out here – laughing and scratching all the time.

MARION: Connie, I think you're going to have to take your husband home and tuck him in – he needs some sleep.

BUDDY: I won't deny it, Marion, I've had a loaded day and the wine has made me sleepy. [MARION *and* BUDDY *stand, he covers a yawn again.*] I can't thank you enough for this wonderful evening. Just the two couples – it's a wonderful balance, two couples. I hope it always stays this way! [*Eagerly*] When I get my vacation, why don't the four of us go some place together?

MARION [*quickly*]: Excuse Madame Kill-Joy, but I'm breaking in a new nurse for Billy. And Buddy's eyes are closing. . . .

BUDDY: I confess – I'll sleep like a log tonight.

CONNIE [*to Charlie*]: Good night, darling. . . .

BUDDY: Good night, Marion. Thanks.

MARION: Good night, dear. . . .

CHARLIE [*with comical twist*]: I'll walk youse out.

[CHARLIE *goes out through the archway with* BUDDY *and* CONNIE. *Alone,* MARION *thoughtfully lights a cigarette and pours herself a small drink.* CHARLIE *returns.*]

MARION: Now that it's over, what was this dinner for?

CHARLIE: I've been ducking him for months. He kinda felt it the other day when Patty Benedict was here! I still can't look him in the eye. . . .

MARION: Yes, I saw. Doesn't Connie know we're separated?

CHARLIE: I don't think she knows. Ain't it dark in here? [*He snaps on another lamp and picks up his drink.*]

MARION: Why do you keep using words like 'ain't'?

CHARLIE [*grinning*]: Ain't 'ain't' a word?

MARION: Not to a man who worked his way through college.

CHARLIE: You know my type, a tight-lipped, reliable, unemotional man of the people – rock-bottom stuff. Can't let my fans down, can I? You wouldn't castigate my catachresis, would you? How's *that* for college? [*Looking intently at her, he laughs to her smile.*] You're looking very austere tonight.

MARION: Tired, I'm afraid.

CHARLIE: Me, too. I'd give three senators and a dozen congressmen for one real night's sleep.

[MARION *holds the Chartreuse up to the light.*]

MARION: Why can't you sleep ... ?

CHARLIE [*soberly*]: For the same reasons you can't. [*Waiting.*] You've buried me so deep, Angel. Are we really ... at the end?

MARION [*reluctantly*]: I think so, Charlie. You've been and gone and done it. You've blown up the bridge ... we can't go back.

CHARLIE: Do you think you're being fair ... ?

MARION: As fair as I can be. Or at least as human and honest as I can be, after twelve glorious years in Hollywood.

CHARLIE: You think I'm dishonest, don't you?

MARION [*with a moue*]: No, but I believe the fairy tale is a lie. In real life no one ever comes to wake us up.

CHARLIE: You go on grieving for the past, like a weeping bird. What the hell was Charlie Cass? A hot-head with clenched fists and a big yammering mouth!

MARION [*sadly*]: I liked him mighty fine. ...

CHARLIE [*annoyed*]: There are lots of attractive things about Hollywood. Could Cass guarantee you next week's meals? I never heard you kick about barbecuing four-inch steaks!

MARION: You're right, there's nothing so habit-forming as money! But that's stupid, as justification.

CHARLIE: What do I have to justify. Do I have to be in politics to hold my head up? What, making money? Is that the sin?

MARION: Your sin is living against your own nature. You're denatured – that's your sin!

CHARLIE: You talk like a fresh, moralistic college kid, who took a course!

MARION: Aren't you the one who says he wants to live a certain way and do a certain kind of work? ... And then pushes a pie in the face of everything he says? Men like Hoff and Coy have their own integrity – they're what they are! The beetle and the fervid Christian can't be equally corrupted! You can laugh – you can snort! But the critic who called you the Van Gogh of the American theatre saw, as I did, that you had a Christian fervour! [*Beginning to cry*] And now you're nothing, common trash – coarsened down to something I don't even recognize! [*Pausing*] Don't think I ever condoned what you did to Buddy. Or my part in what you did! [*Weeping bitterly*] But you're helpless, you're sick and unhappy ... and I go on, trying to help a little, defenceless because you're sick. You feel guilty and it makes you vicious! You've taken the cheap way out – your passion of the heart has become passion of the appetites! Despite your best intentions, you're a horror ... and every day you make me less a woman and more the rug under your feet! And ... and I won't have it, I won't, I can't, I can't ... [*Then, dropping her voice*] I can't ....

[CHARLIE *waits quietly, giving her his handkerchief which she uses.*]

CHARLIE: Take it easy, dear. ....

MARION: Taking it easy is where the trouble begins. ....

CHARLIE [*gently*]: Come on now, be yourself. ....

MARION: That's another good local remark: 'Be yourself', which means, 'Be just like me, *don't* be yourself!'

CHARLIE: Can I get you another drink?

MARION: I don't need another drink. [*Pausing*] Oh, God, I wish the world would get serious so I could be my superficial self again! [*She stands, rubbing her forehead.*] Where did I put my car? Oh ... Hank drove me in. He's supposed to pick me up. What time is it now?

CHARLIE [*looking*]: Ten of one. Is your car bust?

MARION: I was tired and Hank mentioned he was driving in.

[CHARLIE *is really moved by his wife, but as she soon points out, he assumes a light bantering tone now.*]

223

CHARLIE: Marion ... don't you miss me out at the beach, in the wilderness of waves and highway traffic roaring past the door?

MARION [*dryly*]: Poetry at this late hour?

CHARLIE: Why don't you stay here tonight? You can phone Hank, head him off.

[*She smiles at his negligent attitude.*]

MARION: You'd have to want me more than that. ...

CHARLIE: Don't I want you ... ?

MARION: At the moment you want most to keep your easy pose of detachment. Why expose yourself? After all, I might refuse. Could the great Charlie Castle take rejection?

CHARLIE [*lightly ironic*]: So ends my love song. ...

MARION: It's a burp of the ego, not a love song.

CHARLIE: Thanks and thanks. ... [*Shrugging, he drops into a chair.*]

MARION [*pausing*]: I'd tell you something ... but you'd get too excited. [*Then*] The day I was here, the day you renewed with Hoff. ... No, you'd get too excited.

CHARLIE [*smirking*]: Play billiards, Angel, or put the cue down.

[*Sitting on the arm of a chair*]

[*She looks at him with a certain grimness before going on.*]

MARION: The next day I went and had an abortion.

CHARLIE [*turning slowly*]: You went and had ... ? [*Disbelieving*] Why don't you stop it, chum!

MARION [*bitterly, taking his tone*]: Latch on, while I tell you. ...

[*He slowly stands and stares at her, seeing her seriousness.*]

I waited six, long, nervous weeks ... until you signed the contract.

CHARLIE: Why didn't you tell me?

MARION: A husband should know when his wife is three months pregnant. The cook in the kitchen knew.

CHARLIE [*licking his lips*]: All right, I'm a louse. And what about good old Hankus? He knew it, too?

MARION: No ...

[*He stands, looking at her with a menacing quiet, neck stretched, like a snake about to strike. Immobile, after a moment, he crosses and stands behind a heavy chair, gripping it with his hands.]*

CHARLIE: I'm putting this chair between us. Otherwise . . . I might tear your head off. . . . [*Not raising his voice*] You come here and fling this handful of naked pigeons in my face and it's all my fault!

MARION: No, I made my own decisions.

CHARLIE [*not changing his tone*]: How do you feel? Sit down. . . .

MARION: I'm sitting. . . .

CHARLIE: Would it have killed you to have another child?

MARION: I think I did the sensible thing.

CHARLIE [*blowing up*]: Will you, for Chris' sake, not be so goddam awful sensible and objective all the time! Are you such a clever lady? Why don't you fall down and let *me* pick *you* up, for a change? Why the hell don't you go to pieces? [*He begins to prowl like an animal; he turns and shouts*] Do you realize what you did!

MARION: Yes.

CHARLIE [*burning*]: The zeal with which you ran to do it – the ZEAL! [*Then, twisting and turning*] Did it hurt?

MARION: I'll live – there are coonskin caps on my father's side.

CHARLIE [*stopping*]: BUT DO YOU REALIZE WHAT YOU DID?

MARION [*quietly*]: It's all over, Charlie, a week ago. Let's talk about something real. We have a handsome, intelligent boy. What about *his* future?

CHARLIE: You don't get Billy! You're leaving *me*! Then the boy belongs to me!

MARION: Don't be so smug – who told you you're a father? I'd sooner Billy was raised in a bawdy house.

CHARLIE: Is that what you'd tell the judge?

MARION [*temper slipping*]: It's what I'm telling you!

CHARLIE [*abruptly*]: But, Marion, what did you do? What did you go and do?

MARION [*standing*]: Is that the bell?

CHARLIE: I'll go.

MARION: It's probably Hank.

CHARLIE: I said I'll go!

[*He goes quickly. Alone,* MARION *finishes her little drink. She is lipsticking her mouth when* CHARLIE *enters with* 'HANK' TEAGLE *in tow.* HANK, *nearing fifty, limps slightly. He is smiling, tender, and affectionate by nature and experience; his face hides a quiet gaiety and a sharper insight. He is unpretentious, quiet, and mature, with a gift for devotion. A man with his own tremor, he respects a tremor in another. He is a civilized man in the sense that he makes you feel guilty or inadequate on no score whatsoever.*]

HANK: Hello, Marion dear.

MARION: Hello, Hank.

HANK: There's the wonderful Rouault. . . .

[*Sullen,* CHARLIE *hovers near the bar, off balance for the moment.*]

CHARLIE: Drink?

HANK [*with a chortle*]: I'm a convert to water. Didn't you hear?

CHARLIE: How did you manage that?

HANK: With prayer.

CHARLIE [*ironically*]: You believe in prayer?

HANK: I've always believed in prayer. [*Smiling, noting Charlie's sullenness, he turns and asks Marion*] How was your dinner?

MARION: I've been more stimulated in my time! [*Nervously*] How was *your* dinner?

HANK: Well, get seven of Hollywood's intellectual hill-billies at one night-club table and you're in titanic trouble. Men of a thousand causes and quips, not one unpopular or human. And then to be so dull – success has made them all so dull. [*Smiling*] And think of me – dull without success. . . .

[*He looks at Charlie, who now feels he has to say something.*]

CHARLIE: You're leaving for New York, I hear. To write a book.

HANK: Yes, another little book. . . .

CHARLIE [*pausing*]: Marion says you asked her to marry you.

HANK: I did. . . .

CHARLIE: Let me get this straight. Aren't you my friend?

HANK: Yes, but your butler thinks I'm a wine merchant. I called here twice. He thinks I'm selling wine. Or so he says. I thought you were being 'out' to me. [*Quietly*] Marion makes me want to live; most people affect me differently. I'm sorry you're unhappy, but you lost her years ago. In fairness, you can't blame me.

CHARLIE: I'm not fair tonight. But where the hell did you stash your angel wings? Who gave you the right to make decisions here?

HANK: My only right is to make my own decisions.

CHARLIE [*bitterly*]: Nuts to you, dear Beau Heart! Marion isn't leaving me, Hank!

MARION: I'll make my own decisions, too.

CHARLIE: Marion, listen –

MARION: No, I want to go home.

CHARLIE: But, Marion, let me say ten words –! [*Then, morosely*] Sorry, Marion, sometimes I rave and rant as if I had something against you. But you've been only good to me. [*Grimacing, taking off his tie, he steps behind the bar.*] It's all a bleak and bitter dream, a real dish of doves. The only friends I can keep are the classy pimps, like Coy. [*Grimacing*] There's only two ways to forget everything – get drunk or stick a pencil in your eye.

MARION: I'll see the lawyer in the morning. . . .

CHARLIE: Right.

[*She turns and starts for the archway, but* CHARLIE *beats her to it and blocks her way, arms spread out.*]

But I swear I'm innocent, Marion. I swear that while I'm charming the world with my light fantastic . . . I'm bleeding to death under my shirt. Can't you wait, sweetheart, with the lawyer? Am I the worst oaf in the world . . . ?

MARION [*unsteadily*]: The world's a big place . . . but you're the worst one in my life. Good night.

[*She walks around him and disappears.* CHARLIE *slowly drops his arms and looks at Hank.*]

CHARLIE: When are you leaving, Hank?

HANK: Tuesday or Wednesday.

CHARLIE: I'll see you before you go? Is Monday good?

HANK: Any time you say. . . .

CHARLIE: Monday. How can I blame you for loving Marion? Don't think badly of me, Hank.

HANK: I don't.

[*They shake hands.* HANK *limps out, saying, 'Good night.'*]

CHARLIE: Good night. . . .

[CHARLIE *doesn't know what to do with himself. Finally, after sipping his drink, he crosses and dials the phone, but changing his mind, he hangs up. Then he turns sharply at a scratching on the screen door.*]

Who is that?

COY [*outside*]: Charlie . . . ?

[CHARLIE *unhooks the door and lets him in.*]

CHARLIE: For the love of Pete, where were you? Next door?

COY [*smiling*]: Next door. Monty Ritz has a 'shindig' – I looked and left. Don't you hear it?

CHARLIE [*listening*]: No . . .

COY: Breeze is blowing the other way. Bicarbonate. Cracked crab – it's a real heart-burn special.

[COY *walks directly to the bar and mixes himself some bicarbonate of soda.* CHARLIE *takes off his coat.*]

How you feeling, Ella?

CHARLIE: Blue, like my dear baby's eyes. . . .

COY: What did you think of Tess?

CHARLIE [*morosely*]: The redhead? A nice, meaty body on her, but I wasn't in the mood for romance. Yes or no and she said no, and I think I've lost a fan. I came home and read for an hour.

COY: What are you reading?

CHARLIE: I don't remember from day to day. . . . [*Then*] I have to get some larger bulbs in these lamps . . . [*Then*] *Heilige nacht*, it's quiet. . . .

COY: I know you heard about the economizing couple that went to bed early, to save electric light, and it resulted in twins. [*Then*] I saw Tommy Murdoch's new picture last night.

CHARLIE [*listlessly*]: How is it?

COY [*shaking his head*]: I don't think so. [*Then*] Gin rummy?

CHARLIE: I'll play an hour. . . .

[*Getting the cards,* COY *takes them to the card table.* CHARLIE *comes over and sits.*]

COY: What are you dreaming about?

CHARLIE: I'm restless. Marcus have a good trip?

COY: He came back with a cold – everyone in the studio is sneezing.

CHARLIE [*fretfully*]: California, think of it – a place where an honest apple tree won't grow. . . .

COY: What about some fishing?

[*They have begun the hand of gin rummy.*]

CHARLIE: That's a chubby bore. But maybe a few days on a boat.

COY: Marcus isn't using the *Alberta Second*.

CHARLIE: Ahhh . . . it doesn't make much sense to cruise over to Catalina and anchor next to twenty other boats. [*Then*] Hey, you don't want that card. . . .

COY: Purely speculative, Ella. . . .

CHARLIE [*pausing*]: I'm homesick for the East, for the four seasons. . . .

COY: The Chinese say, 'I was angry because I had no shoes. And then I met a man who had no feet. . . .'

[*There is a small flurry of rapid card picking. Faint music is heard from the near-by party.*]

There are only two things in life. The French know that.

CHARLIE [*listlessly*]: What's the second? [*Then*] How old are you, Smiley?

COY: A million, but young enough, to my surprise, to still be losing my temper with a tramp like Dixie Evans.

CHARLIE: What's wrong with her?

COY: Her mouth's too big.

[CHARLIE *stops playing cards and looks questioningly at Coy.*]

She's at Monty's party. Drunk. 'There's my boy,' she says. I turn around and there she sits, cute as a skinned, parboiled ham. 'We know something, don't we, Smiley and me?' she says.

CHARLIE [*slowly*]: I'm trying to get Marion to come back. That's all I need, for Marion to find out I had this girl in the car with me the night of the accident. . . .

COY: She's been hinting like that in quite a few spots.

CHARLIE: Do you think she means any harm?

COY: Who can tell? She's always liked you. Why don't you call her – have her come over? She's worth a few laughs, anyway.

CHARLIE: No, that's not for Mr Castle tonight. Why does she worry you? You can do a thousand things.

COY: Name one. . . .

CHARLIE: Buy her off.

COY: Didn't we buy her off with the contract?

CHARLIE [*smirking*]: But she's dishonest? She won't stay bought?

COY: Ask her over, Charlie.

CHARLIE [*sighing*]: Well . . . anything for my art. Monty's house? I know the number.

[CHARLIE *dials the phone on the bar.* COY *looks through some bottles and takes a drink from a small one.*]

Marion didn't look well tonight. I'll betcha sixty bucks she's lost ten pounds the last month.

COY [*politely*]: Yes, I could see it myself. . . .

CHARLIE [*into the phone*]: Hello? Miss Dixie Evans is there. Evans. Get her, please. [*Waiting*] What do women want from life?

COY [*leaning on the bar*]: Can't say. Don't know. What do *you* think of women?

CHARLIE: I think there's room in the world for them. . . .

COY: There's no satisfying them. Like kids, they're not of our world. I like them for the few tricks they can do, their so-called specialties . . .

CHARLIE [*laughing*]: You're a cruel sonofabitch! [*Into the phone*] Dixie? The old maestro, Charlie Castle. No, I'm not kidding. What are you doing in Monty's Victorian parlour? Come over here – it's modern and functional. Maybe we'll take a swim. [*Listening and nodding*] Uh, huh, um huh . . . I see. Well, come on over ... just east – across and over – that's it. 'Bye, Dimples. [*Yawning and hanging up*] She'll be over. [*Then, stretching*] Catch me a few moths, Smiley. I wanna burn 'em with matches.

COY: Cards?

CHARLIE: Let's sit it out. ...

COY: Be careful what you say to Dixie. Don't give her any more ammunition. Sound her out. There's an outside chance we'll have to get rid of her.

CHARLIE: Have you *offered* to buy her contract up?

COY: Two months ago.

CHARLIE [*impressed*]: She's been blabbing around that long, you mean?

> [COY *is playing with the pin-ball game.*]

COY: Longer. She's a stupid little pus-head with a little power!

CHARLIE: You talked to her? What did she say?

COY: It's a free country and she pays for all her drinks! I'm not saying there's any danger, but her judgement is mighty poor.

CHARLIE: But who would believe a word she said?

COY [*coming to him*]: Ella, look what happened to Georgie Wilson. That wasn't even true, but look what the Press has done to him.

CHARLIE: She doesn't want more money?

COY: That was my last offer. Which same she turned down. I'll tell you what she wants. Are you in the mood for a laugh? I don't say it's what she meant, but she said it twice: 'Charlie should have married me.' [COY *joins* CHARLIE *in his laughter.*] No, that kid doesn't know what she wants. I'm betting even money we have to get rid of her.

CHARLIE: Well, how do you do that?

COY [*shrugging*]: There's no standard procedure. ...

CHARLIE: *She* won't let you drive her out of town.

COY: No, she's all mouth and grab, but she'd never open her mouth again. [*Waving his hand*] Let's wait and see developments.

CHARLIE: I can talk to her, I think. ... [*He is starting for the bar; he stops, turning.*] I'm a little fuzzy there. What do you mean, she'll never open her mouth again?

COY: That's what I mean.

CHARLIE: What's what you mean?

COY: She'll have to be removed. . . .

[CHARLIE, *before laughing, stares at Coy intently.*]

CHARLIE: My mind is fuzzy tonight – my timing is off. For a moment there I really thought you meant that.

COY [*quietly*]: Charlie, she'll have to be removed. . . .

[CHARLIE *continues to the bar and begins mixing a drink before he turns and looks intently at* COY, *who is fiddling with the playing cards.*]

CHARLIE [*softly*]: Tell me . . .

COY: I'm not enjoying this . . . but a fact, like a rock, has solid dimensions. There are certain choices here. . . .

CHARLIE [*pausing*]: For instance . . . ?

COY: Nobody could expect you, for instance, to marry her, could they?

CHARLIE: No.

COY: Then we rule that out. We've gone over the other choices, one by one.

CHARLIE [*stiffly*]: I didn't realize that's what you were doing.

COY: I was. . . . Sorry to throw the raw meat on the floor. [*In a momentary hush the music is heard from the near-by party.*] Was that the bell?

CHARLIE: No.

COY: It's prejudicial for her to find me here. She doesn't like me. In two similar cases, one near home, agents took the girls and smothered them in marriage. Marcus still has privileges to dispense, but where's the agent?

CHARLIE [*uneasily*]: You're saying very funny things, Smiley, but I don't see you grin.

COY [*quietly*]: Life is a queer little man. . . .

CHARLIE [*bursting into laughter*]: Why don't you stop it?

COY [*laughing, too*]: That's what I said before. Let's wait and see what develops.

[CHARLIE *comes down with his drink.*]

CHARLIE: What does Marcus know about this?

COY: Only what he wants to know. There's a reason he pays me seventy-five thousand a year. She'll be here any minute. I'll leave the way I came.

CHARLIE: Don't have any illusions about me, Smiley.

COY [*coming closer*]: Charlie ... you're a fanciful boy. In my end of the business, you have to know types. Take your type: the warrior minstrel of the forlorn hope.

CHARLIE: Good, Smiley, good! Did you make that up?

COY: It's a phrase. The Irish *used* to understand it. Ideals, kid? Nowadays? A lost crusade. . . . [*Smiling*] Don't study life – get used to it.

CHARLIE: You changed the subject. I was –

[COY *cuts him short with a laugh and a waving hand.*]

COY: Are you bothering to remember everything I said tonight? Pleasant dreams, Ella. [*He reaches the screen door and opens it before Charlie can move.*]

CHARLIE: Smiley, listen – !

[COY *is gone.* CHARLIE *starts for the door, stops, thinks, and slowly sips his drink. He listens; again the wind wafts the music of the party here. Hearing a voice he whirls around and sees* RUSSELL, *wearing a robe, standing in the archway.*]

RUSSELL: You call me, Mr Castle?

CHARLIE: No ...

RUSSELL: Thought I heard you ring. Woke me up. Well, anything I can please you with while I'm here?

CHARLIE: No. Yes. Bring down that plaid blanket. Robe and pyjamas, too. I'll lock up myself. Isn't that the robe I gave you?

RUSSELL [*grinning*]: Yes, it is. [RUSSELL *chuckles and starts for the spiral stairs.*] Lucille say she gonna love me all over again in this robe. That the front-door bell?

CHARLIE: It's a young lady. Let her in and go to bed.

[RUSSELL *turns and exits through the archway.* CHARLIE *looks out of the screen door and locks it. He nervously brushes back his hair.* DIXIE EVANS *enters, a little tipsy, gowned, her greetings forced and somewhat shrill because she is nervous. Physically small but attractive, she is a product of a Boston parochial school, a poor family, several years of work in department stores, and finally, four years of Hollywood. Frequently helpless and unconsciously pathetic, she has learned to appear bright and competent; she has shrewd if intuitive flashes of genuine insight.*]

DIXIE: Good evening, Charlie, dear. Long time no see. . . .

CHARLIE: Well, wash out my mouth with whisky! Look who's here! You really look well.

DIXIE [*dropping into a chair*]: Uhh! No, I don't. I'm all 'frowsed up'. It's hot over at Monty's. It's cool here.

CHARLIE: I'm drinking brandy and soda. . . .

DIXIE: If I take one more drink I'll see a snake!

CHARLIE: Take a light one – don't be silly.

DIXIE: All right, you masochist – scotch and soda then. [*Relaxed, she sighs and looks around while* CHARLIE *prepares the drink.*] It's so quiet in this part of the town.

CHARLIE: It's always quiet here. . . .

DIXIE [*sniffing*]: Isn't that heavenly! Night-blooming jasmine, isn't it?

CHARLIE: Lots of it around. . . .

DIXIE: Now I'm relaxed. You must have X-ray eyes. How did you know I was at Monty's?

CHARLIE [*grinning*]: X-ray eyes!

DIXIE [*gaily*]: You're a faker! You're sweet, but I don't trust you! [*Suddenly*] Listen, who's home?

CHARLIE [*bringing her the drink*]: Only the crickets. How old are you?

DIXIE: Girls don't tell. [*Laughing*] Twenty-three!

[CHARLIE *is touched that she is so young.*]

CHARLIE: Why, Dixie, that's money in the bank, to be so young. [*She does not see* RUSSELL *at first, as he comes down the spiral stairs, puts a blanket and other articles on a sofa, and exits.*]

234

RUSSELL: Excuse me. [*He exits.*]

DIXIE: Oh, I didn't see him. . . . [*Then, abruptly*] Charlie, why don't you like me any more? Haven't seen you since the day I sat right here in this room with you and Mr Danziger. [*Slyly*] Didn't I shock him when I asked for the contract?

CHARLIE: Old Nat's been around. . . .

DIXIE [*abruptly*]: In that whole big studio – when I think of some of the things they do and say – !

CHARLIE: Like what?

DIXIE: You'd have to be a girl with a good body to know! I hate those studio bastards, pardon my French! Oh, boy, on rainy afternoons! [*She stands and twirls.*] I'm very small, but I'm perfectly proportioned, aren't I? [CHARLIE *nodding*] Of course, I know that temperament is more important than shape and size. But I still won't get glasses. I can't see across the street, but they're ugly, glasses, aren't they? I won't look any different when I'm sixty. [*Abruptly*] Say, who wound me up? [*Dropping her tempo and sitting*] Well, I wasn't enjoying myself over there and now I am. H'ya, tiger? Can you give me a kiss by radio?

CHARLIE [*beckoning*]: Come over here.

DIXIE [*ditto*]: Come over here. [*He steps over, lifts her and kisses, and runs his hands across her body. She breaks away.*] Hands, Mr Castle, hands! But really, why don't I see you more often in my young and thrilling life?

CHARLIE: Chickie, how you cover ground! Another drink?

DIXIE: Yes, and light, but not too light. I don't care if I see a snake! Although I'm sure I'd rather see a snake than a Hollywood producer! [*She sits at the bar and he makes two drinks.*] Who invented soda? How do they make it? And how do the bubbles get in champagne!

CHARLIE [*laughing, with a mock-threatening gesture*]: You're sweet, you little bitch!

DIXIE [*laughing*]: You're the only one who can call me that. Really! Because I like you – you've been kind and courteous – and that's a very special matter in my special memory box. [*She steps down and does a whirling dance.*] I am going to get a poodle. Do you like poodles?

CHARLIE: Big or little?

DIXIE: The little ones are cute. But the big ones – they're very intelligent, you know. [*Abruptly*] What is that?

CHARLIE [*lifting his head*]: That's an owl.

DIXIE [*surprised*]: A real owl?

CHARLIE: Everything comes to Hollywood. . . .

[*He gives her the drink, leaving the bar. She listens for a moment and it seems that the owl has put a damper on her spirits; her tone changes now.*]

DIXIE: And they give you more protection – the big poodles, I mean. I live alone and like it, but suppose something happened?

CHARLIE: What could happen?

DIXIE: Just the idea of Peeping Toms – you have no idea – it scares me! After all, a dog is faithful. Who else is?

CHARLIE: Alas, Dimples, in that remark, truth.

DIXIE [*listening*]: I never heard an owl before. [*Then*] Molly Murphy, that jasmine is strong! [*Then*] Why's this blanket here?

CHARLIE: If I feel like napping.

DIXIE [*suddenly trembling with tears*]: I'm really very nervous. I'll tell you why. No, don't laugh. When I was sixteen my family threw me out. That makes you very nervous – it makes you touchy. They gave me up for lost. To this day my mother can't tell my father I send them money. Catholics believe in big families, you know. Vaccinated with a Victrola needle, aren't I? It's nerves. People don't realize it's nerves. When you walk in an office, don't have nerves – be a machine. Do I make sense?

CHARLIE [*touched*]: You certainly do. . . .

DIXIE: That's why I like you, Charlie – it's sense to you. But not to them. Oh, no, not to them! Is that good English – 'Aren't I'?

CHARLIE: I believe it is.

DIXIE: I'm saving money now. In government bonds. I'm looking for friend hubby, if I ever meet the guy. But my name is mud in Hollywood. I'm boring you, I know.

CHARLIE: No, don't mind me. I like to hear you talk.

DIXIE: What's the difference? I don't care! [*Then*] I met that Smiley Coy at Monty's party. There's a one!

CHARLIE: He has his good points. . . .

DIXIE: Molly Murphy, I'll make them sweat! Let's see *them* hold in their nerves! [*Abruptly*] I know what you're trying to do, Charlie.

CHARLIE: What . . . ?

DIXIE: Make me forget about the swim you promised! They'd drown me if they could, the studio.

CHARLIE: Why?

DIXIE: Because I needle them, hinting about your accident. It makes them nervous.

CHARLIE: Do you think it's wise . . . ?

DIXIE: I have my contract. They can't hurt me there.

CHARLIE [*sitting up*]: Hoff's a man with an alligator's temper.

DIXIE: Don't tell me about Hoff, calling me 'Child', and one minute later –! You don't see those dogs from the bottom – you're a successful, self-made man.

CHARLIE [*smiling*]: Yep, with the help of a few hundred others, I became a self-made man. Why don't you give *me* a break, Dixie?

DIXIE [*surprised*]: Me? How?

CHARLIE: Well, each time you hint about the accident –

DIXIE: Charlie, don't be like that! You have nothing to fear from me. And I don't talk in my sleep.

CHARLIE: Thanks, but I'm worried, Dimples. Some night you'll have a skinful and inadvertently –

DIXIE: But I have a skinful now. Did I tell you anything that wasn't 'cricket'? That Sammy Burke, for instance! [*She whispers lewdly in his ear.*]

CHARLIE [*soberly*]: You're telling me now.

DIXIE: That's because you asked.

CHARLIE: I didn't ask.

DIXIE: I mean I'm giving you an example. I know where to stop. But I don't see any reason to make it easier for them. I hate them. They signed me up for my body, not to act.

CHARLIE: You've been acting.

DIXIE: You call that acting? Four hat-check girls in three years? All their promises, in every office – with flowers. 'Big part coming up.' 'Testing you next week.' And then a little 'bounce' and next week never comes. They hire girls like me to entertain the visiting sales force. I know how to dress and dance – we borrow clothes from 'wardrobe' – I'm cheaper than a call girl.

[CHARLIE *leans back but he is watching and listening carefully.*]

CHARLIE: Listen . . . to Uncle Collie Dog. Why don't you go back to Boston?

DIXIE: I want to make them crawl and kiss my feet! These damn studios – they louse you up and then they call you louse. Wouldn't you be mad?

[DIXIE *kneels in front of Charlie.*]

CHARLIE [*murmuring*]: Yes . . .

DIXIE: Well, that's my point! And don't think I forgot about my swim. I – [*She stops and peers toward the archway.*] Isn't that . . . someone there . . . ?

[CHARLIE *slowly opens his eyes; then he sits up; then he stands, facing* MARION, *who walks in a few steps. A momentary silence; the party music comes through again.*]

CHARLIE [*rigidly*]: This is my wife. Miss Evans. . . .

DIXIE [*standing*]: How do you do. . . .

[MARION *silently walks across to the bar.*]

We were having a conversation. [*Then*] Charlie, I really have to get back to Monty's party. Thank you for the drink.

CHARLIE: All right, Dixie, thanks – thanks for coming over.

DIXIE [*starting out*]: It's been very pleasant, but I meant everything I said, about the studio. Good night, Mrs Castle.

[DIXIE *leaves helplessly.* MARION *looks at Charlie.*]

MARION: I'm lucky I didn't find Adam and Eve in the swimming pool.

CHARLIE: Marion, you're wrong. She's a little studio contract –

MARION [*sharply*]: I don't care what she is!

CHARLIE: I'm sorry, dear, you're very wrong and I'll bet you sixty bucks you're wrong. I was getting ready to go to bed, but a certain matter came up –

MARION: Why *my* heart should be beating a mile a minute, I don't know! Call a cab. I'll call it myself.

CHARLIE: Marion, can't you look at me and see the truth?

MARION: I arrived a minute too soon and *that's* the truth!

[*She turns and dials the phone. Taking the phone out of her hands, he says, with protesting annoyance:*]

CHARLIE: Did you come back here, Angel, at two a.m. to bang a kettle-drum?

MARION [*angrily*]: I didn't come back, half an hour after I left an inconsolable man, to find him with a blonde piece of consolation!

CHARLIE [*sadly, turning away*]: Grace, in grace, out of grace – disgrace! I can't do anything right. [*Very depressed, he slowly unbuttons his shirt.*]

MARION: I made Hank drive me all the way back from the Brentwood Circle, thinking of how you needed me. I'm sixteen different kinds of fool to give you a second thought.

CHARLIE [*bitterly*]: *Nolo contendere*: I do not contend.

[MARION'S *answer is to dial the phone.* CHARLIE, *without turning, speaks harshly.*]

CHARLIE: What's your hurry, please! Didn't you come all the way back? You can listen! There's all night to call a cab and say goodbye at the marker at the kerb! [*She desists and he turns, gloom intensified.*] You've been a great philosopher about my troubles. . . .

MARION [*coldly*]: I never claimed to be a saint.

CHARLIE: My answer might surprise you. Why not? Is the world so full of saints we can't have more? Sit down.

MARION: Thanks, I'll stand. But if you think –

CHARLIE: No, let me talk – don't push me back to my usual position of self-justification! [*Pausing*] We'll throw away for the moment the rotten bunch of grapes that's me. Although I must say your judgement's gone. You swat the fly on my nose with a hammer. But *your* big trouble, my spouse – for all your talk – the merchant psychology of the country is in your blood, too. You bargain and trifle with your own nature! That's something my Uncle Al never did. I learned that from him. [*Pausing*] Well, that's yesterday, but tonight . . . you're about to possibly destroy your whole life – and maybe mine – by bargaining with your nature, because the object you serve is blemished! Didn't we pick each other out of millions? Can that be bargained away, by saying, like a merchant, that Marion will be herself and love Charlie only if he meets a certain price and conditions? With all your talk, girl, why are you wilfully denaturing yourself? Why? Because *my* integrity's impaired? Because I'm coarsened and listless, dull and burdened? But I struggle – I try to live – don't you see me struggle and resist? I may die in a fight in the street . . . but what about you, with your shopkeeper's bargains? Where's the rich, full-hearted woman I I know you to be? I tell you – I say the hell with bargaining, down with public opinion! Down with not being what we are! The hell with merchants and their tricks. [*Suddenly free and happy*] Marion, I need you, I love you . . . I promise you understanding and devotion, anything I can do. Listen, if I lose you – cross your fingers if you go – in fact, pray for me! But if you stay – if I'm right – I exact conditions: that you fight me back if I'm wrong . . . that you stop reaching for the doorknob. And not the least of these conditions is SILENCE! Because we need silence, all of us. Oh, darling, how we need silence and thought . . . in this noisy, grabbing world!

MARION: You can talk. . . . How you can talk, when you're Charlie Cass! [*Trembling*] I want to beat you. . . .

> [MARION *starts to pound Charlie with her fists –* CHARLIE *grabs her wrists and holds them tightly.* MARION, *broken, next turns away, crying and sobbing bitterly. After a long moment* CHARLIE *takes her*

by the arms and raises her to him; they stand for a moment in an embrace. Then MARION *starts for the spiral stairs saying*]

I'll sleep in my own room. I don't know what I'm doing any more.

CHARLIE: Thanks and thanks. . . .

[*She mounts a few steps before looking down at him.*]

MARION: Do me a favour, Charlie, I beg of you. Grow up . . . before it's too late.

[*With a suspicion of returning sobs, she continues up the stairs. From below,* CHARLIE *is looking up at her.*]

Slow curtain

ACT THREE

SCENE I

Scene: The same.

Time: Late afternoon, a few days later.

[MARION, *sitting at the bar and sipping a cold drink, is marketing by telephone. She is revealing herself now as a bustling housewife, very competent and keen, blithe, performing her duties with snap, precision, and pleasure in functioning.* RUSSELL *stands beside her, wearing a small apron, a shopping list and pencil in his hands.*]

MARION [*into the phone*]: I can't agree, Mr Bower – fourteen dollars for a four-rib roast is impossible. What about calves' liver ... ? [*Laughing*] But what is the world coming to? Well, send three pounds of the liver. [*Warningly*] That's calves' liver, not beef ... good-bye. [*She hangs up and pencil checks the list before her.*] Aren't you thirsty, Russell?

RUSSELL: No, thanks.

MARION: What's the cheese situation in the icebox?

RUSSELL: Nothin' in there but one little cream cheese.

MARION: That sounds lonely. I'll bring some others back. Where's Mr Castle?

RUSSELL: He's still out there in the patio with Mr Nat Danziger. [*Looking through the screen door*] Yep, both of them sittin' under the big, green umbrella. Goodness, both their faces is green!

MARION [*laughing*]: That's the reflection of the umbrella. What kind of beer do we want? [*List in hand,* MARION *swings smartly off the stool; the phone rings.*] I think that covers everything. Take a message if that's for me – I'm not in. [*She lingers, waiting while* RUSSELL *answers the phone.*]

RUSSELL: Castles' residence.... [*Then*] No. He's busy. Yes, still busy. Yes, I will. Good-bye. [*Hanging up*] Mr Coy's secretary – called twice for Mr Castle and Mr Coy's secretary is getting awful mad.

MARION: Give him the message later. Tell him I'll be back in forty minutes, if he asks. [*She starts out briskly but is stopped by* RUSSELL.]

RUSSELL: Mrs Castle ... you know we like it here, Lucille and me. Like it very much.

MARION: Yes ... ?

RUSSELL: But Lucille, she's gettin' awful mad.

MARION: What about?

RUSSELL [*gloomily*]: It's that Sunray Market. She asks them for a uniform-size tomato an' they don't send it. Big and small, you can't stuff 'em if they ain't uniform size.

MARION [*smiling*]: Tell Lucille I'll fix it up.

[*She leaves briskly.* RUSSELL *looks around the room; he crosses, pulling the lever of the pinball game; he is about to leave through the screen door but steps aside, holding it, to let* CHARLIE *and* NAT DANZIGER *enter.*]

RUSSELL: Come in, gentlemen – everything's cool and clean in here.

CHARLIE: Thanks, character. ...

[RUSSELL *leaves with a smile.* NAT *sits, bemused by the heat, fanning himself with his Panama hat;* CHARLIE *goes to the bar.*]

NAT: The evening comes soon ... that's nice. [*Sighing heavily*] When I think of what's happened to the hat industry in this country. ...

CHARLIE: Quench your thirst, darling?

NAT: Something ... anything ... [*Then, as if pained*] Nobody wears garters any more, either. Even I gave up that habit.

CHARLIE: Ginger beer?

NAT: Ginger beer. [*Then, sighing*] Tom Wallace had a check-up at the Mayo Clinic last week. They found a very bad condition – something with the metabolism. ...

CHARLIE: Those damn doves, those mourning doves, they woke me up this morning. Coo-coo-*whoo*, coo-coo-*whoo*. [CHARLIE *hands him his drink.*]

NAT: I'm reminded, I can't leave here without a snack of conversation about the musical script, about which Marcus is dinning in my ears for two weeks now. [CHARLIE *making a horrible face*] You really think it's so bad.

CHARLIE [*annoyed*]: Nat, Hoff-Federated is sailing with a corpse in the cargo!

NAT [*laughing*]: What a boy I manage – one, two, six, he's mad! [CHARLIE *glaring*] Now don't look at me that way – I'll say you're flirting.

CHARLIE: You can sit there, like an adenoidal angel, with your mouth open, from today till tomorrow, but I don't do that script!

NAT: Tell the old man something – is every picture you do a test of your integrity?

CHARLIE: Nat, you're old enough to be my father –

NAT: Older!

CHARLIE: Older! But my God, you're naïve, Nat!

NAT: I may like your integrity, sir, but this picture will sell like bread, like *bread*!

[CHARLIE *dumps the script into his hands and ridicules the whole matter now.*]

CHARLIE: No more pictures for a month or two. Marion and I are thinking of a second honeymoon cruise.

NAT [*gladdened*]: You mean it? I see from your face! Why am I wasting my time? When did this happen?

CHARLIE: A few nights ago. . . .

NAT [*going to him*]: And you held out on the old man like this? Shame on you, shame! Where's Marion I can put my arms around her?

[RUSSELL *enters, puts some bottles behind the bar, and goes, saying:*]

RUSSELL: Mrs Castle is shoppin' but will be back.

NAT: I can't express it to you, Charlie, my commingling of my feelings. Now I can go to Marcus with a human thing, a reconciliation of two of the sweetest mortals God ever put on earth! What can I say? Where can I begin?

CHARLIE [*grinning*]: You can begin by getting the hell outa here so I can change my tennis clothes and shower.

NAT: Okay, I'm going. Give Marion my deepest love – I'll call her later. My dear Charlie . . .

[NAT *happily picks up the script and starts through the archway.* CHARLIE *calls him back quickly when he sees* BUDDY *entering through the screen door.*]

CHARLIE: Nat! . . . Buddy's here. Hello, kid.

BUDDY: I thought you were down at the tennis court.

NAT [*returning*]: And I thought you were going to call me today, Bliss.

BUDDY: I didn't want to bother you. . . .

NAT: Listen to a crazy kid – he didn't wanna bother me! Well, it's all fixed up anyway. The studio don't take orders from Miss Patty Benedict. . . . So relax, son, and enjoy yourself. When in Rome – a word to the wise! 'Bye 'bye . . .

[NAT *waddles out with a self-satisfying wave of the hand, the others calling good-bye.*]

CHARLIE: It's late, kid, don't tell me you come over for tennis? . . .

BUDDY: No, the heat's got me down a bit. I started to paint the house yesterday. . . .

CHARLIE: You're painting the house now, in mid-July? Well! . . . I guess a home is a home!

BUDDY [*gloomily*]: Home? . . . You know how Connie is; unwashed dishes, unmade beds, shoes all over the floor. Just for fun, I counted the dirty towels in the hamper . . . twenty-three!

CHARLIE: You're too serious, Buddy.

BUDDY: But she laughs at everything I say, Charles. . . .

CHARLIE: Well, every marriage is full of bugs. . . .

BUDDY [*troubled*]: She went out yesterday afternoon . . . didn't come back till seven. Tight, too. She laughed and danced around and went to bed at nine o'clock.

CHARLIE: And what did you do?

BUDDY: I went out to the garage and did some work on the Buick.

The way she manhandles that car every day. It makes me sick.

CHARLIE [*wearing thin*]: Look, guy, have a heart. Don't expect everything from one woman. You want an automobile mechanic, too?

BUDDY: Charles . . . I don't think . . . I want you to tell me the truth and I think I can take it. . . . Would Connie, would she cheat on me?

CHARLIE [*carefully*]: Why should she? You're no ogre.

BUDDY: Charles, I want you to . . . [*He stops; on the verge of tears*] I want you to tell me the truth.

CHARLIE: Buddy, I don't know the truth. What do you want me to say?

BUDDY [*lamely*]: I guess . . . I want you to tell me I'm all wet. . . .

CHARLIE: But you are, kid – wet as rain! *So* wet.

BUDDY: I'm afraid to lose her, Charles. I love her and it frightens me. It can ruin me – she can wreck my life!

[CHARLIE, *mixing himself a drink, waits with averted eyes before saying gently:*]

CHARLIE: But . . . anything can ruin us. . . . I guess it's the price of being alive. [*Pausing*] Why don't you both have dinner with us tonight? We're going to Lombrosa's – you really hurt yourself when you eat there.

BUDDY: Connie isn't home . . . I don't know. . . .

CHARLIE: Call us later, when she gets home. [*He walks* BUDDY *to the screen door.*]

BUDDY: My car's down at the court. . . .

CHARLIE: Try to be happy – this isn't a Russian novel.

[*The American male in* BUDDY *shines out again; smiling, he fondly thrusts his hand at Charlie.*]

BUDDY: What a guy . . . [*Then*] I don't know what I'll do if she walks in tight again. . . .

[*He looks unhappily at Charlie and goes. Distressed,* CHARLIE *turns to the phone and begins to dial a number, but quickly puts the phone up when* RUSSELL *enters.*]

RUSSELL: Who was that?

CHARLIE: Mr Bliss. Why?

RUSSELL: Dr Frary is prowlin' around, lookin' for you. Here he is.
[FRARY *enters, a small, elderly pale man, carrying a large bunch of roses. There is a quizzical, chaffing manner about him, a steady twinkle coming out of the eyes almost hidden by heavy, overhanging eyebrows.*]

CHARLIE: Come in, Dr Frary. I don't have to ask you how your garden goes.

FRARY: Where's your wife? Thought she'd like an armful.

CHARLIE: You're a good neighbour, Doctor. I thank you, in the name of my wife. [*He hands the flowers to* RUSSELL, *who leaves.*] How are things with you next door?

FRARY [*mildly*]: Totally uneventful.

CHARLIE [*laughing*]: Politely meaning boring? Why do you stay in California, Doctor? You're retired.

FRARY [*quizzically*]: Would I be unfair, sir, if I said it's really none of your business?
[CHARLIE *laughs.* FRARY *picks up a necktie from a chair.*]
Am I mistaken? Isn't this a very beautiful, artistic tie?

CHARLIE: I'll bet you don't know why we all wear these beautiful, expensive ties in Hollywood.

FRARY: Why?

CHARLIE: It's a military tactic – we hope you won't notice our faces.
[*This time* FRARY *chuckles.*]

FRARY: It's a pity you don't play chess, Castle. You're an amusing boy. I'd be over here more often.

CHARLIE: I'll buy you a highball, Dr Frary.

FRARY: Is it heresy to say that you financial types drink too much?

CHARLIE: No, I sometimes get drunk – take my head off, tuck it under my arm, and run down the midnight, country lane.

FRARY: There's a man standing there, looking right at us. . . . [*He indicates* HANK TEAGLE, *standing in the archway.*]

CHARLIE: Come in, Hank. This is our next-door neighbour, Dr Frary. Mr Teagle – a friend of mine.

HANK [limping in]: Hello . . .

FRARY: Pleased to meet you, sir. That's a strange name – I don't think, in forty years of practice, sir, I've ever met a Teagle.

HANK: They're uncommon. A Teagle, I suppose, is an eagle with one wing. The remark is not improvised.

FRARY [chuckling]: Well, you stay up there in the air, if you can. Our great national bird, the eagle. [He sidles to the screen door.]

CHARLIE: We're always home, Dr Frary.

FRARY [an intense whisper]: Learn chess! [He disappears.]

CHARLIE: An old solid citizen. I admire that type. He reminds me of Marion's father a lot.

[CHARLIE's assumed brightness drops. Without meaning it consciously, he is aloof and jealous of HANK, who himself is wary and tentative at first.]

HANK: He must be old-fashioned to think the eagle is still the American symbol. Of course, it's the cocker spaniel, paws up, saying 'Like me, like me, I'm a good dog, like me!' [Then] How is Marion?

CHARLIE: I think she's shopping.

HANK: She phoned me yesterday . . . about your reconciliation.

CHARLIE [pausing]: Do I hear you offer congratulations?

HANK: Do I read in the papers that you've signed a contract for fourteen years?

CHARLIE [defiantly]: Yes.

HANK [shaking his head]: The Irishman was right: 'Happiness is no laughing matter!'

CHARLIE [temper slipping]: I want you to know that Marion is very happy!

HANK: That remains to be seen. . . .

CHARLIE: You know better?

HANK: I know that Marion stands in your life for your idealism . . . and that you've wounded her and it.

CHARLIE [*about to retort hotly, lapses with a grimace instead*]: When are you leaving, Hank?

HANK: In the morning. [*Smiling*] Maybe I should stay out here and make a fortune, building a toll tunnel from the studios to the race tracks.

CHARLIE: Will the new book be one of your real things?

HANK [*shrugging*]: I still try to write out of Pascal's remark: 'I admire most those writers who tell, with tears in their eyes, what men do to other men.' This book is about a man like you. . . .

CHARLIE [*turning*]: That's a fine, fat subject, but it doesn't smell very average.

HANK: How could a man become a popular movie star without reflecting the average in one way or another?

[CHARLIE, *both pleased and uneasy, crosses to the bar.*]

CHARLIE: And it's really about a guy like me?

HANK: It's a fable about moral values and success.

CHARLIE: You think Marion won't be happy here, don't you?

HANK [*warningly*]: You won't like my answer.

CHARLIE [*promptly*]: Say it!

HANK [*facing him*]: I came here to say good-bye, but I'm too old to be abject. Marion's future interests me deeply. No, I *don't* think she'll be happy here with you! I don't want Marion joining the lonely junked people of our world – millions of them, wasted by the dreams of the life they were promised and the swill they received! *They* are why the whole world, including us, sits bang in the middle of a revolution! Here, of course, that platitude carries with it the breath of treason. I think lots of us are in for a big shot of Vitamin D: defeat, decay, depression, and despair. [*Lapsing off*] Pardon my dust. . . .

CHARLIE: You're eloquent – I give you that – but I don't agree.

HANK: Good enough! Don't agree! Why should you? You're not the man you used to be!

CHARLIE: I'm not?

HANK: No, you're not! You've *sold* out! You'll be here for another fourteen years! Stop torturing yourself, Charlie – don't resist! Your wild, native idealism is a fatal flaw in the context of your life out here. Half-idealism is the peritonitis of the soul – America is full of it! Give up and really march to Hoff's bugle call! Forget what you used to be! That's the only way you'll find a reasonable happiness and pass it on to your wife! No half-man ever made a woman happy!

CHARLIE [*scathingly angry*]: And what are you, a whole man, toots?

HANK [*softly*]: No, I'm toots . . . a crippled man, who needs Marion to help him fight.

CHARLIE: You won't get her, Hank!

HANK: Will you hold her? How?

CHARLIE [*bitterly*]: I'll read your book and find out how!

HANK: You go to hell in the book!

[CHARLIE *wags around the room with wild nervousness before returning to the silent Hank; his voice drops.*]

CHARLIE: And do you say in your book it isn't even easy to go to hell today? That there's nothing left to sin against? [*Then*] Correction! There's health left to sin against! Health – the last, nervous conviction of the time! We're sick at heart, but we'll increase the life span! What for? Nobody knows! . . . [*He crosses muttering, 'What happened to the crowd?' and slumps into a chair, the fight out of him by now.*] You're right, Hank. Your hero's half a man, neither here nor there, dead from the gizzard up. Stick him with a pin and see, psst! No feelings! When I came home from Germany . . . I saw most of the war dead were here, not in Africa and Italy. And Roosevelt was dead . . . and the war was only last week's snowball fight . . . and we plunged ourselves, all of us, into the noble work of making the buck reproduce itself! Oh, those luscious salmon eggs of life! [*He lapses off into silence, with a smirk, exhausted.* HANK *is deeply moved, finally saying gently:*]

HANK: If you feel that deeply . . .

CHARLIE [*staring ahead*]: Get out of here? Does the man in your book get out of here? Where does he go? What, pray tell, does he do? [*Bitterly*] Become a union organizer? [*Turning*] Well, what does he do?

HANK: Charlie ... I can't invent last-act curtains for a world that doesn't have one. You're still an artist, Charlie. ...

CHARLIE: I'll miss you, Hank. Write your book – make it scandalous. Wire me for money any time you need it. Someone has to complete the work he was born to do. Naïve, ain't it?

HANK: Yes, but it's one of your best qualities. ...

CHARLIE: You showed me the rough side of your tongue and I love you for it. [*Wryly*] Why don't you stay here, Hank – be my Horatio. Isn't that a laugh?

HANK: You have Marion. ...

CHARLIE: If she's strong enough. I don't want to hurt her again. She's frail. Women are really 'frails', aren't they? And yet she's the iron hoop that holds my rotten staves together.

HANK [*pausing*]: If you wrestle, Charlie, you may win a blessing. ...
[*Abruptly*, CHARLIE *walks away.*]

CHARLIE: Stand back now, Hank. I don't want to see your face again ... [*Extending his hand*] You're a man with too much courage. Revolution, art – the words you use above ground! Good-bye, Hank. ...

HANK: Give Marion my love. ...
[*Shaking hands, the two men are looking at each other.*]

CHARLIE: Good-bye, bozo. ...
[*Suddenly they are embracing for three tight seconds. Then* HANK *turns and starts out; but he turns, saying:*]

HANK: You rewarded my last visit. You still know that the failure is the best of American life.

CHARLIE [*softly*]: Yes.
[HANK *goes, with a tentative, delicate wave of the hand. It is a long moment before* CHARLIE *turns and puts his glass on the bar.* RUSSELL *enters, announcing* SMILEY COY, *who brushes right past him.*]

RUSSELL: Mr Smiley Coy, in person.

[RUSSELL *misses* COY'S *annoyed look as he goes.* CHARLIE *is in no mood to see Coy and shows it.*]

COY: Hello, Charlie, I just saw that Teagle chap outside. Thought he went back to New York. I'm trying to remember his first name.

CHARLIE: Horatio.

COY [*nibbling peanuts*]: What did he write for us?

[CHARLIE *takes his glass and goes to a chair, leaving Coy at the bar.*]

CHARLIE: The studio paid him one thousand dollars a week for the last four years, and you can't remember his name or what he wrote? [*Gloomily*] My God, those doves – don't you hear them? Coo-coo-whoo-coo-coo-*whoo* . . .

COY [*coming down and listening*]: No. Oh, them. . . . [*Then*] Why didn't you call me back?

CHARLIE: I didn't get any message. Why?

COY [*pausing*]: There's a mess at the studio. I don't know where to begin.

CHARLIE: I told Nat I wouldn't do that script –

COY: I'm not here about a script.

CHARLIE [*mockingly*]: Oh, it's a social visit? Then here's another face! [*He runs an open hand down his solemn face and when the hand comes away, he is smiling broadly.*]

COY: I have to discuss something with you, in private.

CHARLIE: It's private here.

COY [CHARLIE *bent over slightly*]: Cut the caper a moment and listen. Marcus blew his top with Dixie Evans. He'd asked her to come in and see him this afternoon. She arrived one hour late, drunk, lugging in a dog on a leash.

CHARLIE: A poodle?

COY: Yes, but the situation being serious enough, Marcus held his temper. He talked to her like a father. He said –

CHARLIE [*abruptly*]: Let *me* tell *you* what he said. He told her about his boot-black days in Frisco. Next he chimed softly on the 'uneasy-lies-the-head' routine. And before even you knew what was happening, he was smack-dab in the middle of his crying act. And *then* what happened?

COY: She laughed in his face. Told him the whole town knew about his crying and it was time to change the act.

CHARLIE [*unamused*]: He hit her?

COY: Knocked her down and kicked her black and blue. He may have broken one of her ribs – they taped her up at the infirmary. Our story is that the dog – a big sonofabitch – yanked the leash and threw her to the floor. She knows she can't make her assault-and-battery story stick. But she's ready, she says, to spill your story to the Press.

CHARLIE [*stolidly*]: Where is she?

COY: Drinking at The Players' bar. A woman with six Martinis can ruin a city.

[CHARLIE *crosses, stops, and turns.*]

What are you smiling about?

CHARLIE: Am I smiling ... ? [*Waiting*] What's next on our sordid agenda?

COY [*faintly nettled*]: Someone has to saddle the horse. ... I think you'd better get right over there. Get her away from the bar.

CHARLIE: Get her to where?

COY: Her own apartment. You're the only one she'll go with. Don't let her use the phone. Feed her more Martinis – they'll keep her quiet.

CHARLIE: Suppose they don't?

COY: They will. The gin is doctored.

CHARLIE: In her own apartment ... ?

[COY *nods. Surprised,* CHARLIE *stops, looks, and listens; then:*]

Okay, she's on the floor now, on her silly little bottom. What do I do next?

COY: Leave the minute she passes out. You're in the clear from there on. Report back to the studio – you've been there all day, making publicity stills.

CHARLIE [*pausing*]: Smiley, your words have hair on them – your brains are full of lice. . . .

COY [*quietly*]: Now, don't fuss me, Charlie. There's no time to lose. Just keep in mind that the day you first scheme . . . you marry the scheme and the scheme's children. Right this minute . . . everything you are depends on a few drinks in a trollop's guts.

CHARLIE [*flaring*]: But what the hell do you think she is? A moth? A bug?

COY: Speak easy. Keep flexible, Ella. She'll go unremembered by the end of the week. . . .

[*The two men look at each other in silence. Finally:*]

CHARLIE: Where's Marcus?

COY: He doesn't know about this, Charlie.

CHARLIE: Then we'll have to tell him, won't we? You find him, Smiley, while I get Nat.

COY: There is no reason for them to be involved.

CHARLIE: But there's plenty of reason for me to be involved, even deeper than before.

[CHARLIE *laughs curtly and goes to the phone;* COY *stands.*]

COY: I wouldn't do that, Charlie . . . and don't raise your voice again. What are you doing?

CHARLIE [*dialling*]: Don't you remember the 'Warrior minstrel of the forlorn hope'?

[MARION *enters blithely, seeing nothing wrong.* CHARLIE *quickly cradles the phone.*]

MARION: Excuse me – I didn't know you had company.

COY: Hello, Marion. . . .

MARION: I'll get my pop from the kitchen. It's all right. [*She runs out apologetically.*]

COY: What is *she* doing here?

CHARLIE: Cheap serf labour . . . I pay her by the lifetime.

COY: I mean you were separated just the other night.

CHARLIE: I'm waiting – get that good grey weeper here.

COY: Now, Charlie, where's your common sense? Why don't you go upstairs and get some rest! Let *me* handle this.

CHARLIE: Murder is indivisible, Smiley. I'm finding that out. Like chastity, there's no such thing as a small amount of it. I'm finding that out.

COY: Don't blow your wig, scholar. Think . . . just think a minute.

CHARLIE: You know my motto, Smiley – never hit a pimp in the kidneys. Now get me Marcus Hoff!

COY [*soothingly*]: Don't be boyish, Charlie. Do you think you can involve Marcus in a thing like this?

CHARLIE: He's involved up to his neck.

COY: Try to prove it, just try to prove it. For your own sake this is no one else's business. Not even your wife's . . . .

[CHARLIE *goes to the archway and calls* MARION. *She comes quickly, questioning with looks.*]

CHARLIE: Marion, Marion, Smiley Coy wants to tell you something.

COY [*to Marion*]: Charlie's very tight.

CHARLIE: Go on, Smiley, tell her. Go ahead tell her. . . .

COY [*laughing*]: Now don't be boyish and exuberant, Charlie. Watch your step. [*To Marion*] He's not sober enough to discuss a script today. Apparently congratulations are in order. I give them gladly. Charlie needs a long, restful trip. . . .

MARION: ? ? ?

CHARLIE: Don't leave, Smiley. I have certain facts in my hands. If they blow up, I have bleeding stumps left, not hands. But you go, too. Now get me Hoff.

MARION: Charlie, what is it . . . ?

COY [*lightly*]: Charlie gets fanciful ideas about his friends. He's actually accusing me of plotting the murder of a little studio stock player, who was with him in the car, the night of the accident. . . .

[MARION *turns to* CHARLIE, *but he has gone to the phone and is dialling.*]

CHARLIE: I'll explain later, Marion. Take the living-room phone and get Nat here right away!

[MARION *hurries out, after a worried glance at both men.*]

COY: Maybe you know what you're doing. I'll wait. . . .

CHARLIE: Oh, I know you'll wait. You'll wait and wait and wait. . . .

COY [*softly*]: You mishandle your friends, Ella. . . .

CHARLIE [*waiting*]: You're not my friend. That pathetic little girl is my friend – [*Into phone*] Lily? Uncle Hoff, if you please! [*Phone to ear,* CHARLIE *keeps his eyes on Coy, softly whistling, 'Coo-coo-whoo, coo-coo-whoo. . . .'*]

Curtain

SCENE 2

Time: An hour later.

Place: The same.

[*Head bowed,* CHARLIE *is sipping coffee;* MARION *hovers near him.* HOFF, *more suave and reasonable than ever before, is talking with his usual, masked mixture of courtesy and contempt.* COY *listens as he leans against the bar, a highball in one hand. A very distressed and shaken* NAT DANZIGER *listens to one side, his lips pursed heavily. It grows darker as the scene progresses.*]

HOFF: . . . And I know I am expressing not only my views, but yours as well. As far as your idea that Smiley Coy would think in terms of violence and crime . . . with all due credit to what you think you thought, I can't give it credence.

CHARLIE [*lifting his head*]: You're saying Smiley didn't tell me anything? I just dreamed it up?

HOFF: Charlie, I wouldn't be so rash as to say you dream by day. But with a few drinks, isn't it possible –

CHARLIE [*harshly*]: What is possible is exactly what I said!

HOFF [*smoothly*]: Let me round out my thoughts. On the record –

CHARLIE: Don't round out your thoughts. Because –

HOFF: If I may continue. On the record –

256

CHARLIE: I don't want you to continue!

HOFF: As I was trying to say – on the record –

CHARLIE [*jumping up*]: <u>Were you never told the embroidery of your speech is all out of proportion to anything you have to say?</u>

[*HOFF stops dead. He turns and looks at Nat and Smiley. Then he turns back to Charlie and speaks with quiet edge.*]

HOFF [*pausing*]: I'm listening! What do *you* have to say?

[*CHARLIE is unable to resist a cynical, evil smile.*]

CHARLIE: Smiley Coy came here one hour ago. He said there was trouble. He then proposed –

HOFF [*testily interrupting*]: Beyond any cavil of a doubt ... Smiley proposed nothing of the sort. To say that Smiley, a former major of the 27th Division during the first war – friend to the many – I don't know where to begin – George M. Cohan, the late Jimmy Walker – to say that this man plotted murder is to stagger reason! We are wasting valuable time. ...

[*Silence. In the background* COY *is having a brief, whispered conversation on the phone. Tired and frightened,* NAT *comes down.*]

NAT: Marcus, you're a thousand-per-cent right – pneumonia is at the door and we're talking about a headache.

HOFF [*graciously*]: What would *you* do in my place, Nat?

NAT: We have to stop that girl from talking.

HOFF [*most reasonably*]: Yes, but you can't ask me to go into battle with my hands tied. I've always been a simple man. I still make my breakfast on a cup of coffee and a roll, but –

MARION: Mr Hoff, can't you stop talking about yourself?

[*There is an ominous silence which frightens even Marion a little. Finally, sighing jauntily,* HOFF *sits, saying:*]

HOFF: Ah, well, forget it. I'm a clown ... see me as a clown. A little sparkling water, Smiley.

[COY *goes to prepare the water; when he brings it down he will whisper something into Hoff's unturning ear. Now* HOFF *lights his cigar, as if nothing else existed.* NAT *looks helplessly around him before plunging in.*]

257

NAT [*humbly*]: Marcus, nerves are not at their best this minute. No one sees you as a clown, Marcus. That's absurd on the face of it, a remark, to make a remark like that.

HOFF [*sweetly*]: My old friend, Nat Danziger . . . take me by my good right hand and let me follow your judgements and decisions. Is that fair enough?

NAT: I wanna go myself to that girl and make her a cash offer and I think it's feasible. If you'll be good enough to accept half of the burden –

HOFF [*looking at Nat*]: What is our indebtedness to her now, Smiley . . . ?

COY: Three hundred a week, without lay-offs, straight three years, no options.

HOFF [*gravely*]: A mere bagatelle of fifty thousand dollars. I don't think the studio could afford to get involved any deeper there.

NAT: Notwithstanding, I'm willing to talk to her and –

HOFF: No, it's too late for that. The girl is without the fundaments of an education or understanding.

NAT [*earnestly*]: Marcus, where's the percentage in that, for a few dollars to cut off our nose and bite our face?

HOFF: Nat, when I say no I mean no. Arthur Baroni and a few others found that out, too.

[NAT *is about to petition further.*]

CHARLIE: Just a minute. What did Smiley whisper in his ear?

HOFF [*unturning*]: Tell him whatever you said. . . .

COY: Dixie's still at the bar, being amused by a friend of mine.

CHARLIE [*standing*]: If anything happens to her –

COY [*sharply*]: You're selling fish four days old! She's there with Monty Ritz – is he a conspirator, too?

[*Impasse.* NAT *can't find the switch to set the real machinery going.*]

NAT: I honest-to-God don't know what to say any more. . . .

HOFF: Nat, it's been seen fit to dispense with my good offices. I'm not proud. Whose idea is good? Surely the high-calibre people in this room can come to some intelligent solution.

CHARLIE: Not with murder, they can't!

[HOFF *stands, white and swollen, a veritable puff adder.*]

HOFF [*to* NAT]: Nat, your client has to learn how to talk! If you have a boy, teach him manners! [*Turning to Charlie*] We know who is the expert when it comes to murder, Mr Charles Castle! The memory of that accident –!

NAT [*pleadingly*]: Marcus, please! Please!

HOFF: A boy like you, who are you? Snotty aristocracy because the female admissions wanna sleep with you? Who are you, with your dirty, unmanicured finger nails? What are you without Hoff-Federated behind you? I built that studio with my brains and hands – I ripped it out of the world! What are you?

NAT: No, this must stop –!

COY: Marcus ...

[COY *has Hoff by the arm.* HOFF *twists, asking him:*]

HOFF: No, I mean it, Smiley! Do I have to listen to this miserable boy? A man like myself, who's wined and dined with kings and presidents?

NAT: This must stop – it has to stop!

HOFF: Do I have to cater to this?

CHARLIE: One more line of your phoney cathedral eloquence and I'll chop you down like fire-wood!

NAT [*shouting*]: No, please – I beg you – please!

[COY *and* NAT *have their respective men by the arms.*]

HOFF: You are beneath contempt! Wally Cole was better than you! It's a bitter, miserable pity to have to talk to you!

CHARLIE [*shouting*]: There, that's it – that's the deal – no more talk to you!

NAT [*frantically*]: Charlie, Lovey, I beg of you – gentlemen, please!

CHARLIE [*heedless*]: We don't talk to each other from now on.

[*Breathing heavily, both men are silent, staring at each other, held by Coy and Nat.* HOFF *breaks the picture first; he picks up his glass and sips some water.* CHARLIE *turns and goes back to his chair, walking around it in small, crazy circles.*]

NAT: Gentlemen ... this scene must be forgotten. ...

CHARLIE: You're my agent! You meet him – I'll never talk to him again!

HOFF: You won't get in my office!

CHARLIE: Won't I? [*Eyeing him coldly*] *Now let's get down to business!* Don't act bored. Don't sulk – don't put on an act.

HOFF: I'm warning you. You'll drive me too far.

CHARLIE: What's your boiling-point, Uncle Hoff? How much can you take, if you *have* to, instead of terrorizing servile men?

NAT: Charlie, I beg of you, I beg you, Charlie –

COY: He's drunk, Marcus.

CHARLIE: I'm deliberately tampering with your modest ego, Marcus! Because today I see what Marcus Shriner Hoff and his horny partners would do for me: they'd murder! Now ... I realize what I am!

[HOFF *stands. He is cold and quiet now.*]

What, leaving? Don't I get the chance to gaff this monster? Because I'll gaff you, you evil, swollen monster, if it's the last thing I do!

HOFF [*quietly*]: This man buries himself with his mouth.

NAT [*helplessly*]: Charlie ...

CHARLIE: Don't worry. I'm his billion-dollar baby. Look at his mind go: like a lizard – sisst! – sisst! – sisst! I thought I had a crocodile, but it's only a lizard!

HOFF: Smiley, get together with the legal department in the morning, comb through the Castle contract for any outs. Find me a peg to hang my hat on. [*Turning to the others*] All right, Hoff-Federated loses its most valuable male star. An important source of revenue is wiped off our books for ever, I admit. But we're a far-flung empire – we have other stars. But your client is on the verge – he loses everything – it's ruin. The dead child's family and the insurance companies will take the clothes off their backs in any court of the land! So Mr Charles Castle has his choice. Let the girl do her dirty work, or he can call the police himself!

NAT: This is how you feel, Marcus?

[HOFF *turns as if to go;* COY *breaks in quickly.*]

COY: There is one other solution.

CHARLIE [*cynically, to Marion*]: Here it comes – the 'gimmick' – the twist, the switch! There's always a twist – they work in pairs.

COY [*blandly*]: There's an angle to the Dixie problem. It depends on you, Marion.

MARION: Does it?

COY: You've been separated twice in the last three years. Do you love Charlie enough to make a sacrifice?

CHARLIE [*quietly*]: Let him finish, dear. . . .

COY: Dixie Evans would marry Charlie in a minute. It would satisfy all of her dreams. Community property laws automatically take care of you. Half of everything Charlie owns belongs to you.

NAT: Gentlemen, I can't believe my ears!

HOFF [*sharply*]: Why not? Let him finish.

COY: I'm finished. Except to say that Dixie can't legally testify against her own husband. But it would never come to that.

HOFF: Before you jump in, Nat, where it don't concern you, Marion – Mrs Castle – loves a writer we had on the lot till the other day.

MARION: That's untrue!

HOFF: From time to time she slept with him.

[CHARLIE *grabs Marion as she starts for Hoff.*]

CHARLIE: Please, Marion – let me. [*To Hoff*] Of course, you have proof of what you say.

HOFF: Your wife will prove it. We have her conversation on records. With the writer, in his office.

MARION: Don't hold me, Charlie. I have to get this clear. You have recordings of conversations I had in Mr Teagle's office?

HOFF: In his office . . . and on his couch.

NAT [*shocked*]: Marcus, who ordered such recordings to be made?

HOFF: That's out of my hands – I couldn't say. Our police are very active. Certain industrial strife brings such things about.

CHARLIE: Where are these recordings?

HOFF: In my car.

CHARLIE: Get them.

HOFF [*to Coy*]: Get them. . . .

> [COY *goes.* CHARLIE *lights a cigarette and gives it to the nervous Marion.* NAT *clears his throat.*]

CHARLIE: Be quiet, dear. . . .

HOFF: Live and let live was always an important motto with me, Marion. But you never seemed to believe in that. I have nothing against you personally, understand? But I am beholden to our stockholders. They control our every action – they are our invisible but ever-present monitors. Nat, put a little more sparkling water in this glass.

> [NAT *is a pitiful sight as, voice half-strangled for a moment, he slaps the glass out of Hoff's hand.*]

NAT: You don't think so pretty about the stockholders, do you, when you make your sinking funds and hand out executive bonuses? My career is finished and I'm willing, namely. Because you are one of the meanest, dirtiest skunks that God ever put breath into! [*To Marion and Charlie*] This is Mr Hoff, a man that I fall on my knees and thank my God above for one thing – that I don't have to play ball with him any more. [*Trembling and weeping*] You – what are you? Excuse me for crying, Charlie, dear. Don't worry – Charlie and Marion, don't worry. Before he'd let you go in trouble, he'd put his own head on a railroad track.

> [NAT'S *sobbing becomes uncontrollable; he fumbles with his handkerchief;* CHARLIE *takes him in his arms.* COY, *entering with an envelope under one arm, is surprised at the scene, but he says nothing.*]

I'm ashamed to cry.

> [HOFF *nods to* COY, *who gives Charlie the envelope of records.*]

MARION: Charlie, there's nothing to defend about these records. They –

CHARLIE: Be quiet. . . . [*turning to Hoff and Coy*] It's late. Don't you boys ever go home for dinner? Now do that, do that for me, Smiley. [*Coaxingly*] Take Hoff home. Feed him whisky and *keep* him small. [*To Hoff*] You're lucky. I'll betcha sixty bucks if this were a movie you'd have been on the floor ten times. [CHARLIE *slaps him sharply.*] That's only a token.

[HOFF *is pale. He lifts his arm, as if to hurl anathema. Instead he walks to the door, stops there.*]

HOFF: I'll break you like I broke Wally Cole – he was a bigger star. You have pissed away a kingdom today. . . .

[*He walks out.* CHARLIE *breaks the records in the envelope and tosses them behind the bar.*]

COY [*coolly*]: Marcus won't forget today. . . . You'll sit at home, on salary . . . *if legally necessary* . . . for fourteen years or until your liver explodes. But you won't work. In or out of jail, your acting days are over!

CHARLIE: What I told you before, still goes. If anything happens to that girl –

COY: The studio has no further interest in that girl.

[*Nodding stiffly to Marion,* COY *walks out.*]

CHARLIE [*softly*]: All quiet on the Atomic . . . .

NAT [*dolefully*]: It's right, there are things beyond money to that man – but *this* much money not. I don't want you to worry, children.

CHARLIE [*snapping on a lamp*]: Now . . . I realize what I am. . . . [*And he snaps on one more lamp.* MARION *is at the bar.*]

MARION: A drink, Charlie?

CHARLIE: I owe you the deepest apology, Nat, for dragging you into this filth. But I can't go on carrying a musket for Hoff, being his boy.

NAT: Wait a minute, Lovey, first things first. [*Abruptly*] I'll tell you, why don't I take it on my own prerogative to take Miss Dixie Evans home with me and out of my own pocket I'll offer her a ten-thousand-dollar bill?

CHARLIE: You're sweet, darling, but it's too late, from *my* point of view. I can't go on, covering one crime with another. That's Macbeth.

NAT: But, not to rehash an old wound, you didn't commit any crime! You're a good boy – I *know* you're a good boy!

CHARLIE: But Macbeth is an allegory, too: one by one, he kills his better selves. [*Sitting*] My back is stiff. . . . [*Then*] Why am I surprised by them? Isn't every human being a mechanism to them? Don't they slowly, inch by inch, murder everyone they use? Don't they murder the highest dreams and hopes of a whole great people with the movies they make? This whole movie thing is a murder of the people. Only we hit them on the heads, under the hair – nobody sees the marks.

NAT: Charlie, for once I'll tell *you* shut up. Stop wringing your mental hands.

CHARLIE [*quietly*]: You go home, Nat. I'll go over later and speak to Dixie. The worst can happen – she passes out and Monty puts her to bed – he's done it before. I want to think. I'll call you later.

NAT: If you'll call me later, I'll go. . . .

CHARLIE: Around eight, darling. I'll call. Don't worry.

NAT: I'll be at my office very late. The old man is waiting to hear from you, understand?

[CHARLIE *nods and* NAT *picks up his hat.*]

MARION: Good-bye, dear. . . .

NAT: Good-bye, Marion. . . .

[NAT *goes, heavily, reluctant and worried.* CHARLIE *gets up and goes to the bar.*]

CHARLIE: Why did I add this burden to that grotesque, devoted soul? Did you ever notice? He moves his lips when he reads. . . .

[RUSSELL, *with a sense of what has happened, looks in at the archway.*]

RUSSELL: Anything you folks want in here?

CHARLIE: Yes, run a bath for me. Good and hot – I'm stiff.

[RUSSELL *nods and goes up the spiral stairs.* CHARLIE *meantime has picked up a whisky bottle by the neck and begins to lob and scoop up imaginary tennis balls in long graceful strokes.*]

You never slept with Hank, did you . . . ?

MARION: No, because it –

CHARLIE: Don't explain. I believe you. [*Then, delicately scooping up a 'ball'*] Isn't it really time we learnt to bear the strains of living in silence?

MARION: Yes . . .

[CHARLIE *stops his game and sits with the bottle.*]

CHARLIE: Light me a cigarette, dear. [*As she lights the cigarette, he uncorks the bottle, looking at his hands.*] Look how sweaty, my hands. [*He takes one long swig out of the bottle and puts it on the table beside him.* MARION *crosses with the cigarette.*] Sit on my lap. [*She does, giving him the cigarette. There is a snuggling, silent moment.*] What do you think of today?

MARION: I think I can list all the possible roads ahead. . . .

CHARLIE: The alternatives? List them. But, short of murder, we won't silence that girl. It's become the cause of her life. [*Smiling sadly*] You see, everyone needs a cause to touch greatness.

MARION [*quietly*]: You could marry her. . . .

CHARLIE [*gently*]: Could I? [*Then*] Marion, are you my old-time girl?

MARION: Yes . . . and I remember everything.

CHARLIE: Waverly Place?

MARION: Yes . . .

CHARLIE [*pausing*]: Has Hank left yet?

MARION: Not till tomorrow.

CHARLIE: He knows how to think. Why don't we call Hank over? What does he know about all this?

MARION: Nothing.

CHARLIE: Call him, please.

[MARION *immediately goes to the phone and dials.*]

MARION: I think I'll bring Billy back tomorrow.

CHARLIE [*with a warm flush*]: How is the biggest man in town?

[MARION *has to turn abruptly to the phone.* CHARLIE *picks up a photograph of Billy and looks at it, finally leaning back and closing his eyes.*]

MARION: Hello! Hank? This is Marion. Can you come right over here? We need your advice. It's very important. Yes. All right, dear, thanks. [*Hanging up*] He'll be right over. Hey, you, wake up.

CHARLIE [*starting*]: Listen, Billy mustn't grow up to be a rich man's son.

MARION: He won't.

CHARLIE: They're usually made of sponge cake. . . .

MARION [*smiling*]: He won't be. . . .

[*In a warm flush of feeling, CHARLIE goes to Marion at the base of the spiral stairs and puts his arms around her.*]

CHARLIE: Darling . . . Darling . . . You taught me so many things, even how to listen to music. [*Then*] Play some music.

MARION: What?

CHARLIE: Something immortal. [*Wryly*] Anything that's on the machine. [*She snaps on the machine as CHARLIE goes around to the front of the bar.*] Isn't it true? Aren't the times beyond us, cold and lonely? Far away as the stars. [*Pausing*] Nat's alternative is for me to sit tight and let Hoff protect his property. [*Then*] And me . . . I can pick up the telephone . . . and call the police. [*He begins to prowl the room, MARION watching him. He snaps on the lamp.*] Keep meaning to put larger bulbs in these lamps. [*Then, with an abrupt turn, he speaks in panic*] Marion, help me, help me! Hold me tight!

[*In a flash she is up, arms around him.*]

MARION: I'll help you, Charlie, I'll help. . . .

CHARLIE: I can't give myself up! I can't!

MARION: Shhh! Quiet, darling, quiet. . . .

CHARLIE: Hank is right – I mustn't resist! I must make peace here or go out of my mind! I'm caught – Hoff's prisoner. He gave me an appetizing name and now he thinks he'll eat me! My life is sworn away and now they wanna murder for me and I see what I am!

MARION: You be quiet now. . . . I still have Charlie Cass. . . .

CHARLIE [*standing*]: Oh, no! No! [*The phone is ringing; CHARLIE snatches it up.*] Hello . . . [*pausing*] Oh . . . [*then*] Don't cry, Buddy. [*Listening*] No. No. [*Then*] I'll see you in the morning. [*Hanging up and turning to Marion. His voice low and bitter, flat:*] Connie came home tight. ... They had a fight. ... She's leaving Buddy. She brought my name in. ...

[*Here* MARION *understands Charlie's meaning and turns away, momentarily sickened.* CHARLIE *is talking with bitter self-revulsion.*] You see, you have Castle. He murdered Cass. ... I was there. ... I saw him do it! Look at me! Can you face it? Look at this dripping fat of the land? Could you ever know that all my life I yearned for a world and people to call out the best in me? How can life be so empty? But it can't be! It can't! It's proven – statistics and graphs prove it – we are the world's happiest, earth's best. ... [*Stopping*] I'll go up and bathe and change my clothes. ...

[CHARLIE *mounts the spiral stairs. At the top landing he looks down;* MARION *has not moved.*]

CHARLIE: Marion ... [*waiting*] Everything that embitters you ... I pledge you a better future. It begins tonight.

[*He waits a vain moment for a response from her; finally he disappears soundlessly.* MARION *lifts her head and says in a fogged voice:*]

MARION: I'm committed to you. I love you. We won't ... talk about the past. ...

[*She turns and sees that he is gone. She crosses and snaps off the phonograph.* RUSSELL *enters with a large vase of flowers.*]

RUSSELL: These was give to you by Dr Frary. Yes, you just have to throw your arms around a man like that, who is always thinkin' of others.

MARION [*abstracted*]: Ask Lucille if she won't excuse me for such short notice and prepare a light supper for three.

RUSSELL: Sure, that's what we're here for, Mrs Castle.

MARION [*with a half-smile*]: And remind her – no parsley on anything – Mr Castle doesn't like it. Are there bath towels upstairs?

RUSSELL: Think so, but just to make sure, I'll hand him in a few more.

[*He smiles and goes. Looking at her wrist watch, after thinking a moment,* MARION *dials the phone.*]

MARION: Hello? Marie ... ? How is Billy? [*Nodding*] I think I'll drive out tomorrow morning in the station wagon and bring you both back here. Is that Billy? I'll talk to him. ... [*Waiting*] Hello, darling. [*Listening*] Oh, what a shame! All those poor cowboys ... gee whiz ... yes. [*Then*] That's what I wanted to tell you. I'm coming out tomorrow for you and we're coming home. No, goldfish don't need blankets and beds. You bet I will, Billy – you bet! Yes, all right, baby, you have your nice sleep tonight and tomorrow – yes, dear. [*Then*] Marie? Hello? Marie ... ?

[*Evidently* MARIE *has hung up.* MARION *does the same here.* RUSSELL *steps inside the archway, asking sotto voce:*]

RUSSELL: You wanna see Mr Coy? He's here again.

[COY *is in the room before Marion can answer. Ice cold, she looks at him;* RUSSELL *withdraws.*]

COY: I'm sorry for everything, Marion, deeply sorry. May I use your phone? [*He is at the phone before her 'yes' comes, stopping her from leaving the room, by saying:*] Don't go. You'll be interested in what I have to say. [*Having dialled his number he waits a moment, saying into the phone:*] I want the Old Man, Lily. It's important. [*Waiting; to Marion*] Mr Hoff is a very vain man. We have to cater to that a little. Where's Charlie?

MARION: Taking a bath. What do you want, Mr Coy?

COY: I'm nothing more than a sort of memo pad for Mr Hoff and you'd do wrong to – [*He holds up a finger for silence and attention and turns to the phone.*] Marcus? The girl left The Players' bar ten minutes ago and tried to navigate across Sunset Boulevard. Yeah, all that heavy, homegoing traffic. That's the picture! Killed instantly! How do you like that for the luck of the Irish? I'm here, using Charlie's phone. Well, I'll be right back. Good-bye. [*He hangs up and turns to face Marion.*] Before you say anything ... it was a police car that hit her. Changes everything, doesn't it?

MARION: Does it ... ? What a happy coincidence.

COY: But that's not to say that Marcus has forgotten what happened here today. It's a hard-fought battle from which no man returns to tell the tale. Some sort of apology should be arranged – tactfully, of course. And yours is the level head to do it.

MARION: Does a man like you have a memory from one hour to the next?

COY: I'd never forget your kindness for forgetting anything I'm ashamed to remember.

MARION: That's a very gallant speech.

COY: What is that? Water?

MARION: Where?

COY [*pointing*]: Isn't that water dripping through your ceiling?

[COY *walks back,* MARION *with him, both looking at a spot behind the spiral stairs. At the same time a dull thumping is heard from above.* MARION *crosses quickly to the archway and calls, 'Russell! Oh, Russell!' The* BUTLER *appears at the top of the stairs and calls down:*]

RUSSELL: It seems as Mr Castle's bath is runnin' over. I left it turned off.

MARION: Well, tell him!

RUSSELL: I can't get in there – his door is locked and he don't answer!

MARION: It's locked? Did you knock?

RUSSELL: I been beatin' on it! He don't answer!

[*Stock-still a moment, paralysed,* MARION *knows something big in her life has happened.*]

MARION [*weakly*]: Mr Coy ... go up there ...

RUSSELL [*excitedly*]: Come up here – gimme a hand, Mr Coy.

[*Getting a fast idea – as he will tell it later –* COY *bounds up the stairs.* MARION *sucks in a deep gulp of air, forcing dizziness away. She starts for the archway; from there she turns and cuts across to the phone and picks it up; then she drops the phone and cuts over to the screen door and pushes it open with one hand, calling:*]

MARION: Dr Frary! Dr Frary!! [*An echo answering*] Would you come over here right away! Hurry, please!

[*Her voice trails off and she lets the door slam shut. She starts for the spiral stairs, but stops and listens to the sounds from above – a door is*

269

being demolished. She slowly walks to the foot of the stairs but has to stop there to conquer a wave of sickness. After a few seconds, shaking her head clear, she begins to make the awful ascent. The complex of noises from above includes excited, male voices. HANK *enters and looks around. A rapidly breathing* COY *hurries down the stairs. He brushes past* HANK *in his headlong rush to the telephone. He dials agitatedly,* HANK *stepping in toward him.*]

COY: Never in your life ... saw anything so wrong. ... [*Into the phone*] Cut me through to Eddie Frye! [*Savagely*] Break right through! This is Smiley Coy! Well, pull the plugs, you stupid bitch!

[HANK, *eyes and ears on Coy, is inching back to the stairs.* COY, *waiting, is dully banging the bar with a clenched, sickened fist.*]

COY: Eddie! Smiley Coy! Now listen – listen to me with care! don't want to repeat a word – listen! Get Marcus. Get Dr Curley. Send them both here, to Charlie Castle's house right away. Don't ask me any questions – you get here as soon as you do your work and here's your work!

[HANK *is listening to Coy, but reaching the bottom of the stairs, he hears one sound of Marion's voice, a quavering 'Ahh!', which freezes the blood in his veins. He slowly starts up the stairs, but listening to Coy's next block of speech.*]

Write this down, word for word. Charles Castle, the renowned star of fifty Hoff-Federated pictures, died today of a heart attack at his Beverly Hills home at 6.55 Pacific Coast Daylight Saving Time. Present at his bedside were his physician – Curley – his wife, Marion, his five-year-old son, Billy, and ... and his close friend and associate, Marcus S. Hoff.

[HANK *has exited above.* RUSSELL, *wet and rumpled, comes down the stairs and leans against the bar as* COY *concludes on the telephone.*] That goes out on all the wires – A.P., U.P. and all the rest! Don't ask me any questions. Bring a dozen studio cops with you. It's gonna be hell here in a minute! What? Tell Marcus ... he cut himself in three places!

[*He slams down the phone and takes a quick drink. Seeing* RUSSELL *grunting as he leans against the bar,* COY *gives him a drink.*]

Pull yourself together, boy! [*Roughly*] Go wash your hands – change your clothes! Listen! There's a nice piece of change in this for you – get it straight! There'll be an army of reporters here in twenty minutes. But you don't know anything, see? Play dumb, see? Hear me?

[COY *is shaking him hard.* RUSSELL *wrests himself loose from Coy and hurries through the archway.* COY *picks up a bar towel and wipes his hands and a spot on the bar.* MARION *and* HANK *appear at the top of the stairs. She starts down.*]

MARION: Don't help me, Hank. I can walk. . . .

[HANK *watching from above,* MARION *comes down the stairs.* COY *goes to her as she reaches the bottom steps, but she brushes him aside.*] Don't help *me*. . . .

[*The two men watch her.* HANK *slowly inching down the stairs, almost as if not to wake her.* MARION *is moving somnambulistically, strangely collecting the soiled glasses in the room and putting them on the bar. Her light dress is badly stained with blood and water. Helpless,* COY *looks up at Hank.*]

COY [*sotto voce*]: Help her, Horatio – she doesn't like me. Tell her . . . the reporters . . . loads of them any minute.

[HANK *has reached the bottom steps by now. His eyes remain on* MARION, *who now seems obsessed with stacking magazines and tidying the room.*]

HANK: I'll talk to the reporters.

COY: That won't be necessary. We'll be here.

HANK: That's why it's necessary.

[*The scene is dream-like. Neither man has taken his eyes off Marion.* MARION *is lightly weaving her way around the room.*]

COY [*warily*]: Listen, feller, this is no time to get contentious. The photographers –

HANK [*voice full of feeling*]: There will be no photographers, there will be no lies, no display. This is my friend's hour, not the nation's,

271

not Hoff's. Your work is finished here. It won't be smooth, but I'll ... I'll tell the story. He ... killed himself ... because that was the only way he could live. You don't recognize a final ... a final act of faith ... when you see one. ...

[*Having picked up Charlie's coat,* MARION *turns sharply; it seems her consciousness has been touched by the last few words.*]

MARION: Charlie ... ?

[*She stands, pitiful and distressed,* HANK *carefully moving toward her. Several convulsions of her body are expressed with faint 'ahs'. Then her grief bursts, expressing itself in one iterated, pleadingly anguished word:*]

Help! ... Help! ... Help!! ... Help!!! ...

[HANK *has his arms around her, but the word does not stop and it will never stop in this life.*]

Curtain